STUDIES IN IMPERIALISM

General editors: Andrew S. Thompson and Alan Lester

Founding editor: John M. MacKenzie

When the 'Studies in Imperialism' series was founded
by Professor John M. MacKenzie more than thirty
years ago, emphasis was laid upon the conviction that
'imperialism as a cultural phenomenon had as significant
an effect on the dominant as on the subordinate societies'.
With well over a hundred titles now published, this remains
the prime concern of the series. Cross-disciplinary work
has indeed appeared covering the full spectrum of cultural
phenomena, as well as examining aspects of gender and sex,
frontiers and law, science and the environment, language
and literature, migration and patriotic societies, and much
else. Moreover, the series has always wished to present
comparative work on European and American imperialism,
and particularly welcomes the submission of books in these
areas. The fascination with imperialism, in all its aspects,
shows no sign of abating, and this series will continue to
lead the way in encouraging the widest possible range of
studies in the field. 'Studies in Imperialism' is fully organic
in its development, always seeking to be at the cutting edge,
responding to the latest interests of scholars and the needs
of this ever-expanding area of scholarship.

British civic society at the end of empire

MANCHESTER
1824

Manchester University Press

British civic society at the end of empire

**DECOLONISATION, GLOBALISATION, AND
INTERNATIONAL RESPONSIBILITY**

Anna Bocking-Welch

MANCHESTER UNIVERSITY PRESS

Published by MANCHESTER UNIVERSITY PRESS
ALTRINCHAM STREET, MANCHESTER M1 7JA
www.manchesteruniversitypress.co.uk

British Library Cataloguing-in-Publication Data
A catalogue record for this book is available from the British Library

ISBN 978 1 5261 3127 0 hardback

First published 2019

The publisher has no responsibility for the persistence or accuracy of URLs for any external or third-party internet websites referred to in this book, and does not guarantee that any content on such websites is, or will remain, accurate or appropriate.

Typeset
by Toppan Best-set Premedia Limited
Printed in Great Britain
by TJ International Ltd, Padstow

CONTENTS

ACKNOWLEDGEMENTS

I am grateful to the many people who have made this book possible. First I would like to thank the Arts and Humanities Research Council who funded the PhD research that forms the foundation of this book and the World Universities Network who funded the two months I spent at the University of Washington, Seattle. Second, I am thankful to the staff at the libraries and archives I have worked at, in particular those at the Royal Commonwealth Society Archive. Third, I am grateful to all those who have commented on various parts of this book, and for the countless questions and suggestions I have received over the course of this project. I am especially grateful to Richard Huzzey for his generosity, enthusiasm, critical insight, and sharp editorial eye, particularly as I approached the final hurdle. Chris Pearson and Deana Heath, my colleagues at Liverpool, have been particularly kind with their time and advice.

I would like to express my gratitude to Liz Buettner, who was the model of a perfect PhD supervisor and whose own research has offered a constant source of inspiration. Her unwavering enthusiasm, thoughtful advice and meticulous feedback were crucial in helping to mould this project and keep me on track. Thanks also to Mark Roodhouse and Joanna De Groot whose many pointers and suggestions greatly enriched my work, and to Jordanna Bailkin whose incisive comments helped to shape a number of my case studies.

Special thanks to my mum and dad for their support and understanding. Thanks to the York Gang for suffering the PhD alongside me and keeping me sane. Without you there for coffee breaks, long lunches, pot lucks and bike rides, all the hard graft wouldn't have been possible. Thanks to Charlotte Riley and Emily Baughan; you've been a constant source of inspiration and solidarity. My final thanks go to James. For the late nights, the patient questions, the grammar policing and the endless cups of coffee, I owe you a lifetime of tea in bed. Most of all, though, thanks for keeping me company. There's not much I'd want to do without you.

ABBREVIATIONS

BCC   British Council of Churches
CAP   Capricorn Africa Society
CND   Campaign for Nuclear Disarmament
COI   Central Office of Information
FAO   Food and Agricultural Organisation
FFHC   Freedom from Hunger Campaign
ILN   *Illustrated London News*
LEL   League of Empire Loyalists
NFWI   National Federation of Women's Institutes
RCS   Royal Commonwealth Society
RIBI   Rotary International in Great Britain and Ireland
SOAS   School of African and Oriental Studies
UN   United Nations
VSO   Voluntary Service Overseas
WI   Women's Institute

Introduction

In the 1960s the world shrank for the British public. In a literal sense, they lost an empire. The start of the decade marked the most intense period of decolonisation and, by its end, more than twenty-five colonies in Africa, the Caribbean, and the Indian Ocean had gained independence. With each independence ceremony, with each newly hoisted flag, the pink area on the map retreated. But the world was becoming smaller in other ways as well. The 1960s were distinctive not just for the rapid pace of decolonisation, but also for a boom in international mobility and communications, and a concomitant surge in the establishment and growth of international agencies and organisations. As a play produced in 1964 for school children by the humanitarian organisation Christian Aid described it:

> The world we live in has become one. Overnight we have discovered that China is not very far away, that it is easier to fly to Greece ... than it is to drive up the M1 to the North of England. This has been brought about by the rapid growth of travel, satellites in orbit which bring us pictures of Moscow or America as things happen and the on-the-spot commentaries of the commentators as they give us their judgements about a war in Vietnam or a soccer match in Argentina.[1]

This interconnectedness made faraway places, the people that lived in them, and the things that they did there *feel* as if they were closer to Britain than ever before.

Such sentiments may not have been entirely new in the 1960s; similar pronouncements about proximity, accessibility, and interconnectedness were made in 1866 about the establishment of transatlantic telegraph lines, for example, and again in the aftermath of the First World War.[2] Nevertheless, the sense of living in a shrinking world was reinvigorated by the geopolitical shifts of the post-war period and its imagery became a prominent feature of political and associational life

[1]

in the 1960s. In the pages of broadsheet newspapers the world was described as shrinking when markets expanded into new geographical areas, when increased air travel required new international health regulations to stop the spread of disease, and when the threat of nuclear attack made the internal affairs of one country the immediate concern of another.[3] According to R. J. D. Evans, writing in *The Times* in 1959, a shrinking world was a world in which 'most major issues – economic, political and military – [were] ... universal in their import'.[4] But it was also one in which opportunities for real and vicarious travel increased the British public's ability to see and interact with the outside world. Public attitudes towards the wider world were shaped simultaneously by this increasing interconnectedness and by the dissolution of the British Empire. This book is about the paradox of living in these two shrinking worlds – about what it meant that the world felt more visible and accessible to the British public at precisely the moment that Britain lost authority over it – and about the impact of that paradox on the ideas and practices of post-imperial responsibility within middle-class society.

Until at least the mid-1980s, most scholarship on British imperialism assumed that 'empire' was something that happened overseas and was therefore marginal to the lives of most British people.[5] Since then, however, efforts to assess the impact of imperialism on metropolitan societies have moved to the centre of an ever-expanding field.[6] Empire is no longer treated as just a phenomenon 'out there', but as a fact that registered in 'the social fabric, the intellectual discourse, and the life of the imagination'.[7] While the majority of this scholarship deals with the eighteenth and nineteenth centuries, the post-war years of imperial decline also raise important questions about Britain's imperial experience. In 1996 Bill Schwarz published a rallying call, pointing out that conventional histories of decolonisation presented a 'stunning lack of curiosity' about its impact within 'the heartland of England itself'.[8] In the two decades since, scholars have mounted a persuasive challenge to the 'minimal impact thesis', focusing on representations of empire in political discourse and cultural productions (including satire, children's popular literature, commercial films, travel writing, and television programming) to illustrate the effects of decolonisation on domestic life.[9]

This book builds on these existing histories of decolonisation by introducing a cast of actors and a set of spaces understudied in the post-war period. It thinks about the village hall, the clubhouse, the local church, and the small-town assembly room, and it traces the associational and organisational links that connected these spaces to the outside world. By decentring the traditional focus on cultural products in order to analyse civic forms of engagement with the declining empire, this book links a rich scholarly tradition of research on the domestic experience of Britain's Empire to a new and emerging field of research that seeks to understand the institutional and associational makeup of the interconnected post-war world. Popular memories of the 1960s often centre on the increased mobilisation and radicalisation of young and left-wing political activists.[10] Alongside markers of affluence, permissiveness, and transatlantic consumerism, the sit-in and the protest march endure as common symbols of a decade of change. As a result, we have little difficulty in imagining youth or political activists as international actors – as active participants in a globalising world. Yet, as this book shows, it was not just the young and politically active who looked out onto the changing world. The geopolitical changes of the 1960s also opened up new opportunities and created new expectations for international engagement among middle-class, middle-aged members of society with little interest in protest. For many participants in middle-class associational life it became a civic duty to engage, understand, and intervene to help the shrinking world in which they lived. This book uncovers how associations and organisations acted on this sense of duty, developing projects that promoted friendship and hospitality as the foundations of world peace, visions for secular and religious forms of humanitarianism that encouraged relationships of both sympathy and solidarity with those in the global south, and plans to increase international understanding through educative activities.

The experiences of the associational groups uncovered in this book do not simply broaden our sense of those affected by the end of empire, they also require us to rethink how we characterise the domestic impact of decolonisation and the enduring legacies of imperialism. There is a broad consensus that the late 1950s and early 1960s represent a key transitional phase in public attitudes towards the Empire. Stuart Ward suggests that attitudes began to shift after the Suez crisis in 1956, from which point we can see signs of 'a more gradual and ambivalent awareness of British impotence in the world'.[11] John MacKenzie agrees that Suez was significant, but locates the key turning point slightly later, arguing that an illusion of imperial power persisted throughout the 1950s and until the rapid decolonisation of Britain's African colonies in the years between 1959 and 1965. By the end of this process, he suggests, it had become 'cruelly apparent that the British could no longer trade off (in both literal and metaphorical terms) on a richly powerful and imperial past'.[12] Wendy Webster puts similar emphasis on the first half of the decade, arguing that Churchill's funeral in 1965 marked a final public display of heroic visions of martial imperial masculinity that a few decades earlier had been commonplace.[13] There are some significant commonalities between these accounts and the story that this book tells, in particular, the undermining of heroic narratives of empire that these histories detail did filter through to associational life. As expressions of unqualified regret at the dissolution of the Empire were increasingly stigmatised in the early 1960s, there was also a considerable drop-off in appetite for outspoken nostalgia within associational life.

Where this book's findings differ from these existing periodisations is in relation to the high levels of anxiety about decline that they often identify as a key feature of the domestic response to the 1959–65 'implosion' of Empire.[14] This book does not suggest that anxiety and pessimism did not exist. As Stuart Ward has shown, the early 1960s saw a wave of 'state of Britain' writing by journalists, economists, academics, and public commentators, many of who expressed concerns about Britain's declining international status.[15] In his 1963 analysis *A State of England*, for example, Anthony Hartley worried that with no empire and only scraps of programmes and fragments of idealism left – 'a movement of penal reform here and a protest of apartheid there' – there was little left to give the nation a sense of purpose.[16] Writing towards the end of the decade, Michael Adams confidently diagnosed decolonisation as a 'traumatic moment for Britain' because it had required the 'renunciation of a role in the world which had become second nature'.[17] But while the pessimism of these diagnoses may have been a central feature of political discourse and popular culture, it does not hold true for the associations discussed in this book.[18] Indeed, the commonly used vocabulary of absences, amnesia, guilt, shame, and nostalgic longing gives the Empire an emotional charge that was simply not there in many of the ways in which people interacted with the declining and former empire.

As this book shows, the public responded to Britain's changing global role in diverse and often optimistic ways, imagining new futures that sought to tally the receding influence of Britain on a national level with the increased opportunities for international engagement becoming available to the British public on an individual or associational level. Crucially, this optimism was not because participants in associational life were uninterested in or unaware of decolonisation, but because they chose to read it through a pre-existing narrative of global benevolence in which they, as British citizens and participants in associational life, could play an active part. Prior to decolonisation, two imperial narratives had long run parallel to each other.[19] This book shows that while the first – centred on authority, expansionism, and militarised heroism – was dampened by the final implosion of formal Empire in the first half of the 1960s, the second – built on notions of a 'peace' empire of improvement and development – found new purchase among a set of middle-class organisations and associations in this period. For these groups the principles of international goodwill offered a sense of stabilising continuity that made them resistant to pessimistic readings of the 1960s implosion of Empire.

Most of the existing literature that addresses the British public's exposure to, and engagement with, the 'benevolent trusteeship thesis' in the post-war period has focused on the utility of the Commonwealth as its key symbol.[20] In these accounts the development of the idea of the Commonwealth as a symbol of enduring British influence and benevolence is seen to have acted as a potent anaesthetic against the trauma of decolonisation.[21] Historians of the period have tended to share the sense expressed by political commentators at the time that the invention of the Commonwealth saw the public through the most intense period of decolonisation and that, by the mid-1960s, it had mostly served its purpose.[22] In 1967, Bowden wrote a Cabinet memorandum on 'the value of the Commonwealth to Britain' in which he explained, writing pointedly in the past tense, that 'the modern Commonwealth was a triumphant technique to cover the process of decolonialisation, turning "Empire" into "Commonwealth." This both enabled us to extricate ourselves from colonial responsibilities with honour and psychologically cushioned the shock for the people of Britain adjusting to a new era.'[23] The case studies discussed in this book show that the Commonwealth did have *some* appeal in associational settings, but not at the levels imagined by some contemporary commentators.

As this book shows, for many middle-class participants in associational life the crucial 'anaesthetising' element of the 'benevolent trusteeship thesis' was not, as is usually suggested, the ideal of the Commonwealth, but rather a much more flexible conception of international goodwill – a broader faith in British people's desire and ability to do good in the world.[24] There was nothing new in the idea that Britain's responsibilities to humanity might extend beyond empire; the distinction has always been blurred, particularly in relation to humanitarian projects.[25] But in the 1960s the combined processes of decolonisation and globalisation further decoupled 'caring' from 'ruling', making it easier to detach 'benevolence' from specifically imperial responsibilities. Even though the literal geographies of associational benevolence were often still delineated by the boundaries of the former and declining empire, decolonisation made it possible for associations to imagine a world role for themselves that offered the promise of making a difference with neither the burdensome liability of colonial responsibility nor the negative connotations of imperial authority. By the middle of the decade, ideals of international benevolence gained more traction when reworked to apply to humanity as a whole than when limited to the Commonwealth.

Active citizenship and post-imperial responsibility

In this book, I approach associational performances of post-imperial responsibility and international benevolence through the lens of 'active citizenship'. Scholarship on the domestic impact of decolonisation has tended to focus on cultural and political representations of imperial decline. As a result, we are more used to thinking of the public as an audience to decolonisation – as consumers of cultural products and political discourse – than as active participants, shaping their own experiences of the end of empire. Yet, as I show, the combined processes of decolonisation and globalisation prompted civic organisations and members of the public to think through their responsibilities to their local community, their nation, their Commonwealth compatriots, and to the broader global population. Many members of associational life used the imaginative framework of 'active' or 'responsible' citizenship to emphasise the British public – rather than the British state – as key agents of change in a rapidly shrinking world.

A rich body of scholarship shows how the concept of active citizenship shaped associational life in the inter-war period. Organisers used the discourses of active citizenship to defend and give substance to the political rights of citizenship extended to women and working-class men in the aftermath of the First World War. As Helen McCarthy has shown, this period saw rapid growth in non-party mass membership associations, which had 'remarkable success in engaging voters in alternative forms of activism and organised sociability'.[26] Most of these organisations were self-consciously non-radical in their politics and approach, promoting increased civic participation rather than protest as the best route to societal change. As well as informing inward-facing claims for increased rights and representation, the traumas of the First World War also increased consciousness of social, political, and economic problems that transcended borders and contributed to the emergence of internationalism as both foreign policy and civic ideal.[27] In the inter-war period, active citizenship was central to developing projects of civic internationalism that encouraged identification with, and participation in, projects of international collaboration and extended civic responsibility to the international sphere.

As this book illustrates, the principles of active citizenship remained important in 1960s associational life, particularly in relation to international engagement. Yet ideas of active citizenship have been largely absent from research into the impact of decolonisation.[28] Instead, this literature has tended to focus on two other interrelated dimensions of citizenship: first, the political–legal relationship between citizens and the state; and second, the use of citizenship discourse to establish the boundaries of the national community and describe who 'belonged' within it.[29] In relation to the impact of decolonisation, this literature has focused on the intersections between citizenship and race. As Matthew Grant reminds us, 'the history of racial discrimination, and the fight against it, highlights that formal citizenship – the possession of a British passport and political rights – did not in itself define what citizenship was or who was a citizen in post-war Britain'.[30] Yet these are not the only dimensions of citizenship that are relevant to discussions of decolonisation.

Within the circles that this book discusses, those who spoke about civic responsibility were predominantly white and middle class. As such, by the 1960s, the active, performative elements of their citizenship – the specific ways they participated in and contributed to civil society – were underpinned by a legal status and sense of belonging that was never in question. I have not chosen this cohort with the intention of underplaying the significance of race to ideas of belonging in post-imperial Britain. Indeed, this book is indebted to the rich literature that charts the intricate relationship between British identity and racial identity in the post-war period.[31] Instead, I want to show that by temporarily shifting our focus away from debates about status and belonging and towards debates about purpose, we can bring to light underappreciated dimensions of national and civic identity in this period. For the groups discussed here, talking about responsible citizenship offered a way of thinking about Britain's place in the shifting post-war world – thinking, that is, about the kind of influence the nation and its population might exert on the global stage, the relationships they should seek with former colonies and the white British diaspora, and the narratives that should describe this activity. Debates about the best forms of international engagement within civic society bring hierarchical assumptions about Britain's global status into sharp focus; they reveal the influence of state priorities on civic activities; and they illuminate the complex interplay between local, national, and international dimensions of identity.

As well as contributing to debates about the domestic impact of decolonisation, this book also seeks to deepen our understanding of the changing nature of post-war civic society. The meaningful role that discourses of active citizenship played in middle-class associational life in the 1960s does not sit comfortably within traditional narratives about the decline of post-war civic society, which argue that the expansion of the welfare state eroded expectations of civic responsibility and left 'passive' citizens in its wake.[32] Yet nor does it entirely fit within the thrust of scholarship on the globalisation of civic society, which, although it challenges the declinist narrative, has tended to focus either on the rapid expansion of professionalised NGOs or on the confrontational, activist approach of new social movements.[33]

In isolation neither account of post-war civic society fully describes the associational worlds and projects of active citizenship discussed in this book. On the one hand, simplistic narratives of decline have not appreciated the adaptability or diversity of the voluntary sector in this period. Indeed, recent scholarship has challenged the assumption that the decline in traditional forms of civic participation such as church attendance should be read as evidence of the decline of British civic society as a whole. On the basis of the 1959 *Civic Culture Survey* and 1973 *Political Action Survey*, Peter Hall concludes that the average number of associational memberships held by individuals at all levels of educational attainment rose rapidly in the 1960s.[34] Decline in one area was being matched by growth elsewhere.[35] On the other hand, work on the globalisation of civic society and on left-wing new social movements has often overlooked the extent to which, in the 1960s, these new civic activities interacted with – and indeed relied upon – older forms of associational life and discourses of non-activist active citizenship.[36] To date, most work on global civil society has focused on what Matthew Hilton describes as the 'more dramatic forms of campaigning and protests that emerged out of new social movements associated with the 1960s': environmentalism, women's rights, anti-nuclear campaigns, and the anti-apartheid movement.[37] Yet the voluntary sector was 'not the preserve of the radically progressive'.[38] While the growth of NGOs and new politicised social movements did change the face of the voluntary sector in 1960s Britain, many long-standing non-activist associations – including the Women's Institute and Rotary Club, two of the key case studies used in this book – also engaged in the rapid internationalisation of public life, adapting their remits to respond to the shrinking world.

Networks and patterns of associational life

Empires are networked spaces. Flows of people, ideas, and goods have shaped not only the development of the imperial project overseas but also the experiences of those who remained in domestic Britain.[39] Personal, familial, business, and religious networks did not disappear with decolonisation.[40] A central concern of this book is to determine how the organisations and associations of civil society functioned as conduits for the flow of information and ideas between local, national, imperial and global spaces. How did individuals and communities navigate these international networks? Through what frameworks did these networks encourage their members to engage with the Empire? How did the ideological preoccupations and practical limitations of associational organisations shape the local or personal realities of 'experiencing empire'? Civic society was a space in which connections were made and lives opened up. But it was also a space in which identities were formed, boundaries policed, and power exerted. To answer these questions, I focus on 'the social worlds of citizenship' that existed within a set of five non-partisan organisations, each with predominantly (though not exclusively) white and middle-class memberships and supporters.[41] Where Jodi Burkett has shown that the end of empire had a significant impact on the aspirations and activities of progressive, anti-colonial, left-wing extra-parliamentary organisations, this book argues that decolonisation also affected the ostensibly apolitical dimensions of associational life, broadening our sense of who we consider to be international actors.[42]

The five organisations discussed are: the Royal Commonwealth Society (RCS), with a British membership of approximately 8000 made up largely of colonial administrators, retired officers in the colonial civil service, and businessmen with imperial interests; Rotary International in Great Britain and Ireland (RIBI) with a membership of approximately 44,000 middle-class businessmen from across Britain; the Women's Institute (WI) with a membership of approximately half a million women spread across more than 8000 predominantly rural clubs; the humanitarian organisation Christian Aid, whose most active supporters came from existing forms of religious associational life; and the United Nations sponsored Freedom from Hunger Campaign (FFHC), whose British efforts drew on a wide base of support including government, individuals, and existing associations.[43] Collectively the case studies represent a broad section of middle-class society, but their distinct characteristics – their memberships, remits, and access to international networks – also allow us to chart the uneven impact of decolonisation on different sections of the British public. To uncover the distinct trajectories of these organisations and their members, I have used archival and published material produced by the organisations themselves alongside the published material of external commentators, particularly the press, and, where possible, governmental records detailing state interaction with civic activities.

The RCS, WI, and RIBI were, at heart, mechanisms for sociability and service. Their purpose was twofold: to serve the needs of their fee-paying members and to serve the needs of the wider community to which they felt they belonged. For the RCS, this was understood quite narrowly as a responsibility to promote the Commonwealth to the British public while developing collaborative projects with other Commonwealth nations. The RCS was the largest and most senior of a much larger group of associations, including the Victoria League and Royal Over-Seas League, established in the nineteenth and early twentieth centuries in order to serve those with colonial interests while maintaining and strengthening imperial ties. In the 1960s, the RCS served an ageing membership who had once made up the scaffolding of colonial administration, meeting the needs of those who wanted to maintain an intellectual engagement with the changing Commonwealth as well as those who simply wanted the company of like-minded people.[44] While the work of the RCS provides a window onto the impact of decolonisation on those most involved in the Empire – and of their attempts to influence wider British society – the WI's and RIBI's broad spectrum of motivations, activities, and concerns makes them ideal case studies with which to ask: what did the Empire mean to those for whom it did not mean everything?

When Mrs Rachel Wild of the Cliffords Women's Institute in Yorkshire asked her daughter to join the WI in the late 1960s the daughter turned her request down with the exclamation 'oh mother, jams and jellies'.[45] The following extracts from the records of monthly meetings kept by the Burythorpe Women's Institute, also in Yorkshire, do little to challenge such an image.

March 1952:   Competition for the best darn in a sock heel.
June 1952:   Miss Seaton gave a demonstration on salads.
July 1954:   Visit to the Blind Institute in Hull to be arranged. Demonstration on butter icing.
June 1959:   Presentation on the Hoovermatic Washing Machine.
August 1960:   Competition for the best necklace made from garden produce.
June 1961:   Presentation on soft slippers.[46]

Domestic concerns were undoubtedly an important part of members' involvement in the movement, but there was more to the WI than the proverbial jam and Jerusalem. Established in Britain in 1915, by the inter-war period it was one of the few women-only organisations to hold monthly meetings that were partly social, partly educational, and partly a forum for pressure-group politics.[47] As Caitriona Beaumont has shown, the WI provided rural housewives with access to cultural and educational pursuits, and gave them the means to shape British society.[48] Alongside sock darning and salad making, the WI involved itself in a wide range of civic issues in the post-war period, guided by the principles of active citizenship. Some of these activities, such as campaigns on equal pay and family planning provision, directly supported women in their roles as wives, mothers, and workers; others addressed broader concerns such as road safety and littering.[49] Less well known, but also a significant dimension of WI life is the movement's international activity.[50]

Over the course of the 1960s, responding to the decolonising, globalising world, the WI involved itself in a wide range of international issues including international friendship schemes, educational initiatives, and philanthropic fundraising. As one member put it for the WI's monthly magazine *Home and Country* in 1967, 'I can't imagine that any WI member anywhere hasn't had a finger in some international pie or other by now.'[51] These activities make it possible to consider how the 'female space' of the WI shaped its members' experience of decolonisation. As Joanna Lewis summarises, 'European women, whether as wives of administrators, as missionaries, as lobbyists at home, or working overseas as amateur do-gooders, nurses, teachers, welfare officers are now seen as having played an important part' in upholding the imperial project.[52] By studying the international work of the WI in the 1960s we are able to follow the well-plotted trajectory of women's involvement with empire into new territory, beyond the 'end' of empire.

The Rotary Club offered similar opportunities for sociability and active citizenship to business and professional men to those that the WI provided for rural women, but with a greater emphasis on the development of business relationships. The movement had its origins in North American business networking culture; it was founded in 1905 in Chicago as an informal luncheon club and rapidly grew into a global movement.[53] Each Rotary Club was encouraged to admit one individual from each local business or profession with the aim of building a representative community of engaged and responsible citizens. From its early days, Rotary's institutional vision centred on local community service and international engagement with businessmen around the world, seeing little contradiction between these two imperatives.[54] Members were expected to adhere to the principles of 'service before self' in vocational, community, and international spheres. Like the WI, its membership grew rapidly in the inter-war period and, by 1960, there were 40,257 members in clubs spread across Britain, each belonging to the national organising structure Rotary International in Great Britain and Ireland.[55] By considering WI and Rotary participation in local clubs across Britain we can trace how the impact of decolonisation and globalisation registered beyond the nation's more commonly studied urban centres.

The second set of organisations discussed in this book are humanitarian NGOs. These differ from the membership organisations in a number of key ways and therefore allow us to consider the impact of decolonisation across a broader range of civic activity. First, the remit of humanitarian organisations was predominantly outward facing (most of their work was directed at serving the needs of those in the global south); second, their main stated responsibility was to the recipients of aid rather than a fee-paying membership; and, finally, they placed a much higher value on expertise and professionalisation than was generally the case in membership organisations. Existing scholarship on post-war humanitarianism has focused on these elements of NGOs' work, seeking to explain the rapid growth of the sector, detail the changing nature of operational practices, and trace the internal debates that drove these developments.[56] This book builds on this work by thinking about the particular influence of decolonisation on these processes. The FFHC, an international UN sponsored initiative to encourage agricultural development, and Christian Aid, the humanitarian wing of the British Council of Churches, were both at the centre of these changes and illustrate the different ways that humanitarian organisations chose to engage with Britain's imperial past.

This book also differentiates itself from existing scholarship on humanitarianism by integrating its analysis of the ideological debates taking place within Christian Aid and the FFHC with a close examination of the understudied experiences of donor participants. Both organisations were committed to raising public awareness, both generated funds through the organisation of local committees and activities, and both provided diverse opportunities for the public to engage with debates about international aid and development. In these areas there are significant overlaps between the donor side of humanitarian work and older forms of associational life. As well as targeting new NGOs, the FFHC also sought support from a wide range of pre-existing institutions – including the WI and Rotary Club. Christian Aid, one of the new NGOs established at the end of the Second World War, may represent the modernisation and professionalisation of the charity sector, but its fundraising efforts and arguments about post-imperial responsibility were also influenced by longstanding rhythms of religious associational life. Its work reveals how religious organisations adapted in the face of decolonisation, but it also illustrates the extent to which ostensibly 'outward facing' humanitarian activity was determined by local priorities, expertise, and rivalries.

Histories of civic forms of international engagement in the 1960s have tended to focus on its more radical manifestations, feeding into a familiar narrative about the decline of deference and rise of political activism.[57] The Anti-Apartheid Movement, Campaign for Nuclear Disarmament (CND), and anti-Vietnam War movement, for example, all employed the strategies of public protest to challenge the British state to act responsibly on the international stage. In contrast, the organisations that I discuss in this book mobilised members of ostensibly apolitical associational life to support non-confrontational forms of international activity. As Caitriona Beaumont has shown in her work on the domestic efforts of mainstream, non-feminist women's organisations to promote the interests and needs of women in the post-war period, we should not overlook the impact that non-radical organisations might have on public debates about citizenship and public responsibility in this period, nor the significant number of people that they engaged in these debates.[58]

The RCS, WI, and Rotary weren't simply non-radical by comparison to other movements of the time, they incorporated a conscious rejection of radicalism into their institutional identities, consistently discouraging confrontational protest. While Christian Aid and the FFHC made space for political activism, particularly by the end of the 1960s, the majority of their supporters – and the majority of the members of the RCS, WI, and Rotary – participated in ways that did not seek to challenge the political establishment. Where these groups did identify the need for change – for example, in relation to the demand for increased government spending that formed a key element of the FFHC – their approach was reformist rather than reactionary. All five organisations were committed to non-partisanship and generally avoided engaging with parliamentary politics. They saw themselves as acting independently of the state, carrying out work alongside or in addition to it, rather than in partnership with or opposition to it.

This positioning certainly suited the political temperaments of the majority of these groups' members: largely small-c conservatives who felt financially comfortable and secure in their own political rights. Having profited from the political and economic situation as it stood, they had little to gain from any upending of the status quo.[59] But, the anti-radicalism of associational groups was more than a convenience; it was transformed into a largely coherent, though delusional, claim for political neutrality that in turn acted as the ideological underpinning for all the groups' models of international engagement. For the majority of the groups discussed in this book this meant arguing that their work was guided not by political ideology, but dictated by 'common sense' and a commitment to 'service'. Speaking to the Rotary National Conference in 1965, Morris Barr argued that to secure 'Britain's place in international affairs', the assembled Rotarians should 'forget the politics, remember the people. Only the selfish, the beaten, the cynical and the intellectually dishonest fail us, and this sets a task for you and for me [...]. It is a matter of "Service above Self."[60] Members of these organisations had their own political allegiances and inclinations. Broadly speaking, while the diverse groups affiliated to the FFHC occupied a broad range of positions on the political spectrum, RCS, WI, and Rotary members were more likely to be right-leaning, and Christian Aid organisers and participants more likely to be on the centre left. But the concept of service – of limited self-sacrifice and communal endeavour – allowed them to see their active citizenship and international engagements as explicitly separate from these other allegiances. Associations' claims to apolitical neutrality had important implications for the way that they described Britain's relationship with the outside world. As this book shows, discourses of active citizenship often worked in ways that depoliticised the power dynamics of imperialism. While it was empowering for individual members of civic society to focus on civic action, this emphasis also helped to relocate the issue of responsibility away from the political sphere, and from a context in which issues like state culpability, reparations, and compensation might be discussed. This meant that, unlike more politicised campaigns on the left, the associational groups in this book placed their emphasis on the needs rather than the rights of those they sought to help.[61] Rights implied a political rather than a moral responsibility that was not compatible with ideas of apolitical service. The assumptions and practices of outward-facing active citizenship that these organisations established in the 1960s have had an enduring impact on narratives about Britain's international responsibilities into the twenty-first century.

Models of international engagement: the structure of the book

There were three predominant strands of international engagement: those founded on knowledge, those founded on interpersonal relationships, and those founded on philanthropy. All of these forms of engagement shared the same set of underlying assumptions: that responsibility and benevolence were inherently British characteristics; that Britain's experiences as a colonial power had furnished its citizens with a set of skills uniquely suited to make a difference in the post-imperial world; and that Britain should seek to maintain a large global role on the basis of these proficiencies and inclinations. Through each form of international engagement, members of civic society repurposed imperial narratives and networks for a post-imperial age.

In order to map the development of these ideas of international responsibility, benevolence, and exceptionalism, each chapter of this book addresses a distinctive form of international engagement and interrogates the beliefs, practices, and people that informed it. Chapter 1 is about the promotion of the Commonwealth as a model for international cooperation. Using the activities of the Royal Commonwealth Society (RCS), it assesses the afterlife of empire as it was lived by those who had been the most involved. Negotiating the transition from Empire to Commonwealth was a complex process and this chapter, more than any of the others, is about the difficulty of adaptation. This is not a story of triumphant success – the membership of the RCS was an ageing cohort, often more interested in sociability than public engagement. But nor is it a story of outright failure. Many found scope for optimism by reflecting on the possibilities of the new modern Commonwealth. This chapter acts to set up the other four by illustrating what a preoccupation with empire might look like and by illustrating how those with vested interests established discourses that permeated wider circles of associational life.

Chapters 2 and 3 use the Women's Institute and Rotary Club to explore how education and friendship offered different routes to international understanding. Both routes described ways of 'knowing' people from other countries, but where the former promoted detached interest and objective observation, the latter was built on ideas of intimacy, exchange, and direct contact. Chapter 2 shows how imperial decline shaped both the practical and discursive dimensions of educative activities such as film screenings, lectures, and 'International Days'. Global events determined not only which parts of the world were worth investing time in, but also which aspects of foreign life were worth knowing about. Chapter 3 addresses the emotional history of international engagement by focusing on two projects designed to develop familiarity and intimacy across international boundaries: hospitality for foreign visitors to Britain (particularly overseas students) and building friendships with people living overseas. As both chapters illustrate, imperial legacies determined not only the geographies of these connections but also the hierarchical structures through which they were conceived. The precise circumstances in which these different kinds of 'knowing' were brought into play tells us a lot about how members of British society imagined their place in the world.

Chapters 4 and 5 assess secular and religious humanitarian engagements with the decolonising empire. They use the FFHC and Christian Aid as windows onto the changing experience of international philanthropy in the 1960s. Chapter 4 shows how the FFHC became a way to talk about Britain's 'lost vocation' and imagine new forms of benevolent intervention. Chapter 5 uses the work of Christian Aid to address the neglect of religious institutions in histories of the domestic impact of decolonisation. It shows how the complex interplay between domestic and international contexts determined the everyday experiences of religious humanitarian action. By the end of the 1960s, humanitarianism emerged as the dominant form of civic international engagement, attracting far more attention and energy than projects that sought to promote knowledge and friendship. The final two chapters show that three key factors determined this outcome. First, the malleability of humanitarian discourse meant that it was able to support multiple, contradictory narratives about British exceptionalism, ranging from those that were critical of Britain's imperial past to those that were nostalgic about colonial rule. Second, it was driven by an increasingly professionalised infrastructure that recognised the need to embrace both traditional and modern organising strategies in order to engage large numbers of the public. In comparison, friendship and educational projects remained more amateur. Third, it was the most obvious manifestation of the narrative of benevolent Britain that had come to underpin a wide range of international civic engagement. This being the case, why have I not chosen to write a book simply about humanitarianism? Although it came to dominate civic international engagements, humanitarianism did not exist in a vacuum; it always operated alongside other outward facing associational commitments. Associational practices of understanding and friendship were not only important components of narratives about benevolent responsibility, they also made it easier to mobilise crucial networks in support of humanitarian activity.

The concluding chapter brings the five case studies back together to consider how they can help us to understand why narratives of British benevolence and responsibility that had their origins in imperialism have endured into the twenty-first century. The 1960s were a crucial transitional decade in which members of British associational life reasserted, reframed, and repackaged their relationship with the spaces of the Commonwealth and former empire, developing new practices of civic engagement to suit the changing environments of the decolonising world and of domestic associational life. The practices of the WI, the RCS, and the Rotary Club; the supporters of the FFHC and Christian Aid; and the individual enthusiasts that made these organisations work reveal that empire resonated beyond the governing elite. Imperial decline stimulated productive and optimistic discussions – alongside those that were anxious and regretful – within middle-class communities in industrial towns, in isolated villages, in seaside expatriate havens, in churches, chapels, school assembly rooms, town halls, and sitting rooms across Britain.

[16]

Notes

1 School of African and Oriental Studies (hereafter SOAS), Christian Aid archive (hereafter CA) I/5/4 'Our Daily Bread' play *c.*1964, Schools Secretary Bridget Russell 1964–65.

2 Emily S. Rosenberg, *Transnational Currents in a Shrinking World* (London: Harvard University Press, 2014). On responses to increased mobility within the British Empire in the 1840s see Alan Lester, *Imperial networks: Creating Identities in Nineteenth-century South Africa and Britain* (London: Routledge, 2005), p. 179. 'Shrinking World', an 1866 article about the transatlantic telegraph, was reprinted in *The Times* (27 July 1966).

3 'Salesmen "Too Diffident"', *The Times* (9 May 1961); 'New Health Regulations For Air Passengers Predicted', *The Times* (11 February 1966).

4 R. J. D. Evans, 'A Commonwealth Magazine?', *The Times* (13 May 1959).

5 Andrew Thompson (ed.), *Britain's Experience of Empire in the Twentieth Century* (Oxford: Oxford University Press, 2012), p. 2.

6 Antoinette Burton (ed.), *After the Imperial Turn: Thinking With and Through the Nation* (Durham NC: Duke University Press, 2003), p. 2. See also, Catherine Hall, *Civilising Subjects: Metropole and Colony in the English Imagination, 1830–1867* (Cambridge: Polity Press, 2002); Catherine Hall and Sonya O. Rose (eds), *At Home with Empire: Metropolitan Cultures and the Imperial World* (Cambridge: Cambridge University Press, 2006); and the Manchester University Press 'Studies in Imperialism' series.

7 Benita Parry cited in Antoinette Burton, 'Who needs the nation? Interrogating "British" history', *Journal of Historical Sociology*, 10:3 (1997), 232.

8 Bill Schwarz, '"The only white man in there": the re-racialization of England, 1956–1968', *Race & Class*, 38:1 (1996), 65.

9 See, for example, Bill Schwarz, *The White Man's World* (Oxford: Oxford University Press, 2011); Camilla Schofield, *Enoch Powell and the Making of Postcolonial Britain* (Cambridge: Cambridge University Press, 2013); Stuart Ward (ed.), *British Culture and the End of the Empire* (Manchester: Manchester University Press, 2001); Wendy Webster, *Englishness and Empire, 1939–1965* (Oxford: Oxford University Press, 2005); Webster, *Imagining Home: Gender, 'Race' and National Identity, 1945–1964* (London: Taylor & Francis, 1998). Those taking a different and/or broader approach include Jordanna Bailkin, *Afterlife of Empire* (London: University of California Press, 2012); Elizabeth Buettner, *Europe after Empire: Decolonisation, Society, and Culture* (Cambridge: Cambridge University Press, 2016); Jodi Burkett, *Constructing Post-imperial Britain: Britishness, 'Race' and the Radical Left in the 1960s* (London: Palgrave Macmillan, 2013).

10 See, for example, Caroline Hoefferle, *British Student Activism in the Long Sixties* (Abingdon: Routledge, 2013); Burkett, *Constructing Post-imperial Britain*; Lent, *British Social Movements Since 1945*; Celia Hughes, *Young Lives on the Left: Sixties Activism and the Liberation of the Self* (Oxford: Oxford University Press, 2015).

11 Ward (ed.), *British Culture and the End of Empire*, p. 8.

12 John M. MacKenzie, 'The persistence of Empire in metropolitan culture', in Ward (ed.), *British Culture and the End of Empire*, pp. 21–36. Bailkin, *Afterlife of Empire* also focuses on 1958–62 as a key transitional period.

13 Webster, *Englishness and Empire*, p. 184. On changing attitudes towards imperial masculinity see Jeffrey Richards, 'Imperial heroes for a post-imperial age: films and the end of empire', in Ward (ed.), *British Culture and the End of Empire*, pp. 128–44; Max Jones *et al.*, 'Decolonising imperial heroes: Britain and France', *Journal of Imperial and Commonwealth History*, 42 (2014), 787–825.

14 For further discussions of decline and decolonisation see: Dan Rebellato, 'Look back at Empire: British theatre and imperial decline', in Ward (ed.), *British Culture and the End of Empire*, pp. 86–7; Ward, 'No nation could be broker', in Ward (ed.), *British Culture and the End of Empire*, p. 108.

15 Ward (ed.), *British Culture and the End of Empire*, pp. 9–11.

16 *Ibid.*, p. 13.

17 *Ibid.*, pp. 23–4.

18 On the interdependence of optimism and pessimism, see Bailkin, *Afterlife of Empire*, p. 21; on left-wing optimism see Burkett, *Constructing Post-Imperial Britain.*

19 Peter Hansen, 'Coronation Everest: The Empire and Commonwealth in the "second Elizabethan age"', in Ward (ed.), *British Culture and the End of Empire*, p. 58.

20 Rebellato, 'Look back at Empire', p. 86.

21 John Darwin, 'The fear of falling: British politics and imperial decline since 1900', *Transactions of the Royal Historical Society*, 36 (1986), 42. This interpretation has been repeated and endorsed by others including Rebellato, 'Look back at Empire', p. 86; Hansen, 'Coronation Everest', p. 69; Craggs, 'Hospitality in geopolitics', 93; K. Srinivasan, *The Rise, Decline, and Future of the British Commonwealth* (London: Palgrave Macmillan, 2015), p. 116; Burkett, *Constructing Post-Imperial Britain*, pp. 68–72.

22 For discussion of the Commonwealth in political discourse see Buettner, *Europe After Empire*, pp. 67–77. See also, Enoch Powell's anonymous contribution to *The Times* in which the Commonwealth was a project of 'self-deception' that had 'been employed on the grand scale' but that, in 1964, had 'served [its] purpose'. 'Now the wounds have almost healed and the skin formed again beneath the plaster and bandages, and they can come off' in 'Patriotism based on reality not on dreams', *The Times* (2 April 1964). For further discussion of Powell see Schofield, *Enoch Powell.*

23 'The Value of the Commonwealth to Britain' Cabinet memorandum by Mr Bowden, Annex, 24 April 1967 NA, CAB 129/129, C(67)59 reprinted in S.R. Ashton and Wm. Roger Louis (eds), *East of Suez and the Commonwealth 1964–1971*, Part II *Europe, Rhodesia, Commonwealth* (*British Documents on the End of Empire*, Series A, Volume 4) (London 2004), 418–29. Also discussed in Buettner, *Europe After Empire*, p. 71.

24 On the role of morality in left-wing international activism in this period, see Burkett, *Constructing Post-Imperial Britain*, p. 20.

25 Richard Huzzey, 'Minding civilisation and humanity in 1867: A case study in British imperial culture and Victorian anti-slavery', *The Journal of Imperial and Commonwealth History*, 40:5 (2012), 807–25. See also Emily Baughan, 'The Imperial War Relief Fund and the All British Appeal: Commonwealth, conflict and Conservatism within the British humanitarian movement, 1920–25', *The Journal of Imperial and Commonwealth History*, 40:5 (2012), 845–61.

26 Helen McCarthy, 'Parties, voluntary associations, and democratic politics in interwar Britain', *The Historical Journal*, 50:4 (2007), 892.

27 Daniel Gorman, 'Empire, internationalism, and the Campaign Against the Traffic in Women and Children in the 1920s', *Twentieth Century British History*, 19 (2008), 189.

28 The most significant exception is Jodi Burkett's work on anti-colonial, left-wing civic organizations. Burkett, *Constructing Post-imperial Britain.*

29 For a summary of this literature see Matthew Grant, 'Historicising citizenship in post-war Britain', *Historical Journal*, 59:4 (2016), 1187–206. See also, Kathleen Paul, *Whitewashing Britain: Race and Citizenship in the Post-war Era* (Ithaca, NY: Cornell University Press, 1997).

30 Grant, 'Historicising citizenship', 1193. See also Kennetta Hammond Parry, *London is the Place for Me: Black Britons, Citizenship, and the Politics of Race* (Oxford: Oxford University Press, 2016).

31 See, for example, Schwarz, *White Man's World*; Schofield, *Enoch Powell*; Webster *Imagining Home*; Paul, *Whitewashing Britain.*

32 For example, Frank Prochaska, *Christianity and Social Service in Modern Britain: The Disinherited Spirit* (Oxford: Oxford University Press, 2006). For statistics on membership figures see Matthew Hilton *et al., A Historical Guide to NGOs:*

Charities, Civil Society and the Voluntary Sector Since 1945 (Basingstoke: Palgrave Macmillan, 2012), pp. 22–5.

33 For example, Akira Iriye, *Global Community: The Role of International Organizations in the Making of the Contemporary World* (London: University of London Press, 2002); Adam Lent, *British Social Movements Since 1945: Sex, Colour, Peace and Power* (Basingstoke: Palgrave Macmillan, 2001); Håkan Thörn, *Anti-Apartheid and the Emergence of a Global Civil Society* (Basingstoke: Palgrave Macmillan, 2006).

34 P. A. Hall, 'Social capital in Britain', *British Journal of Politics*, 29 (1999), 417–16.

35 Hilton *et al.*, *A Historical Guide to NGOs*, p. 22.

36 For a discussion of this interplay in relation to human rights campaigning see Chris Moores, *Civil Liberties and Human Rights in Twentieth-Century Britain* (Cambridge: Cambridge University Press, 2017).

37 Matthew Hilton, 'Politics is ordinary: non-governmental organizations and political participation in contemporary Britain', *Twentieth Century British History*, 22:2 (2011), 240.

38 Caitriona Beaumont, 'Housewives, workers and citizens: voluntary women's organizations and the Campaign for Women's rights in England and Wales during the post-war period', in Nick Crowson, Matthew Hilton and James McKay (eds), *NGOs in Contemporary Britain: Non-state Actors in Society and Politics since 1945* (London: Springer, 2009), p. 61. See also, Lawrence Black, *Redefining British Politics: Culture, Consumerism and Participation, 1954–70* (London: Springer, 2010).

39 See, for example, Alan Lester, 'Imperial circuits and networks: geographies of the British Empire', *History Compass*, 4:1 (2006), 124–41.

40 For a discussion of these networks see Andrew Thompson with Meaghan Kowalsky, 'Social life and cultural representation: Empire in the public imagination', in Thompson (ed.), *Britain's Experience of Empire*, pp. 251–97.

41 Grant uses the phrase 'social world of citizenship' in Grant, 'Historicizing citizenship', 1205.

42 Burkett, *Constructing Post-imperial Britain*.

43 Women's Institute, 'History of the W.I.: 1960s', www.thewi.org.uk/standard.aspx?id=63 (accessed 1 May 2010); *1965 Proceedings: Fifty-sixth Annual Convention of Rotary International* (Rotary International, 1965), p. 260.

44 Ruth Craggs, 'Cultural Geographies of the Modern Commonwealth from 1947 to 1973' (PhD dissertation, University of Nottingham, 2009), p. 69.

45 'We can play politics now', *Guardian* (9 June 1971).

46 Borthwick Institute for Archives, York (hereafter Borthwick), PR.BUR, 42–3, Burythorpe Parish Minutes, 11 March 1952, 22 June 1952, 13 July 1954, June 1959, August 1960, June 1961.

47 Maggie Andrews, *The Acceptable Face of Feminism: The Women's Institute as a Social Movement, 1915–1960* (London: Lawrence & Wishart, 1997), p. 154.

48 Beaumont, 'Housewives, workers and citizens' in Crowson, Hilton and McKay (eds), *NGOs in Contemporary Britain*, p. 59.

49 Beaumont, 'Housewives, workers and citizens'.

50 Discussed in Sophie Skelton, 'From Peace to Development: a Reconstitution of British Women's International Politics, c.1945–1970' (Phd dissertation, University of Birmingham, 2014); Andrews, *Acceptable Face of Feminism*.

51 *Home and Country* (October 1967).

52 Joanna Lewis, *Empire State Building: War and Welfare in Kenya, 1925–52* (Oxford: Oxford University Press, 2000), p. 11.

53 McCarthy, 'Parties, voluntary associations', 895.

54 Brendan Goff, 'The Heartland abroad: The Rotary Club's Mission of Civic Internationalism' (PhD dissertation, University of Michigan, 2008), p. 13.

55 *1960 Proceedings: Fifty-First Annual Convention of Rotary International* (Rotary International, 1960), p. 264.

56 Michael Barnett, *Empire of Humanity: A History of Humanitarianism* (Ithaca, NY: Cornell University Press, 2011); Matthew Hilton, 'Ken Loach and the Save the Children film: humanitarianism, imperialism, and the changing role of charity in

post-war Britain', *The Journal of Modern History*, 87:2 (2015), 357–94; Andrew Jones, 'The Disasters Emergency Committee (DEC) and the humanitarian industry in Britain, 1963–85', *Twentieth Century British History*, 26:4 (2014), 573–601.

57 For a critique of decline of deference narratives see Frank Mort, 'The Ben Pimlott memorial lecture 2010: The permissive society revisited', *Twentieth Century British History*, 22:2 (2011), 269–98.

58 Caitriona Beaumont, *Housewives and Citizens: Domesticity and the Women's Movement in England, 1928–64* (Oxford: Oxford University Press, 2013).

59 For analysis of the political nature of apolitical organisations in the interwar period see Ross McKibbin, *Classes and cultures: England 1918–1951* (Oxford: Oxford University Press, 1998).

60 Morris Barr, *Rotary* (May 1965), p. 141.

61 Moores, *Civil Liberties and Human Rights*.

CHAPTER ONE

Imperial lives and Commonwealth visions

Commonwealth societies and emotional storehouses

In 1969, the Deputy Secretary-General of the Commonwealth Secretariat, A. L. Adu, gave a speech at the Royal Commonwealth Society (RCS) on 'the reality and potential capacity of the Commonwealth'. Adu was from Ghana – the first British colony in sub-Saharan Africa to gain independence – and he spoke to his predominantly white British audience as a representative of the multiracial 'New Commonwealth'. He used his platform at the RCS not only to set out the work of the Commonwealth Secretariat, but also to critique what he saw as Britain's problematic emotional connection to its imperial past. 'I am uncommitted to the past', he argued,

> to the weight of British colonial history, to the curious store-houses of emotion and reflex about colonial rule and the British Empire. I do not feel guilty about the Commonwealth. I do not see it as a relic of empire ... I do not feel sentimental about the Commonwealth ... Naturally I am not untouched by the Commonwealth's past but I, unlike others in this country in particular, am not intimately bound up in it. I have, I hope, no weight of feeling to shift from one shoulder to the other before I can think clearly about it.[1]

Whether rooted in guilt or nostalgia, Adu had determined, the British public's unprocessed memories of empire prevented them from thinking clearly about the Commonwealth's present-day possibilities.

Was Adu right about the weight of feeling that he saw resting on his audience's shoulders? At the time and since, the Commonwealth has often been disregarded as an accidental relic of the past, as 'the ghost or dilution of empire'.[2] John Darwin, for instance, has echoed Enoch Powell's argument that the Commonwealth provided an 'anaesthetizing rhetoric' that helped Britain come to terms with the loss of the Empire.[3] Writing in 1967, Sir Paul Gore-Booth, Permanent Under-Secretary of

State at the Foreign Office, drew on religious imagery to explain that the Commonwealth had 'temper[ed] the wind to the shorn lamb of British public opinion'.[4] Though the Commonwealth may offer few practical advantages, Gore-Booth suggested, it had served an important psychological function by protecting a vulnerable national psyche from the trauma of losing its empire. While we should be wary of pathologising national responses to imperial decline in such broad terms, mapping specific public reactions to the changing Commonwealth can offer important insights into the domestic experience of decolonisation.

Like Adu, I am interested in how those whose lives had been 'intimately bound up' in Empire engaged with the changing Commonwealth. It is highly likely that the majority of those in attendance at Adu's talk would have had direct connections to the British Empire. RCS membership included men such as Arthur Barton (1892–1983), who had worked in Imperial Customs and Excise since 1912, with posts in Kenya, Guiana, Jamaica, Trinidad and Tobago, and Nigeria, and Roger Barltrop (1930–2009), who held posts in Nigeria, Rhodesia, and Ankara as well as working between 1960 and 1969 at the Foreign and Commonwealth Office.[5] It also included those who became involved in the Empire through other means, such as Herbert Barnell (1907–73), who held the post of Chief Scientific Adviser for the Ministry of Agriculture, but had worked as a biochemist in Trinidad in the 1930s; Edith Batten (1905–85), who had not worked overseas or in an official capacity, but was organising secretary of the British Association of Residential Settlements in the 1930s; Reverend John Gilbert Hindley (1910–86), who worked in Hong Kong and London and was General Secretary of the Church Assembly Overseas Council from 1955 to 1963; and George Bilainkin (1903–81), who worked at the *Jamaica Daily Gleaner* and the *Straits Daily Echo* in Malaysia in the inter-war period before returning to England to become a diplomatic correspondent for the *Star*.[6]

This ex-imperial composition makes the RCS a key point of access to expatriates returning to Britain at the end of empire. Despite the fact that an estimated five to seven million people were repatriated to Europe during the thirty-five years of decolonisation following the Second World War, relatively little has been written about the experiences or impact of these migrations.[7] For many returning Britons, the repatriate experience was profoundly unsatisfying. As Elizabeth Buettner has shown, narratives of the ennui experienced by men once they reached the civil service retirement age of 55 had been well established since the Victorian era.[8] These experiences were often exacerbated by decolonisation, which engendered a sense of resentment among expatriates at Britain's apparent betrayal of what they had worked to achieve in the Empire.[9] As Frederick Cooper reminds us, not everyone who returned to Britain in the wake of decolonisation 'sought refuge in the collective identification of colonial repatriate – some simply wanted to get on with their lives'.[10] However, faced with disillusionment, many did find relief in the form of rediscovered companions from overseas, forming communities that allowed them to associate with others of a similar background.

The RCS is one of many organisations that provided an associational framework for these interactions. Since its inception as the Royal Colonial Institute in 1868, the society aimed to provide a meeting place for those 'connected with the colonies' or 'taking an interest' in colonial affairs.[11] To become a member was to self-identify as a sym-pathiser with the Empire, the Commonwealth, or both. People joined, suggests former RCS Secretary-General Stuart Mole, 'almost like adding one of those plastic badges to your lapel as a strand of your beliefs or your identity'.[12] This chapter uses the society as a window on to a group of people who had not only been involved in the imperial project, but whose interest in the Empire and Commonwealth was sufficient to inform their social as well as working lives.

As well as offering us insights into the experiences of those most invested in the imperial project, organisations like the RCS are also important for our understanding of the wider impact of decolonisation. As Elizabeth Buettner has argued, former participants in the imperial project played a key role in shaping how the Empire was understood among the wider public.[13] The RCS had an explicit remit not only to serve the needs of its paying members, but also to foster 'Commonwealth Consciousness' in the British public as a whole. While a considerable body of scholarship shows the significant contribution that imperial organisations made to domestic imperial culture in the early twentieth century, we know very little about their responses to the end of empire.[14]

The late 1950s and 1960s were a crucial transitional period for once-imperial organisations like the RCS. Not only did they have to come to terms with the loss of the Empire – making what one member described as a 'mental somersault' – they also needed to get to grips with what was replacing it.[15] The Commonwealth that Adu referred to in 1969 was a significantly different organisation from that which had existed in the inter-war period. Once the preserve of white dominions – bound together by ties of kith and kin – the makeup of the post-war Commonwealth was dramatically altered by decolonisation. The addition of India and Pakistan in 1947 marked the beginning of a 'New' mul-tiracial Commonwealth. Over the next two decades, the vast majority of those British colonies that gained independence joined the Com-monwealth as nation-states, rapidly expanding its ranks. By the end of the 1960s, the pre-Second World War club of cooperative and comfortable informality between white dominions was contained within a much larger New Commonwealth, dominated in number by multiracial and newly independent nations. This transition was neither smooth nor straightforward. Writing in 1964, Guy Arnold declared that the 'modern' Commonwealth was an organisation with which Britain appeared 'to have little idea what to do'.[16] In the same year, John Hope, Chairman of the Royal Commonwealth Society Council, explained that the new Commonwealth was still 'finding its feet'.[17] For most of the 1960s, so too were the associational organisations that sought to support it.

For organisations established at the height of the British Empire, much of the decade was spent trying to figure out how to stay relevant in the context of decolonisation. Many imperial organisations were unable or unwilling to adapt to the new circumstances. *Corona*, the Journal of Overseas Colonial Service, decided to cease publication in 1962 rather than seek a new audience, concluding that their colonial connections 'might be an embarrassment to those who had not shared our origins with us'.[18] The Society for the Overseas Settlement of British Women, which had supported female emigration to the British Empire since 1919, was forced to close in 1964 when the Treasury withdrew its financial support. Despite its attempts to adapt to changing circumstances – in particular, by broadening its work to include the support of short-term migrants working in the field of international development – the society's continuing focus on 'old Commonwealth' countries no longer met the British state's diplomatic needs.[19]

Other Empire and Commonwealth societies were better able to weather the storm, either by adapting the services that they provided or by redefining their relationship to the changing Commonwealth. The Victoria League, English Speaking Union, Royal Over-Seas League, and RCS have survived into the twenty-first century. As Alex May argues, for those organisations that 'emerged from the end of empire committed to the new Commonwealth, it was a very different world from that in which they had been conceived'.[20] Rather than offer a shallow survey of the adaptations that each of these different organisations underwent, this chapter provides a detailed case study of the experiences of the RCS and its members. In particular, it is important to identify the varied roles played by the 8000–11,000 UK members, its nine regional branches, and the central administrative committees based at its London headquarters. This chapter uncovers the dilemmas and conflicts that arose in the pursuit of the society's aims and objectives, given the different constituencies and perspectives that constituted the institution. The RCS may have outlasted the end of empire but how did an organisation that was so tied up with the Empire deal with its demise? How did they carry what Adu called the 'weight of British colonial history', deal with the 'store houses of emotion and reflex' and process the guilt and sentiment supposedly born of their complicated relationship with the Commonwealth? What responsibility did they feel towards the Empire, Commonwealth and wider world? And what impact did all of this have on the wider British population?

Urgency and adaptation: defining the New Commonwealth

The RCS is distinct among the case studies discussed here because it was the only one to explicitly and consistently discuss the impact of decolonisation and relevance of empire to British life. By tracking the ways in which the RCS described the New Commonwealth and sought to explain their role within it, we can assess how the organisation made sense of the changing circumstances of decolonisation. In 1958, following consultation with its members, the Royal Empire Society (formerly the Royal Colonial Institute) changed its name to the Royal Commonwealth Society. This decision was the outcome of a debate that had been ongoing since 1947 and it represented the society's recognition of the changing relationship between Britain, its former colonies, and the territories still under its control.[21] As Earl De La Warr, the Society's Chairman explained, '[w]hat has happened to-day ... is not a retreat but a direct fulfilment of the noble work done by our fathers and grandfathers in taking our traditions of liberal law and material progress to every quarter of the globe. All we are doing is recognizing reality. Our old name was holding up our development in the new Commonwealth territories.'[22] The symbolic significance of this gesture was amplified by the government's decision to rebrand the Imperial Institute as the Commonwealth Institute in the same year. While on the surface these new names may have indicated a break from Britain's imperial past, the linguistic shift from Empire to Commonwealth, as Ruth Craggs has argued, did not necessarily represent a parallel shift in discourses, practices or ideas about the association of countries that came under the imperial/commonwealth umbrella.[23]

Arthur Bryant's weekly column for the Illustrated London News (*ILN*) illustrates how resistance to change played out in wider public discourse. Born in 1899 and educated at Harrow, Bryant refused to be anything other than a product of his upbringing. He was, he declared, 'an unregenerate imperialist', 'brought up in [his] nursery to believe in the British Empire', and unwaveringly proud of all that it had achieved. Bryant frequently used his *ILN* column to celebrate the achievements

[25]

of the British Empire and defend its legacy, railing against what he described as 'the false and distorted view of the past that sees "the expansion of England" merely as a shameful essay in greed, aggression, pomposity and hypocrisy'.[24] The precise terms in which Bryant was willing to discuss the Commonwealth illustrate the symbolic significance renaming could hold. Rather than embracing the new phraseology, Bryant consistently couched it in language that reasserted the imperial past, referring to it either as the 'British Commonwealth' (despite the fact that it had been formally known as the 'Commonwealth of Nations' since 1949) or as that 'which used to be called the British Empire and which is now known as the Commonwealth'.[25] For Bryant, a new name did not – and should not – mean a fresh start or a new thing.

Bryant's reaction to changing terminology is illustrative of the sentimental 'reflex' that Adu critiqued in his speech at the RCS. His desire to preserve continuity was shared by many, including James P. Brander who, in writing to *The Times*, expressed his concern that the term 'Commonwealth' had 'no pride of ancestry'. He saw the new name not as a sign of a new, more equal organisation, but as 'a symbol of disintegration'.[26] Complaints such as these fold neatly into existing historical narratives about the Commonwealth, which tend to see it as little more than a buffer for those who were loath to give up the Empire.[27] While there is little doubt that some members of the RCS would have been sympathetic to their views, Bryant and Brander are not representative of the diverse range of responses to the changing Commonwealth that developed over the course of the 1960s.

In addition to the retrenchment of old white Commonwealth ideals of kith and kin by those seeking to shore up the remaining vestiges of the Empire, the RCS also provided forums for discussion in which new forms of Commonwealth identity took shape. Throughout the 1960s the society held regular lunchtime meetings at which invited guests gave talks on a wide variety of topics. In October and November of 1961 the society hosted lunchtime meetings on the following topics: 'Prospects and Progress in the Federation of Rhodesia and Nyasaland' presented by the Director of the Institute of Race Relations and held in conjunction with the Royal African Society; 'The Significance of West Indian Independence' presented by the Commissioner for the West Indies; 'Britain's Place in the World' presented by Labour politician Denis Healey; 'Aviation in Africa' presented by an adviser on African Affairs to BOAC; 'Basic Democracies in Pakistan' by the historian Rushbrook Williams; and a joint meeting on 'Technical Cooperation Overseas' hosted with the London Chamber of Commerce.[28] This fairly typical programme is indicative of the geographical spread of RCS talks and of the wide pool of speakers from which it drew, including representatives from industry, government, the Commonwealth Office, and other invested institutions. Topics under discussion addressed the full geographical range of the Commonwealth – both Old and New – as well as issues such as Britain's entry into the European Economic Community, which were thought to reflect on the status of the Commonwealth.

The RCS prided itself on being able to accommodate political difference and stimulate informed debate. As Ruth Craggs has shown, those speaking at the society in the 1960s represented a much wider range of heritages, interests, and ideologies than they had in the 1940s and 1950s.[29] The increasing prominence of speakers such as Adu reinvigorated interest in the Commonwealth and stimulated new ideas of multiracial partnership and cooperation. The examples discussed in the following paragraphs confirm how important it is to move beyond the polarised stereotypes of nostalgia and amnesia that characterised some of the early analyses of the domestic impact of decolonisation.

Some RCS members and speakers positioned themselves in direct opposition to figures like Bryant and sought to challenge nostalgic narratives of imperial pride. Speaking at the society in 1968, leader of the Liberal Party Jeremy Thorpe said that the future of the Commonwealth depends on 'recognising that what is past, is past … It is still possible and eminently desirable', he argued, 'to make of the Commonwealth something more than a club for addicts of nostalgia.'[30] Other speakers made more specific demands. One of the most controversial speakers of the 1960s was Kenneth Kaunda, President of Zambia. Kaunda spoke about Rhodesia, directly criticised British policy, and advocated the use of force by the oppressed population. For younger RCS members such as Prunella Scarlett, the event 'was a great coup', but Scarlett also acknowledged that 'others thought it was appalling'. Writing about the event later, Derek Ingram, another relatively young member of the society's Central Council, described how the walls 'almost trembled', such was the reaction of some of the audience to Kaunda's address.[31] Scarlett saw these events as part of the society's overall modernisation, outlining how the racist attitudes of some members might be challenged through exposure to wide-ranging opinions:

> we'd embarrass them by inviting them to come and listen to a particular speaker who would then provide an eloquent and interesting talk with which it was hard to disagree. Many times I remember people coming up to me afterwards and admitting that they had perhaps been a little hasty in their judgement.[32]

While it may have given a platform to those who directly challenged British policy, the RCS was also careful to give space to those who sought to defend the legacies of empire and the nature of Britain's interest in its former colonies. The views of one member, Vincent Powell-Smith, which were published in the *Commonwealth Journal*, contradicted the otherwise positive attitude with which the RCS spoke about the member states of the New Commonwealth:

> I am wondering whether it is the mother country which is to blame. The current fashion among the emergent African nations seems to be to blame Britain for anything that goes wrong; wild accusations of 'imperialist exploitation' and the like are made frequently against us by African politicians ... It is significant that those who are most vociferous in the condemnation of Britain's role in the Commonwealth have not yet put their own house in order.[33]

It is significant that the RCS, which was striving at this time to recast itself as a modern, forward-thinking institution, still made space for such attitudes in its publications and lecture programming.

Just as important as explicit defences of colonialism were the significant silences that existed, even within a diverse programme. The violence of colonial encounters, for example, and particularly that which characterised the imperial endgame in countries such as Kenya and Malaya, was given little discussion either in lectures or in the pages of the *Commonwealth Journal*. The likely participation of some members of the society in the more violent and controversial dimensions of decolonisation presumably helped to reinforce this taboo. This was particularly evident in the appointment of Alan Lennox-Boyd as chairman in 1961. Lennox-Boyd had been Secretary of State for the Colonies in the Conservative government between 1954 and 1959. He was a protégé of Lord Beaverbrook, outspoken about protectionist 'empire free trade', and had, for much of his time at the Colonial Office, warned against granting independence prematurely on economic grounds.[34] As Secretary of State for the Colonies he was the government face of a series of significant controversies in the late 1950s including the management of the Central African Federation, the detention of Dr Hastings Banda, and the Hola Camp massacre in Kenya. When introducing Lennox-Boyd to RCS members, *The Commonwealth Journal*, not surprisingly, chose to overlook these episodes. Instead, it celebrated his career by framing it within a popular narrative of coherent, well-directed decolonisation. As the article introducing him to members jokingly put it, in his role as Secretary of State for the Colonies he 'was so very busy *reducing* the Department's jurisdiction'.[35]

Debates at the RCS were also shaped by the broader discussions about the Commonwealth taking place in the public press. In order to fulfil its self-appointed mandate as an advocate for the Commonwealth, the society was compelled to respond to articles that called the Commonwealth a 'gigantic farce' and a 'lively corpse'.[36] It did not run away from this role, but rather engaged with the terms of these public critiques. Many issues of the *Commonwealth Journal* included articles that explicitly discussed the problems and relevance of the modern Commonwealth with titles such as 'Some sombre thoughts on the depressing divisions in the Commonwealth today' and 'Some thoughts on the Commonwealth's formidable difficulties'.[37] By the mid-1960s, those speeches and articles that focused on the limitations of the Commonwealth repeatedly concluded that it would not function as a comprehensive political, economic, or defensive alliance, and that the 'pressures of nationalist feeling' undermined its potential to be an association of peoples sharing the values of liberty, parliamentary democracy, and allegiance to the Crown.[38] This is not the behaviour of a society in denial about the loss of the Empire, but rather of a group of individuals taking a pragmatic (if somewhat pessimistic) interest in the problems raised by decolonisation.

While those speaking at the society seemed confident in determining what the Commonwealth was not, the society often found it difficult to articulate in precise terms what purpose it did serve and how it should determine Britain's relationship with the 'outside world'.[39] In the Examiners' Report for the society's 1966 Schools Group Project Competition students were said to be using their essays as an opportunity 'to fit themselves mentally, emotionally, and spiritually to live up to the transcendence that springs from the Commonwealth idea. They could never disclose this in words but their works declared "the glory and the dream"'.[40]

Yet for all that the idea of 'transcendence' cast the Commonwealth in a positive light, it failed to provide the RCS with a functioning definition that they could use to justify their ongoing existence and activity. For this, the society increasingly relied on the rhetoric of the People's Commonwealth. The idea of the People's Commonwealth rested on two key principles: that the Commonwealth was sustained by the actions of individuals rather than governments, and that it was uniquely suited to 'surmounting barriers of race, ignorance, and prejudice'.[41] These principles were not entirely new – the Queen's Coronation Tour in 1953 had depicted the Commonwealth as a 'multiracial community of equal nations'[42] – but they solidified and gained prominence over the course of the 1960s as both membership of the New Commonwealth and tensions between member states steadily increased.

In the early 1960s the modern Commonwealth had reached what John Chadwick described as a 'nadir of disillusion'; 'political like-mindedness, shared defence interests, and economic co-operation had seemingly been broken on the altars of racism, regional polarisation and through abhorrence for [...] neo-colonialism'.[43] By focusing on positive examples of person-to-person interaction the society embraced an alternative identity for the Commonwealth that was more likely to survive the political turmoil and flux of decolonisation.[44] One member described the Commonwealth as 'an epic in which the idealism of explorers, doctors, missionaries, magistrates and scientists is interwoven with the expediency of soldiers, merchants, engineers and farmers'.[45] Another argued that 'the Commonwealth is not just to do with nations; it is to do with human beings',[46] while Chadwick described it as 'an international idea rather than an organization, a *modus Vivendi* rather than a constitutional entity'.[47] By the Society's centenary in 1968, William Kirkham concluded that the 'recognition of the fact that the Commonwealth is primarily an association of peoples, not governments, [was] a first important step in understanding the reality of the modern Commonwealth relationship'.[48]

The rhetoric of the 'People's Commonwealth' empowered associational organisations like the RCS as key actors in the 'making' of the modern Commonwealth. As *The Times* Commonwealth Correspondent explained, the RCS, Victoria League, English Speaking Union, and the Royal Over-seas League were 'uniquely poised' to 'underpin, or substitute, with personal bonds and a sense of cultural citizenship, the disintegrating political and official structure of the Commonwealth association'.[49] Rather than undermining these civic organisations, pessimistic diagnoses of the political Commonwealth helped to justify their significance, giving them a sense of purpose at a time when many dismissed them as colonial relics. 'Though the old Empire may or may not have been created in an absence of mind,' wrote Norman Jeffries, 'the sustenance of the Commonwealth today stems from its presence of mind.'[50] As Arnold Smith, Commonwealth Secretary-General explained, 'the Commonwealth is what we think it is. It can be what we make it'.[51] Put by another member who was more attuned to the difficult task faced by the society: the trouble with the Commonwealth was that 'nobody [was] working hard enough at it'.[52] Adjusting to the modern Commonwealth was not simply a matter of establishing a vibrant new rhetoric of multiracial inclusivity and individual action; the society also faced the considerable challenge of putting this new identity into practice.

Club life and the People's Commonwealth

How successfully did the society's membership model the behaviours and characteristics of the People's Commonwealth that were advocated in its own publications? Throughout the 1960s, articles in the *Commonwealth Journal* drew on the rhetoric of the 'People's Commonwealth' to present the New Commonwealth as a progressive tool for multiracial cooperation. Advocates repeatedly emphasised what they saw as the Commonwealth's specific suitability for international cooperation, particularly when compared to other international organisations such as the United Nations. 'The national society is too narrow', explained member Philip Birkinshaw, 'the world society is still too large, incoherent, distracted and vague. The Commonwealth is an intermediate and working expression of international citizenship and goodwill.'[53] Writing to *The Times*, the Chairman of the Society Council, John Hope, promised that the Commonwealth could 'become a unique instrument of racial cooperation over the whole field of human endeavour'.[54] Such pronouncements were easy to make, but the RCS's ability to match itself to the image of a dynamic and multiracial Commonwealth was severely limited by the white, ageing demographic of its membership.

As Earl De La Warr observed in 1961, 'the words multi-racial and non-racial can be a kind of parrot cry which we all periodically utter, but which mean very little in practice'.[55] 'It must be admitted by all our Societies', De La Warr explained, referring to the English Speaking Union, Victoria League, and Royal Over-Seas League alongside the RCS, 'that we still see only a comparatively limited number of coloured faces in our headquarters or branch buildings'.[56] Recognising the problem was not, however, the same as solving it. Twelve years on from De La Warr's warning, the society acknowledged that on 'the human side' they were still far from being a Commonwealth-wide society; they were almost unknown in many Commonwealth countries and, in others, were considered to be a conservative Anglo- or post-imperial organisation.[57] They could not shake what *The Times* Commonwealth Correspondent described as the '"aura of white dominiondom" that clung to them'.[58]

The majority of overseas RCS branches were in the old dominions, undermining society claims that they were part of the new modern Commonwealth and not a 'small, rich man's, white man's club'.[59] Even those branches in 'new' Commonwealth countries failed to attract a diverse membership. Prohibitively high membership fees excluded most of the non-white populations of recently independent nations. In 1963 the Ceylon branch, for example, was described by the Commonwealth Relations Office as an elderly group of persons with 'wholly pre-1948 connections, who look backward to the glorious past of which they were an important part, but not forward to what they regard as an inglorious future in which they are being trampled underfoot by the mob of the shirtless'.[60] Such a group had little interest in representing a post-imperial Commonwealth based on racial equality.

Branches in the UK followed a similar pattern. Few branch locations were in areas with significant black and Asian communities and those that were often had smaller memberships than those in the Home Counties; compare, for example, the 597 members of the Hants and Dorset branch to the 153 in Liverpool.[61] Most UK branches were located in areas where returning imperial officers and administrators tended to retire. In 1967, 8 per cent of British members lived in either Guernsey or Jersey where the branches had a combined membership of 806.[62] The Sussex branch drew members from coastal towns such as Brighton and Eastbourne, which, since the mid-nineteenth century, had held reputations as fashionable watering holes for returned colonials, providing leisure facilities, a warmer climate, and numerous private schools.[63] Similarly, it is likely that the branches in Bath and in Bristol, which in 1967 had a fairly high combined membership of 724, serviced not only their own immediate populations but also the wider South West area and in particular Cheltenham Spa, the best-known British-Indian enclave in the metropole.[64] Branches that did exist in close proximity to student and migrant communities often failed to engage with them. The Cambridge branch, for example, repeatedly failed to take advantage of the potential for diversity offered by the university's Commonwealth student population.

The high average age of society members exacerbated these problems, undermining discourses that identified youth as the future of the Commonwealth. The RCS faced a constant uphill struggle to move beyond its conspicuously ageing membership. A questionnaire conducted in 1973 revealed that the majority of British resident members were white male professionals or retired professionals, of whom the vast majority were over 40 and more than a third of whom were over 55.[65] Anecdotal evidence suggests that overall membership and branch level administration were stagnant and that members lost through old age or death were not replaced by a new young cohort. Hants and Dorset, for example, reported that 'age and infirmity' prevented a 'steadily increasing number of cases' from supporting social and other activities.[66]

Despite its non-party principle and the presence of a number of Labour members on the central council and list of vice-presidents, the RCS retained the image of a conservative and Conservative organisation. This image was recognised as a hindrance when trying to attract younger, non-white members to the society.[67] An exception was Prunella Scarlett; in her twenties in the 1960s and Public Affairs Officer for the society between 1965 and 1999, she only proved the general rule when she described the majority of the membership as 'distinctly ancient and dusty'.[68]

This created self-perpetuating problems for a society seeking to promote the modern Commonwealth. As Charles Carrington, who, at 66, was a member of this 'dusty' majority, explained:

> Young active people in the prime of life are too busy to give much time to it and it therefore falls into the hands of the retired old fogies who have time to spare; with the further consequence that the 'cause' gets written off as an old fogie's superannuated notion. I am dreadfully afraid that the Commonwealth is so regarded by a great many younger people.[69]

John Chadwick confirmed this view, suggesting that those who were 'near the biblical limits' – and for Chadwick this seems to be anyone over the age of 60 – were seen to have backward yearnings for empire.[70]

Although the RCS's own membership may not have reflected the diversity of the Commonwealth, the society did try to act as a hospitable venue for New Commonwealth collaboration. By the 1960s the RCS promoted itself as a safe space for Commonwealth hospitality where black and Asian guests 'could eat, drink, meet, and talk without fear of discrimination'.[71] As Craggs describes, citing an interview with Prunella Scarlett, corporate members such as Barclays and trading companies took advantage of this atmosphere, wanting 'their bright spark from wherever to walk into a prejudice free place where they would feel at home'.[72] In 1963 the Speakers and Public Relations Office reported that the society was increasingly being asked by the Central Office of Information to arrange lunches and entertainment for touring visitors from the Commonwealth including editors, trade unionists, and youth club leaders.[73]

While these interactions did help to dispel stereotypes of the RCS as an imperial hangover, we should not overestimate their importance to the everyday experience of society members. A market research questionnaire completed by ninety-four members in 1973 revealed the uncomfortable truth that the society's restaurants were of more importance to members than the interaction with 'Commonwealth People' and access to Commonwealth 'affairs'.[74] By this point members and others who came into contact with the society tended to regard it as 'quite a good inexpensive Commonwealth club' and 'a sound but ineffective Commonwealth Affairs institute'.[75] There was significant scope for a member to be an active participant in the society without ever engaging critically with the changing Commonwealth. The Sussex branch's lecture programmes for 1961–62 and 1964–65 reveal a persistent lack of critical engagement with the pressing issues of the developing modern Commonwealth.[76] Dominated by talks on issues such as 'Dutch Interior Paintings', 'Highlights of Moorish Spain', and British Railways colour films, Sussex offered little on the political or economic dimensions of Commonwealth countries and little that addressed the purpose or meaning of the New Commonwealth. Along similar lines, in London, the active Social Committee organised visits to Battersea Dogs' Home, the Bank of England, Frogmore Gardens, Woburn Abbey, and Ascot.[77] In the course of the 1960s a Royal Commonwealth Motor Group was established and the Billiards Committee saw users of the billiards room increase from twelve to around one hundred. Similar trends are apparent at branch level: so successful was the Hants and Dorset Bridge Circle that they had to introduce a second afternoon each week to avoid overcrowding.[78]

While the use of the society's accommodation and bars remained consistently high, by the early 1970s it acknowledged that only a handful of members had the time or interest to attend weekly lunchtime meetings.[79] In 1969, low attendance forced headquarters to reduce the these meetings from weekly to fortnightly events.[80] If not for the invited audience of corporate members and the staff of high commissions, embassies and the press, commented a memorandum, 'the speaker would often be facing an almost empty hall'.[81] These issues were exacerbated by branch level mismanagement. The 1969 Annual General Meeting of the Cambridgeshire branch, for instance, revealed that so much had been spent on a party for the visiting Australian cricket team, in the hope of attracting new members, that it had been impossible to afford much else for the rest of the year.[82]

Over the course of the 1960s, the society's central committees grew increasingly concerned about the balance between its club and educational functions. As early as 1961, Headquarters accused the Sussex Branch of failing to play an 'important part in promoting the main objects of the Society' and of 'carrying out the Commonwealth work of the Society with insufficient effort and initiative and with insufficient relevance to the modern Commonwealth'.[83] In 1963, Lord Casey echoing similar concerns, argued that 'many of the Society's social and other activities [...] represent[ed] nostalgic recollections of the glories of the past, not anxious constructive looking-forward into the future of the Commonwealth'.[84] As Reese warned in the society's centenary history, social activity was important, but it 'could not alone form a durable and worthwhile basis for a society that wished to be taken seriously'.[85]

By the end of the decade, the Commonwealth Affairs Committee warned that 'the society was more and more in danger of becoming merely an inexpensive club with an Empire aura and a tendency to be emotionally involved in rather vague Commonwealth ideals without enough vital contact with politics, economics and people of the Commonwealth to carry conviction'.[86] Similar appraisals were again levelled at the society's branches overseas, some of which were described as 'little more than loose groupings of members of the Society who happen to live in the area, who come together once or twice a year on some occasion which is primarily social but has a Commonwealth flavour' and others which were criticised for being 'to all intents and purposes social clubs, relying for their appeal on distinguished patronage and social cachet'.[87]

Social functions at the RCS helped to recreate the atmosphere of the imperial club back home in Britain. As John Darwin discusses, for upper-class British residents overseas, the club was a key site of community and sociability where residents were brought together through sport, the card table, or seasonal jollity.[88] By offering similar services, the RCS provided a haven where returning civil servants could take refuge in the company of other repatriates. For many members, the society brought together a community of like-minded people at a time when popular opinion was increasingly unenthusiastic about the Commonwealth. Far from being a conduit for wider Commonwealth consciousness, this social space worked to temporarily isolate repatriates and their shared recollections from the rest of the public. As in the clubs attended by British communities overseas, the society's bars and dining rooms were exclusive. There were strict rules about who could use which of the society's facilities, and although a number of guests were hosted by the society, these were generally already converts to the Commonwealth cause. Regardless of how open-minded or outward-looking the conversations held at the society's bars and restaurants might have been, they rarely touched the wider British population.

Taking the Commonwealth to the people

To fulfil the promise of the People's Commonwealth so frequently advocated in its publications, the RCS had to look beyond its own bars and dining rooms. Putting the People's Commonwealth into practice required those who were already invested to reach out and engage the public. Although the majority of RCS members may have been inactive in this field – interested in the organisation only for the club services and like-minded company that it provided – an active minority sought to use the society's resources to build 'Commonwealth consciousness' in the wider public. The society's efforts in this area were determined, to a considerable degree, by the other forms of Commonwealth promotion that also existed in the period, and by the availability of receptive audiences.

There is now a significant body of research detailing the myriad factors that fed into the public's sense of an imperial identity in the nineteenth and twentieth centuries. Since the nineteenth century, specific groups and individuals have sought to actively promote the Empire and Commonwealth to the British population. Their efforts have included friendship schemes, educative talks, celebratory events, and great public exhibitions.[89] Although the existence of such schemes is not in itself a reliable indicator of public attitudes to the Empire, they do give us a sense of the changing motivations and concerns of those invested in the Empire. Empire and Commonwealth propaganda in the post-war period is best characterised as a series of peaks and troughs in which the first half of the 1960s stands out as a period of significant reinvestment and reinvention. Prior to this, state promotion of the Empire and Commonwealth had last peaked in the early 1950s, coinciding with a period of reinvestment in British Africa and the Coronation of Elizabeth II in 1953.

At the Coronation, the wartime rhetoric of the People's War was repurposed to promote the People's Commonwealth, representing a significant shift in the way the Commonwealth was promoted to the British public. As Webster describes, 'the image of an empire/Commonwealth rejoicing at the crowning of the Queen elaborated the wartime idea of unity between diverse peoples'.[90] The spirit of the multiracial People's Commonwealth was given further ammunition by the successful ascent to the summit of Everest, announced on the same day as the Coronation. Edmund Hillary, a New Zealander, and Tenzing Norgay, an Indian-Nepalese Sherpa, were promoted as symbols of the multiracial partnership of the New Commonwealth. These images of cooperation were consolidated by the Royal tour of the Commonwealth in 1953–54 and by the Queen's Christmas Day message in 1953, when she pledged to 'give myself, heart and soul' to the 'new conception of an equal partnership of nations and races'.[91] Though the rhetoric of the People's Commonwealth survived this period of optimism, the large-scale pageantry did not.

The celebratory years of 1953–54 were followed until the end of the decade by a period of minimal state involvement in the domestic promotion of the Commonwealth. In the latter half of the 1950s there was no individual ministerial responsibility for the promotion of the Commonwealth in Britain; the Commonwealth Relations Office had no funds to directly promote the Commonwealth; the Colonial Office spent only a few thousand pounds on pamphlets and visual aids; and the Ministry of Education was constrained by an overcrowded curriculum and professional resistance to teaching the Commonwealth as a separate subject.[92] The reduction in state efforts to promote the Commonwealth was matched by a decline in civic pageantry. Empire Day – which had been widely celebrated in the first half of the century – was dismissed as 'moribund' in 1957 by the Commonwealth Relations Office. Its successor, Commonwealth Day, attracted little public support. On 24 May 1961, the *Yorkshire Post* somewhat mournfully asked its readers: 'who, except the printers of diaries, remembers that this is Commonwealth Day?'[93] For much of the 1950s, S. C. Leslie concluded in *The Round Table*, the Commonwealth was 'not much thought about or discussed'.[94] As a result of this neglect, the level of public knowledge about the form and function of the New Commonwealth was low.

The momentum changed again in the first half of the 1960s, driven by the increasing pace of decolonisation. These years, MacKenzie argues, marked the point at which the illusion of imperial power was no longer sustainable.[95] Rather than leading to a further decline in Commonwealth consciousness-raising, the increasing inevitability of end of the Empire reinvigorated attempts by state and non-state organisations to promote the New Commonwealth as its replacement. Rapid changes to the nature of the Commonwealth prompted urgent appraisals of existing efforts to develop Commonwealth consciousness. In 1960 an interdepartmental working party concluded that the 'lack of forceful promotion of knowledge and interest in the Commonwealth' was starting to limit the options available to Commonwealth policymakers. While many members of the public 'refuse[d] to think about the Commonwealth at all', the report observed, 'others were susceptible to 'propagandists against "imperialism" and "colonialism"'.[96] In the absence of efforts to promote its 'positive and multicultural' side, the Commonwealth was increasingly thought of only in relation to the 'immigration problem'. Without intervention, advisers warned in 1962, the 'mood of pessimism' would continue to grow.[97]

This sense of urgency was shared by voluntary organisations. While the RCS had been fairly complacent about outreach in the mid-1950s, by 1961 when they announced the handover of the Chairmanship from De La Warr to Lennox-Boyd they warned that 'time is running out; the Society's work is urgent and must be done quickly'.[98] These appraisals highlight the push–pull between optimism and pessimism that characterises this period. Writing in the *Commonwealth Journal* in 1962 one member argued optimistically that 'a true live Commonwealth could be an example to all the world' but concluded there was 'no proper machinery, no Ministry to develop in. There is nothing to give it a soul.'[99]

On the basis of these worrying realisations, public funding for projects that aimed to 're-insert the Commonwealth into the national imagination' increased significantly in the first half of the 1960s.[100] The two biggest state-sponsored projects were the new Commonwealth Institute (formerly the Imperial Institute), which opened in a specially commissioned building in Holland Park in 1962, and the Commonwealth Arts Festival, which was held at sites across the country in 1965.[101] Both initiatives aimed to generate awareness, understanding and goodwill towards the Commonwealth by promoting its cultural diversity. By 1967 the Commonwealth Institute was being visited by more than half a million visitors each year, including over 7000 school visits.[102] Though it attracted large numbers of primary school children through its doors, the Institute was less successful at reaching the adult population. Organisers of the Arts Festival hoped to attract a much wider audience to events held in port-cities across the country. The Commonwealth Relations Office stressed that it should 'not be confined to the relatively few people who always follow cultural events but that it should have wide public impact'.[103] In addition to lunchtime displays of music and dance in Trafalgar Square, the Associated Television production 'The Commonwealth Entertains' was broadcast to 15 million viewers in Britain.[104] Despite hopes for a second festival, however, the Commonwealth Arts Festival was the only large-scale event of its kind.

While large-scale initiatives like the Arts Festival attracted the most press, we should not overlook the smaller-scale but more consistent work of voluntary organisations in promoting Commonwealth consciousness in this period. Voluntary organisations had long played a significant role in the promotion of the Empire. By the late 1950s, however, state attitudes towards the contribution that voluntary organisations might make towards Commonwealth consciousness were ambivalent. In 1958, the Secretary of State for Commonwealth Relations reported that voluntary organisations were 'jealous of each other' and could not be relied upon for a 'successful initiative'.[105] Such concerns seem to have been confirmed by the fiasco surrounding the Commonwealth Day Movement at the turn of the decade. In 1961 the Commonwealth Relations Office felt it necessary to intervene to rescue the movement from the hands of enthusiastic but misguided retired Air Marshall Sir Victor Goddard. Between 1958 and 1961, Goddard had written and distributed a series of nonsensical Commonwealth Day messages that were so out of step with the rhetoric of the modern Commonwealth that they were seen as a liability to public perceptions of the Commonwealth.[106]

The RCS, in contrast, was trusted as a safer pair of hands and a useful mechanism for coordinating the '200 little voices' of organisations concerned with the Commonwealth.[107] Its London headquarters acted as a centre for coordinating and encouraging other Commonwealth organisations, hosting the Round Table, the Commonwealth Youth Exchange Council, the Commonwealth Human Ecology Council, and the Council for Education in the Commonwealth. Other large-scale collaborative efforts included the frequent joint meetings held with the Royal African Society, which, in the 1960s, was also resident in the RCS offices; and the Joint Commonwealth Societies Conference at which the society agreed to work together in the 'new countries' with the Victoria League, the Royal Over-Seas League, and the English-Speaking Union.

Although the RCS was rich in physical space and affiliations, it had limited financial resources with which to carry out outreach activities. While its total assets exceeded £325,000 in the 1960s, most of this was tied up in property and by 1968 their annual expenditure was exceeding revenue by about £16,000.[108] The society was funded almost entirely by its membership fees and in the 1960s there was a severe shortfall in revenue from annual subscriptions. In part this can be ascribed to the loss of fees from the grant of autonomy to international branches, but declining UK membership also played a part. Most significantly, the society failed to replace the many members lost to death and old age with a younger cohort. In 1968 the Duke of Devonshire, then chairman of the society, announced that the society was facing 'a very serious financial crisis'.[109] At a time when the society saw their work as particularly urgent, the decline in funds and members created substantial pressure to limit activities and increase efficiency.

In light of its increasingly limited resources, the RCS chose to focus on educative outreach activities, capitalising on its history as a learned body. In 1957 the Imperial Studies Committee reported that the educational activities of the society should be a priority and that 'any other activities on which [the society] may be engaged are subordinate'.[110] In 1968 the committee reaffirmed that one of the society's key objects was to 'spread interest or knowledge of the Commonwealth', noting that 'whilst the other societies all had excellent social programmes, the Royal Commonwealth Society was the only one with a good educational programme'.[111] The reach of the society's educational efforts was determined not only by money available to support these initiatives, but also by the willingness of members to contribute labour and expertise, and the availability of receptive audiences.

As I discuss in greater detail in Chapter 2, throughout the 1960s many associational audiences actively sought out the types of knowledge and expertise that RCS members had gained through their work in empire-related fields. In 1963 the society reported that it was increasingly being asked to promote Commonwealth-related issues to the wider public through courses and conferences. In 1969, for example, they held a short residential course on 'New Perspectives on Race Relations in Britain', organised jointly with the Commonwealth Institute. Intended to attempt an objective assessment of the economic, social, and cultural effects of the presence of new communities from other Commonwealth countries, the course was attended by forty-seven people including probation officers, community relations officers, and staff of Commonwealth high commissions and the Foreign and Commonwealth Office.[112] Smaller-scale outreach events ranged from briefing students from Minnesota before a trip to Tanganyika, to organising a two-day conference on West Africa at Canford independent school.[113]

During 1968 and 1969 the society met at least forty-five requests for speakers from external groups including schools, Rotary Clubs, women's organisations, and political groups.[114] These requests were often fielded through local branch networks, rather than through society headquarters, emphasising the importance of local connections. In Hants and Dorset, for example, the chairman gave a speech on the royal family and the Commonwealth to the Bournemouth branch of the Young Conservatives, while another member, Commander C .J. Charlewood spoke to the Beckenham Mothers' Union about Australia's capital cities.[115] This method of organisation suggests that members of the public living in areas with a high proportion of empire repatriates were likely to have had greater exposure to imperial and Commonwealth concerns than those who lived in other parts of Britain.

In 1958 the society decided that although the most valuable educational function it could perform lay in the creation of an informed public opinion, its limited resources necessitated that it concentrate on the 15–20 age group.[116] When the society re-stated their objectives in 1964 they included a specific goal to encourage 'mutual interest in Commonwealth countries among young people'.[117] In doing so, the RCS tapped into wider discourses on youth and emphasised the importance of educating the young as heirs to the new multiracial Commonwealth. This sector of the public had, for a long time, been seen as a crucial one in which to establish imperial sentiment. Lord Meath, the founder of Empire Day in Britain, had been devoted to making children aware of their responsibilities as 'citizens of the greatest Empire in the world in the interwar period'.[118] Within wider debates about sport, militarism, and national character, organisations such as the Boy Scouts also sought to foster a sense of imperial duty in their young members.[119] In the inter-war period the School Empire Tour Committee, the Overseas Education League, and the Overseas

Settlement of British Women sent groups of children to different parts of the Empire in an effort to develop their imperial education and commitment.[120]

These kinds of commitments did not disappear after empire; if anything, youth outreach became even more important in a post-imperial context. By 1963, there were 800,000 more teenagers among the British population than there had been the decade before.[121] Anxieties about declining deference, consumerism, counterculture, and the 'generation gap' pushed this cohort under the sociological and political lens and into the public eye. This constellation of concerns was also balanced with optimism about the role of the young as internationally minded citizens of tomorrow. As Joanna Bailkin has shown, youth became an issue of international relations – one that was particularly fitting to the environment of imperial decline.[122] For the RCS, the rhetoric of youth was perfectly suited to the needs of the modern Commonwealth. By repeatedly referring to the modern Commonwealth as a young association the society worked to bypass some of the problematic legacies of imperialism.[123]

The RCS never had the resources to compete with the Commonwealth Institute's youth work, nor were they ever inclined to try. Instead they provided a supplementary service, centred on educational projects that encouraged critical engagement. Of these activities, the two largest and most direct forms of outreach were a Commonwealth-wide essay and group project competition and study conferences hosted for sixth-form students by headquarters in London and by a number of branches across the country. Both schemes significantly pre-dated the 1960s (the essay competition had been instituted in 1883), but both were adapted to encourage participants to latch on to the idea of the modern, People's Commonwealth. In the early 1960s, sixth-form study conferences were modified so that, rather than dealing with the general background of a colonial territory and an 'old' dominion, they presented the Commonwealth as something more than the sum of its parts.[124] For the essay competition, open to school students across the Commonwealth, students in the eldest age category were prompted to engage critically with questions such as the following:

> The Commonwealth is not a static organism. The product of evolution, it is capable of adapting itself, as it has done successfully in the past, to changing circumstances and needs. To what extent do you agree?[125]

The 1961 Study Conference organised by society headquarters for 265 sixth formers clearly illustrates the society's broad-ranging and critical approach to youth outreach in this period. Speakers at the conference were the Bishop of Johannesburg, who reflected on problems in South Africa; the editor of the newsletter *Africa 1960*, Charles Janson, who spoke about Ghana and Guinea in the context of the struggle for West African Leadership and J. Z. Gumede, a Matabele headmaster from Southern Rhodesia who spoke on the future of the Central African Federation. In addition to the educative critical engagement with the modern Commonwealth encouraged by these three talks, students at the Study Conference were also encouraged to involve themselves more actively in the People's Commonwealth. They were addressed not only by returning Voluntary Service Overseas volunteers but also by the Commonwealth Service Group who talked about the social welfare initiatives that they undertook among non-student West Indian immigrants.[126] Through its balance of outreach, education, action, and interaction, this conference embodies the society's key aims and practices as they appeared in the records of the central administration and in its publications.

Although the competitions and conferences that the RCS organised in the 1960s encouraged their participants to examine the role that young people themselves might play in influencing the future of the Commonwealth, they did not necessarily reach new, untouched portions of the population. The central society sixth-form conference was limited to two hundred London students each year. Although many branches also ran their own sixth-form conferences, reaching a greater number and wider geographical range of school-age children, the conferences remained relatively limited in the range of schools and children they attracted. A *Guardian* article on the society's 1960 Sixth-Form Study Conference described the audience as composed of 'fairly studious children from families "pretty well up the social scale"'. It was, the article argues, 'a case almost of preaching to the converted rather than attracting a new type of audience'.[127]

Like state-run initiatives such as the Commonwealth Institute and Commonwealth Arts Festival, the RCS's efforts to promote the Commonwealth struggled against what many members saw as an apathetic public. It is very difficult to measure the 'effectiveness' of either the state or the RCS's attempts to promote Commonwealth consciousness, but we do have a sense of how each assessed the broader climate of public opinion. In the early 1960s the RCS described the pursuit of their aims as 'long and difficult'.[128] In 1967 the Foreign and Commonwealth Office remained concerned that there was 'widespread doubt' about the value of the Commonwealth.[129] In the same year, the RCS swallowed what they described as a particularly 'bitter pill' when the Postmaster General rejected their proposal for a centenary stamp in favour of one commemorating a half century of votes for women.[130]

This strain of frustrated pessimism acted as an important counterbalance to the idealistic enthusiasm often expressed in the *Commonwealth Journal*. It reminds us of the difficulty in matching reality to rhetoric. The international work of the Women's Institute and Rotary Club, discussed in the following chapters, shows that some of these assessments may have been overly pessimistic. Despite the RCS's and Foreign and Commonwealth Office's perceived failure to influence public opinion, the frameworks and narratives of the People's Commonwealth were still meaningful to other sections of British society, particularly when linked to projects of international friendship.

Making a difference or 'making a nuisance': politics at the Royal Commonwealth Society

Despite the RCS's clear enthusiasm for study and education, this was not the only means by which the society and its members engaged with the Commonwealth. For many members, their responsibility towards the preservation of the Commonwealth extended beyond lunchtime talks and educative outreach programmes, neither of which seemed to quite catch the sense of urgency with which they felt the society ought to be acting. In 1962, a speech given at society headquarters by Lord Casey, an Australian politician involved in Commonwealth Affairs, was published in the *Commonwealth Journal* under the exclamatory heading 'Awake! Awake!' Casey called for the RCS to become a 'militant fighting body' and 'do something before it is too late'. The society was, Casey argued, 'ideally situated by [its] membership and prestige to take a much more militant attitude in respect of the Commonwealth: asking awkward questions, making a nuisance of [itself], pointing out in simple understandable language what is at stake and what might be done'.[131] Though he did not say so, Casey was urging the RCS to join a messy field.

The efforts of pro-Commonwealth interest groups like the RCS were complicated by those, such as the League of Empire Loyalists (LEL), who sought to preserve the formal Empire. Formed in 1954 and chaired by G. K. Chesterton, the LEL sat on the far right of the political spectrum. Under the label of 'patriotism' they aimed for 'the maintenance and, where necessary, the recovery of the sovereign independence of British Peoples throughout the world' and 'the conscientious development of the British Colonial Empire under British direction and local British leadership'.[132] Far from endorsing the image of a multiracial new Commonwealth, the LEL associated it with the 'immigration problem' and argued that black immigration to Britain needed to be 'drastically curtailed' to prevent 'a mulatto Britain of the future'.[133]

The influence of the LEL as a pro-empire lobby declined in the early 1960s, but they remained an influential force in immigration and race relations debates, joining with the British National Party in 1967 to form the National Front. In the mid-1960s, the space on the right that the shrinking LEL had occupied was largely filled by the rapid rise of the Monday Club within the Conservative Party. Established in 1961 and named after the so-called 'Black Monday' on which Harold Macmillan gave his 'Wind of Change' speech in South Africa, the Monday Club became an important base for the Rhodesia 'settler lobby' in the mid-1960s and eventually also argued for a racially 'pure' Britain unpolluted by the peoples of her former empire.[134] The trajectory of the Monday Club – from an organisation that, in 1961, promoted principles of multiracial paternalism, to a more fringe organisation advocating a restrictive immigration policy – highlights some of the temptations and difficulties of participating in the pro-Empire/Commonwealth lobby. In 1962, Lennox-Boyd, while chairman of the RCS, accepted a role as a patron of the Monday Club, presumably recognising that it offered greater political influence than the RCS. By 1968, however, he resigned his post over the Club's decision to support Enoch Powell's stance on immigration.[135]

Given this complicated political climate, RCS members were in disagreement over whether the society should join the fray and engage openly in political debates about either immigration or the future of the Commonwealth. The society's own commitment to non-partisanship and inclusivity meant that political action was not only difficult to coordinate among the different views of its membership, but also went against the RCS's efforts to present a neutral approach to the Commonwealth. Some rejected outright Casey's suggestion that the society become a lobbying organisation. One member explained that 'in these precarious times perhaps the only sure foundation the Commonwealth can count on is genteel collaboration, based on enlightened self-interest; and any Royal Commonwealth Society agitation or effort [...] will be regarded in many quarters as a vain attack by the "Old Guard" to recover some of the shorn glory, if not the power'.[136] Such a statement highlights members' awareness of the awkward climate in which they operated and their particular concerns about accusations of nostalgia.

Others were less pessimistic, however, and used the momentum generated by Casey's call to arms to set up new initiatives. One such initiative was the Commonwealth Purpose Group, established by Charles Carrington in 1962 as a private dining club in which to air general views about the Commonwealth and consider the best ways that society members could help in promoting Commonwealth cooperation.

Carrington (1897–1990), Professor of British Commonwealth Relations at the Royal Institute of International Affairs, secured the participation of a number of prominent RCS members including Kenneth Kirkwood and Lord Walston, both heavily involved in the Institute for Race Relations; James Coltart, director of Thompson's publishing company, which owned *The Times*; and John Turnbull, an influential information officer in the Civil Service. Yet despite early bombast the group achieved very little. In his own words, Carrington was 'not clever at managing people with whom [he did not] see eye to eye' and the meetings soon petered out with his concluding in a letter to David Whatley, 'I don't want to be a political organiser; I want to be an elderly literary man, reading and writing and lecturing about the Commonwealth as quietly as my nature permits.'[137] The failings of the inappropriately named Purpose Group indicate how difficult it could be to turn aspirations into concrete action and reveal the gulf that often existed between rhetoric and reality. Carrington's journey of self-discovery also emphasises how crucial the skillsets, networks, and attitudes of individual instigators were to the success or failure of society projects. Carrington may have been well connected, but he was clearly not an organiser.

Though Whatley was encouraged by Carrington to continue the work of the Purpose Group, it was not until 1967 that he took up the mantle, heading a new and active committee called Nudge. Nudge was the most vociferous and demanding manifestation of the RCS, and from its inception came much closer to Casey's vision of militancy than the Purpose Group had ever done. Formed in order to 'combat the growing apathy towards the Commonwealth from the Government and the people of Britain', the group aimed to do so by giving 'a sharp shove whenever and wherever it is needed'.[138] Nudge spoke out against the trebling of the Commonwealth press cable rate, against entry to the European Common Market, on Commonwealth citizenship, on racial discrimination in Rhodesia, and on forms of commercial cooperation. Although the group was sponsored by the society, Nudge press statements came with the disclaimer that they 'did not necessarily represent [the views] of the Society'.[139] Nudge's approach – often taking significant action without consulting the executive committee or council of the society – unnerved members of the society's central council. In a letter to Stephen Leslie, then chairman of the Nudge Committee, the secretary-general of the society wrote that he was 'worried' about Nudge's actions and particularly concerned that a letter that had been sent without consultation by the group to a number of Commonwealth prime ministers would be 'regarded as just a piece of damn cheek!'[140] The Central Council's efforts to rein in the Nudge Committee and their blunt comment that 'we must either control it or disown it', reveal the society's broader unease with political activism and the message that it might send.[141] If it pushed too hard it would be regarded as troublesome, but if it did not champion the Commonwealth, who would?

As Elizabeth Buettner discusses, ex-colonials could either brood from the side-lines as empire was forgotten (propped up, perhaps, at a RCS bar) or take on roles as interpreters for the wider population.[142] The RCS survived because it made it possible for its members to do either. It was adaptive to the New Commonwealth and built a reputation as a source of information and expertise, but it also accommodated those who were not willing, able, or interested in adjusting. Members clearly responded to decolonisation and bore the 'weight of feeling' that A. L. Adu saw resting on their shoulders in very different ways. Yes, there was a gulf between the active outlook of the society's committees and the majority of the members who were content use the RCS as a social club where they could be with like-minded people. But the fees of inactive members sustained the society and its outreach activities, even as their behaviour frustrated those sitting on central committees.

What was distinctive about the RCS's approach to the Commonwealth in the 1960s – and this is particularly true of the first two-thirds of the decade – was its constant toing and froing between optimism and pessimism. The Commonwealth could offer a path to global peace, if it did not collapse by the end of the year; the British could be a shining example to the Commonwealth, if only its population would acknowledge the Commonwealth's existence; the society could be a militant player in Commonwealth affairs, if only its members were interested in more than billiards. By the end of the 1960s the more extreme permutations of the society's optimistic *and* pessimistic impulses had been tempered by a more pragmatic approach, one that recognised the limitations to what the Commonwealth could achieve, reined in the society's ambitions, and committed them to persevere in the areas where they had the expertise and resources to do so. As David McIntyre wrote in 1977, the end of the 1960s marked the commencement of 'a new age of realism' in which 'the Commonwealth continued, was taken for granted, but did not have too much expected of it'.[143] Don Taylor encapsulated the society's attitude of resilience and perseverance in these circumstances in a speech at the Branches Conference in 1968. Responding to suggestions that the Commonwealth might collapse, Taylor argued that even if it did the RCS would continue to be 'the guardian of the principles, traditions and contacts with the people with whom Great Britain had had such a long connection'.[144] Though often expressed differently, similar principles of continuity and preservation inform many of the international engagement activities discussed in the rest of this book.

Notes

1 A. L. Adu, 'The reality and potential capacity of the Commonwealth', *Commonwealth Journal*, 12 (February 1969), 12.
2 Arnold Smith in Harry Miller (ed.), *Royal Commonwealth Society Centenary, 1868–1968* (London: Royal Commonwealth Society, 1968), p. 63.
3 John Darwin, 'The fear of falling: British politics and imperial decline since 1900', *Transactions of the Royal Historical Society*, 36 (1985), 27–43.
4 The National Archives (hereafter TNA), FCO 49/155, no. 8, 'Value of the Commonwealth to Britain', letter from Sir P. Gore-Booth to Sir S. Garner on draft of a Commonwealth Office Paper 15 Feb. 1967. Reproduced in S. R. Ashton and Wm Roger Louis (eds), *British Documents on the End of Empire*, Series A, Volume 5, East of Suez and the Commonwealth 1964–1971, Part II Europe, Rhodesia, Commonwealth (London: Institute for Commonwealth Studies, 2004) p. 407.
5 'BARTON, Arthur Edward Victor', *Who Was Who*, A. & C. Black, 1920–2008; online edn, Oxford University Press, Dec. 2007, www.ukwhoswho.com/view/article/oupww/whowaswho/U161808 (accessed 24 February 2011); 'BARLTROP, Roger Arnold Rowlandson', *Who Was Who*, www.ukwhoswho.com/view/article/oupww/whowaswho/U6521 (accessed 24 February 2011).
6 'BILAINKIN, George', *Who Was Who*, www.ukwhoswho.com/view/article/oupww/whowaswho/U162013 (accessed 24 February 2011); BATTEN, Edith Mary', *Who Was Who*, www.ukwhoswho.com/view/article/oupww/whowaswho/U161835 (accessed 24 February 2011); 'BARNELL, Herbert Rex', *Who Was Who*, www.ukwhoswho.com/view/article/oupww/whowaswho/U152040 (accessed 24 February 2011).
7 Andrea Smith (ed.), *Europe's Invisible Migrants: Consequences of the Colonists' Return* (Chicago: University of Chicago Press, 2002), p. 9.
8 Elizabeth Buettner, 'Imperial Britons back home', in R. Bickers (ed.), *Settlers and Expatriates: Britons Over the Seas* (Oxford: Oxford University Press, 2010), p. 315.
9 Buettner, 'Imperial Britons back home', pp. 312–23.
10 Frederick Cooper, 'Postcolonial peoples: a commentary' in Smith (ed.), *Europe's Invisible Migrants* p. 169.
11 'Objects of the Royal Colonial Institute, founded 1868', Appendix A in Trevor R. Reese, *The History of the Royal Commonwealth Society, 1868–1968* (London: Oxford University Press, 1968), p. 259.
12 Stuart Mole, from an interview conducted by Ruth Craggs, 14 July 2003, cited in Ruth Craggs, 'Cultural geographies of the Modern Commonwealth from 1947 to 1973' (PhD dissertation, University of Nottingham, 2009), p. 69.
13 Elizabeth Buettner, 'Cemeteries, public memory and Raj nostalgia in postcolonial Britain and India', *History & Memory*, 18:1 (2006), 17.
14 John MacKenzie, *Propaganda and Empire: The Manipulation of Public Opinion 1880–1960* (Manchester: Manchester University Press 1986), pp. 147–73; Barbara Bush, 'Britain's conscience on Africa: white women, race and imperial politics in inter-war Britain', in Clare Midgley (ed.), *Gender and Imperialism* (Manchester: Manchester University Press, 1998), pp. 200–24; Clare Midgley, 'Bringing the Empire home: women activists in imperial Britain, 1790–1930', in Hall and Rose, *At Home with Empire*, pp. 230–50; J. O. Springhall, 'Lord Meath, youth and Empire', *Journal of Contemporary History*, 5:4 (1970), 97–111. Despite its long history and the great potential offered by its substantial archival records there have been very few detailed studies of the Royal Commonwealth Society. Ruth Craggs's 2009 doctoral thesis 'Cultural geographies of the Modern Commonwealth from 1947 to 1973' is the first concerted engagement with the society's institutional archives since

Trevor Reese's *The History of the Royal Commonwealth Society* was commissioned for the society's centenary in 1968.

15 John Chadwick, 'A very lively corpse', *Commonwealth Journal*, 6:1 (1968), 19.
16 Guy Arnold, *Towards Peace and a Multiracial Commonwealth* (London: Chapman and Hall, 1964), p. 24.
17 'A party finding its feet', *The Times* (4 April 1964).
18 *Corona* (August 1962), p. 8.
19 Jean P. Smith, '"The women's branch of the Commonwealth Relations Office": the Society for the Overseas Settlement of British Women and the long life of empire migration', *Women's History Review*, 25:4 (2016), 529.
20 Alex May, 'Empire loyalists and "Commonwealth men": the Round Table and the end of Empire', in Ward (ed.) *British Culture and the End of Empire*, p. 53.
21 Craggs, 'Cultural geographies', p. 77.
22 'New name of Royal Empire Society', *The Times* (9 May 1958).
23 Craggs, 'Cultural geographies', p. 17.
24 Arthur Bryant, *Illustrated London News* (5 November 1960).
25 Arthur Bryant, *Illustrated London News* (30 May 1964).
26 *The Times* (22 June 1957). It is highly likely that this is the same James P. Brander who wrote letters to the *Eugenics Review*.
27 For a summary of more recent attitudes see K. Ford and S. Katwala, *Reinventing the Commonwealth* (London: Foreign Policy Centre, 1999), pp. 50–1.
28 'Coming Events at H.Q.', *Commonwealth Journal*, 4:5 (1961), 247.
29 Craggs, 'Cultural geographies', p. 104.
30 *Ibid.*, p. 96.
31 *Ibid.*, p. 102.
32 *Ibid.*, p. 104.
33 Vincent Powell-Smith, *Commonwealth Journal*, 5:5 (1962), 228.
34 Philip Murphy, *Party Politics and Decolonisation: The Conservative Party and British Colonial Policy in Tropical Africa, 1951–1964* (Oxford: Oxford University Press, 1995), pp. 53, 197.
35 *Commonwealth Journal*, 4:1 (1961), 4. Italics in original.
36 Enoch Powell called the Commonwealth a 'gigantic farce' in an anonymous article in *The Times* (2 April 1964).
37 *Commonwealth Journal*, 8:5 (1965), 259; *Commonwealth Journal*, 9:1 (1966), 1.
38 Duke of Devonshire in *Royal Commonwealth Society Centenary*, p. 25.
39 Arnold, *Towards Peace*, p. 24.
40 Royal Commonwealth Society Archive, Cambridge University Library (hereafter RCS), Commonwealth Study Committee, Committee Papers 1966–1969, Group Project Competition, Examiners Report 1966.
41 *Commonwealth Journal*, 10:3 (1967), 118.
42 Webster, *Englishness and Empire*, p. 104.
43 John Chadwick, *The Unofficial Commonwealth: The Story of the Commonwealth Foundation, 1965–1980* (London: Allen & Unwin, 1982), p. 45.
44 Margaret Ball, *The 'Open' Commonwealth* (Durham, NC: Duke University Press, 1971), pp. 78–79.
45 *Commonwealth Journal*, 5:6 (1962), 299.
46 Earl De La Warr, 'Commonwealth Day Message', *Commonwealth Journal*, 4:4 (1963), 49.
47 Chadwick, 'Lively Corpse', *Commonwealth Journal*, 21.
48 William Kirkham in *Royal Commonwealth Centenary*, pp. 73–5.
49 *The Times* (10 June 1966).
50 Norman Jeffries in *Royal Commonwealth Society Centenary*, p. 92.
51 Arnold Smith in *Royal Commonwealth Society Centenary*, p. 61.
52 RCS, Nudge Miscellaneous, Nudge Memorandum for Central Council, 20 February 1968.
53 Letter from Philip Birkinshaw, *Commonwealth Journal*, 5:6 (1962), 299.
54 *The Times* (4 April 1964).

55 Earl De La Warr, 'The work of the Commonwealth Societies', *Journal of the Royal Society of the Arts*, 109:5062 (1961), 802.
56 De La Warr, 'The work of the Commonwealth Societies', 82.
57 RCS, Public Affairs, May 1969-May 1977, Memorandum: a Critical Appraisal of the Society, 9 January 1973.
58 Commonwealth Correspondent, *The Times* (10 June 1966).
59 Smith in *Royal Commonwealth Society Centenary*, p. 61; Kirkman in *Royal Commonwealth Society Centenary*, p. 73.
60 TNA, DO 191/149, G. D. Anderson, Memo to General Bishop, 18 March 1963.
61 Report of Central Council for year ended 31 December 1967, *Commonwealth Journal* (1968).
62 RCS, Council Minutes 1868–1947, Minutes, 27 July 1967.
63 Elizabeth Buettner, *Empire Families: Britons and Late Imperial India* (Oxford: Oxford University Press, 2004), pp. 212, 227–9.
64 Buettner, *Empire Families*, p. 222.
65 RCS, Commonwealth Affairs Committee Papers, Pilot Scheme on Market Research, 28 February 1973.
66 RCS, Hants and Dorset, Annual Report for the year 1966 and Annual Report for the year 1967.
67 Reese, *Royal Commonwealth Society*, p. 234.
68 RCS, Public Affairs May 1969–1977, Market Research 28 February 1973; Craggs, 'Cultural geographies,' p. 107.
69 RCS, Commonwealth Purpose Group 1963–4, C. Carrington to David Whatley, 29 October 1963.
70 Chadwick, 'Lively corpse', p. 18.
71 Craggs, 'Cultural geographies', p. 110.
72 *Ibid.*, p. 111.
73 RCS, Council Minutes, Council Minutes, 24 October 1963.
74 RCS, Commonwealth Affairs Committee Papers, Pilot Scheme on Market Research, 28 February 1973. (Over half of the respondents identified the society's restaurants and bars as the aspect of the society that was of highest personal value to them.)
75 RCS, Public Affairs, May 1969–May 1977, Memorandum: A Critical Appraisal of the Society, 9 January 1973.
76 RCS, Branch Records, Sussex, Lecture Programme 1961–62 and 1964–65.
77 *Commonwealth Journal*, 4:3 (1961), 144.
78 RCS, Branch Records, Hants and Dorset, Chairman's Report for 1958.
79 RCS, Public Affairs, Memorandum on Lunchtime Meetings, 13 November 1973.
80 RCS, Commonwealth Affairs Committee, Agendas and Minutes Review of Past and Current Activities, 5 May 1969.
81 *Ibid.*
82 RCS, Cambridgeshire Branch Minutes, AGM, 25 April 1969.
83 RCS, Sussex Branch, Sussex Branch Overview from Central RCS, Deputy Chairman of Council to Sir William Sullivan, 11 November 1961.
84 Lord Casey, *The Future of the Commonwealth* (London: F. Muller, 1963), p. 38.
85 Reese, *Royal Commonwealth Society*, p. 257.
86 RCS, Commonwealth Affairs Committee Agendas and Minutes May 1969–February 1962, Future Policy Agenda, 9 June 1970.
87 RCS, Financial and Administrative Arrangements with Branches Guidance to Branches Overseas, 30 September 1970.
88 John Darwin, 'Orphans of Empire', in Thompson (ed.), *Britain's Experience of Empire*, p.339.
89 MacKenzie, *Propaganda and Empire*; Bush, 'Britain's conscience'; Midgley, 'Bringing the Empire home'; Springhall, 'Lord Meath, Youth and Empire'.
90 Webster, *Englishness and Empire*, p. 92.
91 Cited in Peter Hansen, 'Coronation Everest: the Empire and Commonwealth in the "second Elizabethan age"', in Ward (ed.), *British Culture and the End of Empire*, p. 68.

92 TNA, DO 35/8232, Summary of Report of an Interdepartmental Working Party on the Projection of the Commonwealth in the United Kingdom, no date, c. 1960.
93 *Yorkshire Post* (24 May 1961).
94 S. C. Leslie, 'British attitudes to the commonwealth', *Round Table*, 63:251 (1973), 364.
95 John MacKenzie, 'The persistence of empire in metropolitan culture', in Ward (ed.), *British Culture and the End of Empire*, p. 32.
96 TNA, DO 35/8232, Summary of Report of an Interdepartmental Working Party on the Projection of the Commonwealth in the United Kingdom, no date, c.1960.
97 TNA, DO 191/11, Minutes Executive Committee, 25 January 1962, Commonwealth Institute Education Executive and Managing Committees meetings.
98 'Au Revoir', *Commonwealth Journal*, 4:1 (1961), 43.
99 Brigadeer Johnson, *Commonwealth Journal*, 5:6 (1962), 300.
100 Ruth Craggs, 'The Commonwealth Institute and the Commonwealth Arts Festival: architecture, performance and multiculturalism in late-imperial London', *The London Journal*, 36:3 (2011), 248.
101 Gail Low, 'At home? Discoursing on the Commonwealth at the 1965 Commonwealth Arts Festival', *Journal of Commonwealth Literature*, 48:1 (2013), 97–111; Radhika Natarajan, 'Performing multiculturalism: the Commonwealth Arts Festival of 1965', *Journal of British Studies*, 53 (2014), 705–33; Craggs, 'The Commonwealth Institute and the Commonwealth Arts Festival'.
102 TNA, ED 121/1048, O&M Report on the Institute, August 1967.
103 TNA, WORK 20/346, Mr J.T. Hughes, Commonwealth Relations Office, to Mr R. W. Barrow, Ministry of Public Building and Works, 20 January 1965, cited in Low, 'At home?', p. 98.
104 Natarajan, 'Performing multiculturalism', p. 731; Low, 'At home?', p. 99.
105 TNA, CAB 129/95 Memorandum by the Secretary of State for Commonwealth Relations and the Chancellor of the Duchy of Lancaster, 13 December 1958.
106 TNA, DO 191/149 N. Pritchard to Mr Braine, 19 June 1961.
107 RCS, Commonwealth Affairs Committee, Review of Past and Current Activities, 5 May 1969.
108 Reese, *Royal Commonwealth Society*, p. 232.
109 RCS, Council Minutes, Council Minutes, 25 July 1968.
110 RCS, Commonwealth Studies Foundation, Memorandum by Secretary-General on Report of Committee, 30 July 1957.
111 RCS, Commonwealth Studies Foundation, Minutes of the Commonwealth Study Committee, 10 October 1968.
112 RCS, Public Affairs, Press release on New Perspectives on Race Relations in Britain, 14 August 1969.
113 RCS, Council Minutes, Council Minutes, 27 June 1963.
114 RCS, Commonwealth Affair Committee Agendas and Minutes, Review of Past and Current Activities, 5 May 1969.
115 RCS, Branch Reports, Hants and Dorset, Chairman's Report for 1958.
116 RCS, Commonwealth Studies Foundation, Memorandum on Possible Activities of the Commonwealth Studies Foundation, September 1958.
117 Reese, *Royal Commonwealth Society*, p. 260.
118 Springhall, 'Lord Meath, youth and empire', p. 103.
119 *Ibid.*
120 M. Harper, '"Personal contact is worth a ton of text-books": educational tours of the Empire, 1926–39', *Journal of Imperial and Commonwealth History*, 32:3 (2004), 48–76.
121 Jonathon Green, *All Dressed Up: The Sixties and the Counterculture* (London: Vintage, 1999), pp. 2–3.
122 Bailkin, *Afterlife of Empire*, pp. 19, 55–132.
123 RCS, Council Minutes, Council Minutes, 24 February 1966.
124 *Commonwealth Journal*, 4:1 (1961), 43.

125 RCS, Commonwealth Studies Committee Minutes, Committee Minutes, 2 February 1969.
126 Alec Dickson, *Commonwealth Journal*, 4:1 (1961), 47.
127 'Holiday Lectures', *Guardian* (30 December 1960).
128 *Commonwealth Journal*, 6:2 (1963), 45.
129 TNA, FCO 49/155, no. 8, 'Value of the Commonwealth to Britain': letter from Sir P. Gore-Booth to Sir S Garner on draft of a Commonwealth Office Paper 15 Feb 1967. Reproduced in S. R. Ashton and Wm Roger Louis (eds). *British Documents on the End of Empire*, Series A, Volume 5, East of Suez and the Commonwealth 1964–1971, Part II Europe, Rhodesia, Commonwealth (London: Institute for Commonwealth Studies, 2004), p. 408.
130 *Commonwealth Journal*, 6:6 (1967), 225.
131 Lord Casey, 'Awake! Awake!', *Commonwealth Journal*, 5:4 (1962), 168.
132 Capricorn Africa Society, Borthwick Institute for Archives, York (hereafter CAP), League of Empire Loyalists, 'Policy for Patriots' *c.*1957.
133 *Ibid.*
134 Murphy, *Party Politics and Decolonisation*, pp. 203–8.
135 Murphy, *Party Politics and Decolonisation*, p. 225.
136 RCS, Commonwealth Purpose Group 1963–4, Gerald Graham to Hilary Blood 27 September 1962.
137 RCS, Commonwealth Purpose Group 1963–64, Carrington to Whatley, 24 October 1963.
138 RCS, Nudge Miscellaneous, David Whatley, Chair of Nudge Committee 'What is Nudge about?' 1967.
139 RCS, Nudge Miscellaneous, Press Statement by Nudge Committee, 1 May 1967.
140 RCS, Nudge Miscellaneous, A. S. H. Kemp, Secretary-General of RCS to Stephen Leslie, Chairman of the Nudge Committee, 14 October 1968.
141 *Ibid.*
142 Buettner, 'Britons back home', p. 324.
143 W. David McIntyre, *Commonwealth of Nations: Origins and Impact 1869–1971* (Minneapolis: University of Minnesota Press, 1977), p. 474.
144 RCS, Commonwealth Studies Committee, Committee Papers 1966–1969, Branches Conference, 24 June 1968.

CHAPTER TWO

International mobility and the pursuit of informed understanding

Domestic cultures of international mobility

In 1962 Air India ran an advertisement in *The Times* that made the bold declaration: 'Look out Mr. World. I'm coming to see you with jets jetting.'[1] Referring to the rapid expansion of commercial air travel that had been taking place since the 1950s, the advertisement also tapped into the widespread excitement that surrounded global mobility in this period – mobility in which members of the British public were ever more able to participate. In the immediate post-war years, international travel opportunities had been largely restricted to an elite class of diplomats, politicians, officials, businessmen, and foreign contractors.[2] By the early 1960s, advancements in jet propulsion had allowed lower-cost carriers to open up the globe to British tourists on a new scale.[3] Britain's main airline BOAC boasted that it would 'unfold the world' and, for affluent tourists now able to fly as far as India, East Africa, Australia, and America, this must have rung true.[4] As *Rotary*, the magazine of RIBI, put it in 1964, 'never in the course of human history have so many men and women from every walk of life spent their holidays in countries other than that of their own origin'.[5] Travel provided opportunities for relaxation and escapism, but for many – and particularly for those who travelled further afield – it was also regarded as an edifying tool for cross-cultural understanding. Through travel, *Rotary* explained, 'much of the rumour and prejudice which once surrounded nations which men could never hope to visit has been torn away'.[6] As one member's wife expanded, 'while the aeroplane, like a modern magic carpet, by shrinking time and distance, has given us a vision of a single home for the human family, it has also enabled us to see how excitingly different we are'.[7] This narrative of travel was not new, but it was given new meaning in the post-war period in the context of decolonisation and the Cold War.

Crucially, not all members of British society were equal participants in this mobility. Even with the increasing democratisation of tourism, international flights remained prohibitively expensive for the majority of the population. The average holiday was more likely to be reached by car or boat than by plane, and most holidays took place within rather than beyond the European continent.[8] Until the 1970s first-hand touristic experiences of the 'unfolding world' remained the privilege of the upper and upper middle classes. Within associations like the WI, this inequality of opportunity continued inter-war trends. As Linda Ambrose describes, grass-roots members could only 'watch from the side lines and try to imagine the experiences' that elite mobile members 'enjoyed as they recounted to their membership their exciting tales of luxurious international travel adventures'.[9]

But while international travel itself may have been limited to these affluent members of society, the cultural impact of transcontinental mobility on 1960s Britain had a much wider reach. Research on post-war mobility has tended to focus on the experience of physical travel itself. But, as opportunities for 'real' travel increased, so too did those for 'virtual' or 'vicarious' travel.[10] As the WI told their members, 'even if it is not possible for you to go far afield from your village, let alone visit another country, you, too, can travel through the minds of others and get to know people and places all over the world'.[11] Associational organisations such as the WI and Rotary Club provided important spaces for this kind of virtual travel, their international remits working to bring cultures of international mobility into everyday British life. This chapter shows that, far from being a minority issue, increased mobility shaped how less mobile members of the British public imagined both their place in the decolonising world and their responsibilities towards it.

British responses to the rapidly globalising world of the 1960s always contained strong elements of both optimism and anxiety. These were not separate responses to separate issues – not a list of simple pros and cons – rather the perceived positives of globalisation carried with them their own negatives. Though increased contact with foreign peoples and places offered the possibility for international understanding, it also raised the spectre of potential misunderstanding – misunderstandings that could hardly be afforded at a time when global stability appeared increasingly fragile. While increases in mobility were celebrated for the freedom and leisure opportunities that they presented to individuals, they came with warnings about the need for collective responsibility that extended beyond those who could afford to travel. As a WI handbook on international work explained, 'because the world has grown "smaller" our own lives are more closely linked with the peoples of other nations and woven with theirs to the intricate pattern of international affairs. It is, therefore, vitally important that we learn all we can about them.'[12] Those who could not travel themselves were nevertheless expected to take advantage of the opportunities for vicarious travel offered by associational life. The WI told its members that 'to reach out, from the village into the world beyond is a golden opportunity well within every member's grasp'.[13] It was not only their mobile members who these organisations expected to live international lives.

This chapter and the next are about how members of associational life acted on this sense of responsibility and made use of different networks of mobility in order to 'get to know' the decolonising world. They explore the impact of decolonisation and globalisation on not only the different types of international experience to which members of the WI and Rotary had access in the 1960s, but also the different values that these organisations assigned to those experiences. While this chapter focuses on the pursuit of knowledge about foreign places and peoples, the next is concerned with intimate and affective relationships formed with those from overseas. Understanding how knowledge works in imperial contexts has been a central concern of scholarship on colonialism since the late 1980s. Informed by Foucault's account of the relationship between knowledge and power, this research has focused on the social construction of knowledge and its impact on the relationship between coloniser and colonised.[14] It has shown that the universalising claims of technical and scientific superiority were a central feature of the legitimising discourse of colonialism (and, indeed, of neo-colonialism). As well as functioning as a mechanism of colonial rule, socially constructed knowledge about the Empire has also shaped the 'imaginative geographies' of those in the metropole, building a picture of the wider world and their relationship to it.[15]

Within Britain, supporters of imperialism have tended to assume a strong connection between knowledge about, and loyalty towards, the British Empire. As discussed in Chapter 1, the post-war Commonwealth societies that committed themselves to creating an informed public followed in the footsteps of nineteenth- and early twentieth-century imperial propagandists. In 1904 Lord Meath, founder of the Empire Day movement, wrote that youth ought to be acquiring a

> thorough knowledge of the history, extent, power and resources of the great Empire to which they belong, of the conditions, moral and physical, which rule in different portions of that empire, of the nature of the climates, productions, commerce, trade and manufactures, and of the characteristics, religion, customs, and habits of thought of the various races, peoples, creeds and classes, which owe a common allegiance to King Edward.[16]

Meath may have set the bar rather high, but his assumptions about the relationship between knowing and caring are shared by some historians of Britain who have suggested that because the British public knew little about the Empire it neither mattered to them nor impacted on their lives.[17] This chapter is not primarily concerned with judging *what* members of the WI and Rotary knew about the declining empire (not least because it is difficult to determine this with any precision), but rather with understanding how they approached the pursuit of knowledge – what did they think it important to know about and why? In her work on the impact of decolonisation on the welfare state, Jordanna Bailkin has shown the tremendous insights we can gain from re-evaluating this period in terms of its 'competing modes of knowledge'. Meath's list gives a clear indication of the broad range of knowledge that was deemed useful at the start of the twentieth century. But what 'new ways of knowing' were demanded by the British public in the post-war world?[18]

This chapter traces how different claims to authority and sources of 'knowledge' circulated within WI and Rotary associational life and assesses what impact they were likely to have had on members' understandings of the world. Tourism may have been widely discussed as a new form of international mobility, but it was not the only form of mobility that shaped experiences within associational life. Many others were influenced directly by decolonisation and informed a set of competing visions of the declining empire, wider world, and Britain's place within it. The choices that the WI and Rotary made about how to utilise available forms of international knowledge tell us about the different kinds of relationship they imagined with the outside world. What expectations did these associations have for their members' international engagement? What were members expected to know in order to fulfil their responsibility as internationally engaged citizens? And to what extent did WI and Rotary decisions perpetuate material and imagined networks of imperialism?

These questions do not have straightforward answers. There is no such thing as the WI or Rotary position on the British Empire. Neither organisation's activities can be said to represent any kind of sustained analyses of decolonisation, Britain's imperial past, or plans for a post-imperial future. Instead, Rotary and WI practices of international engagement and the discourses that accompanied them are best characterised as messy, incomplete, inconsistent, and often contradictory. The attitudes and activities promoted varied dramatically, within each organisation's official magazine – *Home and Country* for the WI and *Rotary* for RIBI – as well as between individual clubs and institutes. What follows is not, therefore, an exhaustive account of this complexity in all its different variations, but an attempt to trace the ideas and practices that surface most often and to explain the significance of the common assumptions that underpinned them.

International remits for an international age

The primary function of Rotary Clubs and Women's Institutes was not to serve international causes. The WI was, at its heart, a mechanism for rural sociability. As Caitriona Beaumont sets out, its original purpose was to give rural women 'the opportunity to study home economies and to stimulate their interest in agricultural industries'.[19] Typical meetings included handicrafts, music, drama, and agricultural pursuits, emphasising women's responsibilities to their local community and to the nation.[20] By the WI's own admission, it was an 'insular' movement prior to the inter-war period.[21] Although the Rotary movement became international very quickly – expanding from its US origins to include clubs in London, Dublin, Belfast, Manchester, and Glasgow by 1912 – this network was initially seen only in terms of the business and trading opportunities that it provided.[22] In its early years, Rotary had two key objectives: the promotion of the business interests of its members and service to the local community.[23] Before the start of the First World War, therefore, Rotary was an international organisation that thought little about international responsibilities. Yet, by the 1960s all members of both organisations were expected to think and act as global citizens. How and why did this transformation take place?

Internationalist ideas started to emerge at the end of the nineteenth century but it was not until the inter-war period that they really took root. The traumas of the First World War created a greater consciousness of social, political, and economic problems that transcended borders, which in turn led to the emergence of internationalism as both foreign policy and civic ideal.[24] Advocate of the League of Nations Willoughby Dickinson wrote that nations would gradually draw together and 'by cooperating constantly for the good of all they will develop a new internationalist spirit'.[25] Beyond the state, associational, religious, and humanitarian groups also began to discuss the best means to restore and preserve harmony. This was, Arsan, Lewis, and Richard argue, 'a period of unprecedented popular enthusiasm for transnational associational life, in which various competing calls to global affinity ... jostled and clamoured for the attention of men and women from North America and western Europe to India and Southeast Asia'.[26] Already an international organisation, Rotary took steps towards increased cooperation within its own movement. In 1921 at their annual convention members voted to support what is now Rotary's Fourth Objective: 'The advancement of international understanding, goodwill and peace through a world fellowship of business and professional persons united in the ideal of service'. As Goff describes, in the inter-war period '"service" became an ideological common denominator for local civic activism as well as international strides towards peace'.[27]

Within Britain, this popular internationalism took a range of different forms but, as Helen McCarthy has shown, it largely 'drew its succour' from the League of Nations. League supporters used public ritual and pageantry to embed the movement in wider civil society, encouraging Britons to 'see themselves as members of an international community, as well as citizens of an imperial nation state'.[28] Both the WI and Rotary encouraged their members to participate in League of Nations activity. In 1921 the WI, who described how they had been 'shaken out of ourselves' by the First World War, pledged to study the principles underlying the League of Nations.[29] In this period, imperial propagandists also sought to capitalise on associations' increased interest in the outside world. The Victoria League specifically targeted the WI in an attempt to bolster interest in empire among newly enfranchised rural women, while the Empire Marketing Board also sent representatives to Rotary and WI meetings.[30] At a Saltford WI meeting in 1926, for example, Eldred Walker spoke to members about butter from New Zealand, cheese from Australia, fruit from South Africa, and wheat from Canada. In 1933, members of Pendeen WI in Cornwall combined a talk by Nancy Williams on the 'Common Empire' with a competition to draw the 'best sketch of Hitler on a blackboard'.[31]

Rotary and the WI set important precedents for international engagement in the inter-war period, both in terms of the commitments that they made to preserving peace and the types of international activity that some members began to participate in. But the real, practical growth in their international remits and activity did not take place until after the Second World War. Two key changes characterise this shift. First, both organisations increased the expectations they placed on individual members to uphold their organisational commitments to internationalism and international understanding. By the mid-1950s the WI explained that education in international affairs should be 'part of the general pattern of work in every WI' and added a clause to its local and national rules 'to promote international understanding among countrywomen'.[32] In 1964 Fred Longden, chairman of RIBI's International Service committee set out similar expectations: 'In this troubled world of ours "understanding" and the desire to understand are of paramount importance.' It was the job of the International Service Committee, he explained, to ensure that 'every Rotarian is filled with the desire to understand'.[33] Both organisations spent the 1960s putting in place networks and practices that would allow their members to meet these increased expectations.

The second significant difference between both organisations' inter-war and post-war internationalism lay in the set of global challenges that drove this work. Where peace in Europe had been the priority in the inter-war period, the challenges that WI and Rotary described and the responsibilities that they assumed in the post-war period were much more global. Alongside references to a generalised sense of living in a shrinking world, a set of more specific issues recur throughout Rotary and WI discussions of internationalism in the 1960s: poverty, the Cold War, new-state formation, and racial conflict. International activities within both organisations did address other issues; for example, in the late 1950s and 1960s the Yorkshire Federation International Subcommittee of the WI organised International Days on Holland, America, Spain, Italy, Iceland, Greece, Canada, and Japan.[34] Collectively, however, these challenges shifted both movements' attention towards the global South. For example, the WI's Denman College ran a popular week-long course on 'South Africa from the Boer War to Apartheid', which addressed questions about contemporary race relations as well as providing a historical narrative, and another on 'Africa and the New Emergent Countries', with an emphasis on agricultural and community development.[35] Many of these events built on the assumption that instability in these regions was now the greatest threat to world peace. For example, the President of RIBI sought to persuade Rotarians that developing nations must be saved from potential disaster: 'If there is to be peace in the world their standard of living must be constantly raised.'[36] Each of these issues was also understood as a global concern – one with global implications and in need of a collaborative global solution. As the WI explained, 'the movement as a whole appears increasingly aware that its aims to improve conditions of rural life cannot now be worked out in one country in isolation from the rest of the world'.[37]

How did the WI and Rotary expect their members to respond to these new global challenges? Both organisations' international remits were underpinned by the belief that international stability was increasingly reliant upon international understanding. President of RIBI John Little explained that 'if the problems of the world are to be solved, they must be solved by more and more people thinking seriously about them and then trying to understand them, and discussing them in a sympathetic and friendly way'.[38] 'If our work with other nations is to serve a useful purpose and so help towards a peaceful future,' echoed the WI, 'we must *think internationally*.'[39] Both organisations did participate in schemes that made specific practical interventions to address global poverty, but they also stressed that developing members' international understanding was a necessary precursor to other forms of international action. The WI described understanding as an essential precondition for effective assistance: 'we really must get to know the background of their lives before we can offer constructive help'.[40] In very similar language, Rotary explained that 'knowledge of the situation in ... underdeveloped countries was a necessary forerunner to enlightened action'.[41]

To build this foundation of international understanding both organisations assigned their members two interrelated responsibilities. The first of these, and the focus of this chapter, was what Rotary described as 'world thinking' and the WI as 'the education of the WI member in international matters'.[42] This required members to build up their knowledge about the wider world. 'To qualify themselves to advance international understanding', the international magazine *Rotarian* explained, 'Rotarians must first become informed on great issues in the area of international affairs', or, as the Women's Institute put it, members needed to learn to 'be world wise with the WIs'.[43] The second key component of international understanding was what Rotary described as 'world fellowship' and the WI as 'international friendship'.[44] This built on the foundation of world thinking to establish empathetic and reciprocal relationships with people living in other parts of the world. This affective model of international understanding is the focus of Chapter 3.

Although the principles of international understanding were widely endorsed by countries on both sides of the Iron Curtain in the post-war period, its celebration and practice had distinctive national permutations. British approaches were shaped by the country's imperial past and decolonising present. As Helen McCarthy suggests, the model of international community dramatised so effectively by liberal internationalists between the wars rested on the assumption of Britain's premier status as a global power.[45] The empire was to be '*the* great example of the sort of international cooperation on which a stable system of organised world relations can be erected'.[46] Decolonisation, the Cold War, the events of the Suez crisis, and Britain's declining global status made it increasingly difficult to hold together the multiple images of Britain as a historic English nation, a great imperial power, and a responsible member of the international community – though some still clearly tried.[47]

In 1960s Britain, the skills required to practise cultural diplomacy were frequently discussed in relation to the country's imperial past. Writing in *Rotary*, member J. E. Parry explained the unique contribution that Britain could make to global peace and understanding: 'The world, in this hour of menace, has never needed so much our British experience in world affairs, our tradition of tolerance and firmness in adversity, our wealth of understanding of the races and creeds of our far-flung if evanescing Empire.' Parry's claims that Britain understood its Empire and its peoples echoed broader affirming narratives that described decolonisation as an orderly and amicable transfer of power.[48] His article illustrates the anxieties about Britain's global role that were circulating at this time – 'lately there has been a tendency for us to disparage ourselves and talk in a defeatist vein, and then we wonder that other nations take us at our own valuation' – but it also shows how readily Britain's imperial past could be invoked to describe an optimistic future in which Britain maintained power and influence on the global stage. As Parry explained, 'we in Britain can still exercise a tremendous force in the world, and we owe our prestige to our past history'.[49] In this narrative, Britain's imperial past and post-imperial future were folded together as part of the same project of international understanding.

Parry's advice to Rotarians is indicative of the broader discursive dynamics of post-imperial responsibility within associational life. In Rotary and WI publications, the challenges of the Cold War, new-state formation, global poverty, and racial tension were described as belonging not to Britain, but to the entire international community. By focusing on the global nature of the challenges faced, Rotary and the WI over-looked the causal role that centuries of colonial rule had played in shaping the global inequalities of the 1960s. For example, although the dynamics of decolonisation were central to each of the global challenges that the WI and Rotary described, they were rarely mentioned in associational discussions of international responsibility. The same was not true at state level: the Foreign Office, Colonial Office, and Commonwealth Relations Office treated them as interlinked issues. In the early 1960s the decision to grant independence with majority rule to British colonies in Sub-Saharan Africa was driven, in part, by the desire to limit the advance of Communism in this region, while efforts to address poverty and underdevelopment were also part of Britain's broader post-imperial strategy to maintain influence in newly independent African states.[50] It is difficult to judge precisely why these connections did not register in associational life, but their absence had important implications for the ways in which the WI and Rotary imagined their members' international responsibilities. At the same time that they overlooked British culpability for these problems, com-mentators such as Parry also suggested that Britain's unique skills – developed as an imperial power – ought to give the nation and its population increased *status* in the search for solutions, and increased *credit* when favourable changes took place.

As with the People's Commonwealth, citizens were at the centre of this project. When Parry spoke about the collective prestige of the British nation he placed responsibility for that prestige not with the state but with its citizens. 'Though Britain has a mighty quota to add to the pool of international understanding', he wrote, 'that contribution can only be made by individual citizens'.[51] This emphasis on 'ordinary' individuals also echoed principles of cultural diplomacy endorsed by the British state in the decades after the Second World War. At an international level, efforts to improve nations' reputations overseas increasingly emphasised cultural exchange and interaction over more traditional methods of propaganda.[52] In Britain, an increasing number of state-funded organisations and projects – most notably the British Council, established in 1934 – sought forms of international influence that could avoid 'the taint of political propaganda' as well as negative associations with the political turmoil of decolonisation and the Cold War.[53] These state initiatives gave greater impetus to similar activities taking place in associational life.

But what were individual citizens expected to do in order to fulfil the responsibilities that their associations had claimed for them? Rotary and WI members' 'education' in international issues occurred through two primary channels: speakers giving presentations at regular club and institute meetings and the organisation of larger-scale, publicly attended International Days. Both organisations' international education programmes were reactive, in the sense that they relied on the availability of people willing to speak to them. But they are also illustrative of the active role that associations and individual members of associational life played in shaping their own experiences of decolonisation. The international remits of both organisations may have rested on the broad assumption that increased knowledge led to increased international understanding, but each had specific ideas about what, precisely, their members ought to know in order to 'accept the challenges of this new age of mass communication and travel'.[54] These institutional records do not give us direct access to the motivations of individual members and, for the most part, they give little insight into the content of these talks. But they do allow us to observe revealing patterns in local WI and Rotary activity as each organisation made determinations about what was worth knowing about. They indicate which parts of the world and which kinds of knowledge were most relevant to the specific global challenges that they had identified.

As I discuss throughout this chapter and the next, Rotarian and WI attitudes towards knowledge and understanding both perpetuated and challenged what we might characterise as imperial approaches to representing and engaging with foreign others. Some elements of their international work continued colonial traditions of knowledge acquisition, endorsing the imposition of expertise on foreign populations, while others indicate a growing interest in modes of knowledge formation that emphasised mutual understanding as the foundation of collaborative endeavours. The rest of this chapter is divided into three sections, each addressing distinct forms of international knowledge that circulated in associational life. These examine the experiences of tourists and amateur enthusiasts; white British citizens with first-hand experience working or volunteering in the British Empire; and 'representatives' of foreign countries visiting Britain. Each of these groups either claimed or was granted a distinct kind of authority based on the nature of their overseas experiences, and each contributed their own perspective on Britain's relationship with the declining empire and wider world.

Tourism and the amateur enthusiast

A considerable body of scholarship has shown the crucial role played by travel in shaping narratives of British identity and imperialism, particularly in the Victorian era. While research does consider the impact of decolonisation on these narratives, studies have tended to focus on the experiences of 'literary adventurers' and their published travel texts or television documentaries.[55] While professional travel narratives undoubtedly played an important role in shaping (post-) imperial consciousness back home in Britain, they tell us little about how travel as leisure pursuit – as opposed to professional endeavour – provided the British public with experiences of imperialism and decolonisation. And yet, by the 1960s, amateur tourists were increasingly able to share their travel experiences with the wider public. Three key factors made this possible. First, increased aero-mobility enabled the relatively affluent to travel to the kinds of faraway destinations that had previously been the preserve of the professional traveller; second, improvements in cine-camera technology made it easier for tourists to record their experiences overseas; finally, the growing international programmes of associations like the WI and Rotary meant that there were increasing opportunities for tourists to share their experiences once back in Britain. As the WI suggested, in 1957 the travel talk was 'probably the most popular way of introducing foreign lands'.[56]

By the 1960s, most club and institute programmes included at least one travel talk a year, and many organised considerably more, drawing on the touristic experiences of their own members as well as external speakers offering their services.[57] While these talks covered a wide geographical range – including many accounts of trips to Europe and North America – it is notable that travel talks about countries within the former and declining British Empire seem to have increased in the 1960s as it became easier for tourists to travel further afield. Between 1966 and 1968, for example, *Home and Country* reported on talks given at local institutes by members who had travelled to Barbados, Jamaica, Uganda, South Africa, and Kenya.[58] It is reasonable to expect that a significant number of similar talks went unreported.

A case study of Charles Chislett, a retired bank manager, a prolific amateur filmmaker, a Rotarian, and an active member of the Rotherham community illustrates the impact that increased tourist mobility could have on associational practices of international understanding. Touristic experiences often leave little archival trace, so Chislett's records, held at the Yorkshire Film Archive and Rotherham Archives, offer a rare opportunity to consider the impact of increased mobility on an individual tourist and his local community.[59] Before the Second World War, Chislett had travelled domestically and within Europe, but in the 1960s his travel horizons expanded dramatically: in 1962 he embarked on a thousand-mile cruise up the Nile, following this a year later with a Middle Eastern air cruise that stopped in Syria, Lebanon, and Jordan. In early 1965 he took a boat cruise along the East coast of Africa from Tanzania to Suez and in September of that year he left again for Africa for a four-month holiday. In his final trip of the decade he spent a month travelling across Asia, taking in India, Bangkok, Hong Kong, Singapore, and Malaysia. Chislett returned from these journeys with hours of film footage and a collection of experiences that shaped and informed his understanding of the changing world.[60]

Though Chislett did not comment on the geographic distribution of his travels, it is noteworthy that these trips took place almost exclusively within the bounds of the former British Empire. As well as relying on the increasing affordability of jet travel, touristic experiences in the 1960s also rode, to borrow Hsu-Ming Teo's phrase, 'on the coat-tails of colonization'.[61] In many Commonwealth and post-colonial nations the tourist industry was inescapably intertwined with the legacy of imperialism – shaped not only by its organisational infrastructure, but also by imperial fantasies of exotic travel that the industry knowingly tapped into.[62] Chislett explained that his decision to travel to Africa was shaped partly by Rider Haggard's fantastical stories of exotic African adventures, first published in the late nineteenth and early twentieth centuries.[63] When reviewing Haggard's autobiography in 1926, Horace G. Hutchinson wrote that it was 'not to be doubted that Haggard's South African romances filled many young fellows with longing to go into the wide spaces of those lands and see their marvels for themselves'.[64] As Chislett's enthusiasm reveals, these same narratives continued to be meaningful to a new generation of men in the post-war era of decolonisation. But while the language of heroics did survive the end of empire, it became considerably less prominent in the 1960s, particularly in the associational circles that I discuss in this book.[65]

Although touristic experiences were influenced by the tropes of professional travel and adventure narratives, they were not bound by them. For example, while Chislett was certainly attracted to the romance of adventure, his frequent celebration of the tourist experience (and repeated use of Thomas Cook tours) differs significantly from the disdainful attempts to avoid tourist practices so prevalent in travel writing dating from the same period. Many self-styled literary travellers went out of their way to avoid the beaten track and, as Hsu-Ming Teo describes, an astonishing number of travel writers expressed a 'nostalgic sense of loss ... for the possibilities of "real" travel' in the decades after decolonisation.[66] Yet for non-professional travellers such as Chislett who were not constrained by the expected tropes of published travel writing, the increased aero-mobility of the 1960s offered expanding rather than diminishing opportunities to experience and understand the shrinking world. Chislett's enthusiasm for touristic experiences not only offers an important counterpoint to narratives of post-imperial decline and inward-facing parochialism, it also illustrates the increasing acceptability of non-heroic modes of travel in the 1960s.[67]

As argued above, the impact of touristic mobility frequently resonated beyond the individual experiences of those who were able to travel overseas. Alongside locally focused charitable work – including support for a children's convalescent home, the St John's Ambulance Brigade, and Church and Pastoral Aid – Chislett was heavily involved in promoting international engagement among Rotherham citizens. He did this by taking on official roles within existing organisations – such as the chair of Rotherham Rotary's International Service Committee – but also as an individual enthusiast, seeking to reach as wide an audience as possible.[68] Chislett published accounts of his travels in *Rotary in the Ridings*, the quarterly publication of his Rotary district and, more significantly, in the first half of the 1960s he gave around 150 lectures and screenings about his travels to local and national audiences.[69] As Norris Nicholson explains, these amateur activities were not entirely new, but rather extended the conventions of the nineteenth-century illustrated travel lecture in which professional travellers toured the country delivering talks and slide shows.[70] As had the commercial travel lecturers that went before him, Chislett hoped to entertain his audiences, but he also stressed the educational purpose of his endeavours. Echoing Rotarian principles of international understanding, Chislett explained that he hoped 'to increase the knowledge of overseas countries and their peoples, and so to help to build friendship on understanding'.[71]

Chislett's self-appointed role as an amateur gave him the flexibility to approach issues of decolonisation from a range of different – and at times contradictory – perspectives.[72] Following broader trends in post-imperial travel writing, he frequently spoke of a desire to experience something of the pre-imperial past. He titled the film of his Nile cruise, *Egypt 2,000,000 Days Ago*, for example, and described how in Jordan '"Old Testament" land and life was all about [him]'.[73] It was a paradox that for many former colonies the transition to independence was often also a period of increased 'westernisation', prompting nostalgia among tourists for the loss of uniqueness, exoticism, and primitivism that empire had done away with.[74] Yet while Chislett clearly mourned the loss of 'primitive life', he failed to hold colonialism accountable for its role in this loss. Such an act of oversight closely conforms to Renate Rosaldo's characterisation of 'imperialist nostalgia'.[75] As well as showing an interest in what came before it, Chislett was also nostalgic about the imperial era itself. His description of Wadi Halfa in Sudan illustrates his tendency to gravitate towards heroic moments from the late-nineteenth century: 'the parade grounds are silent and deserted in the blazing sun, but you half expect to hear the imperative summons of a bugle, or meet a squad of pith helmeted sweat-stained khaki figures arguing about Gordon or Kitchener'.[76]

The account of imperialism and decolonisation that Chislett offered to associational audiences both included and transcended these more typical nostalgias of travel writing. Unlike published writers such as Lévi-Strauss, whose obsessive preoccupation with the past left him, in his own words, 'groaning among the shadows', Chislett also showed a keen interest in contemporary development.[77] For every wistful comment that Chislett made about the past, he made another that engaged critically with the post-colonial present; for every shot of rural life, he filmed another of a busy city. Juxtapositions between 'traditional' life and bustling modernity were a prominent feature of the appropriately titled *Africa Old and New*, which contrasted shots of unpeopled open plains with footage of cities such as Nairobi and Dar es Salaam where the buildings are decked in advertisements for international brands and modern cars line the kerb. As well as celebrating modernity, Chislett was also critical of what he identified as local and general problems in the post-colonial African continent. These included 'chips on shoulder re white help [*sic*]', 'evil propaganda', 'nationalism – often quite illogical', 'power of witch doctors', and 'Africans unwilling to prepare for future', as well as more specific examples such as the 1963–67 secessionist Shifta War in Kenya, 'problems in Uganda' (presumably referring to separatist Bugandan revolts), and the Rhodesian Unilateral Declaration of Independence in 1965, all events that occurred either during or immediately before his trip.[78]

The indeterminacies in Chislett's attitudes towards empire – variously praising modernisation, primitiveness, imperial influence, and authentic untouched culture – are evidence not just of inconsistency but also of the wide range of different frameworks and tropes – all shared in associational settings – that shaped Britons' experiences of decolonisation. They illustrate that at the end of empire, as had been the case in its heyday, there was no 'no uniform imperial impact, no joined-up or monolithic ideology of imperialism, no single source of enthusiasm or propaganda for the empire, no cohesive imperial movement'.[79] As Chislett's approach confirms, individuals within Britain have always embraced selectively those dimensions of the Empire that most suited their own desires and interests.

While the role of the amateur tourist afforded flexibility to those seeking to share their experiences, it also left them open to criticism about lack of rigour. This is illustrated in a 1961 *Guardian* profile of 60-year-old Hester Marsden-Smedley, a wealthy and well-travelled Chelsea resident who often gave public talks about her experiences in Africa, including to the WI. Having introduced Marsden-Smedley as a 'non-specialist', the article explained:

> She leaves you breathless as she rattles on talking about Kasavubu [the first president of the Republic of the Congo] and Tshombe [the first president of secessionist Katanga]; about Jesuit priests and Moslem dignitaries in Tehad; about Guinea's president, Sékou Touré, whose signed photograph occupies a place of honour in her cluttered study.[80]

For the author of the profile, Marsden-Smedley's amateur status as an outside observer made her an accessible and engaging speaker, but it was also a source of criticism. The *Guardian* concluded that her 'strength, as well as her weakness perhaps, is that she sees international relations in terms of human relations'. Such an approach might lead to colourful anecdotes – such as one about meeting the President of the Republic of the Congo and showing him a photograph of her husband, Basil, in his mayoral gown – but, implied the *Guardian* interviewer, it lacked the critical insight necessary to make a valuable contribution to the public's understanding of international relations.

While Rotary and the WI acknowledged that travel talks were a popular, enjoyable, and readily available point of access to foreign places, they also expressed reservations about their suitability as a tool for increasing international understanding. To be of 'real value', the WI told members, travel talks must 'be more than mere holiday reminiscences'.[81] Chislett's talks, we can presume, would have passed the test, full as they were of details about environmental conditions, political situations, and conversations with people Chislett met on his travels. But members of Rotary and the WI were encouraged to be critical audiences, capable of recognising the partiality of travel talks and films, particularly when provided by lending bodies such as tourist boards.[82] In the mid-1950s the WI had already concluded that the travel talk 'so much enjoyed by all WIs may prove a possible beginning, but it is not now always sufficient to satisfy the interest in international affairs which exists among WI members'.[83] Rotary and the WI did not suggest that learning about foreign spaces could not continue to be entertaining; meetings were always approached as opportunities for enjoyment as well as self-improvement. But, over the course of the 1960s, they did place increasing emphasis on both the depth and usability of the knowledge that members were expected to acquire through international engagement activities.

Usable knowledge: colonial know-how, professional expertise and voluntary experience

By the mid-1960s it was commonly accepted that the global challenges that most attracted the WI and Rotary's attention – poverty, new state formation, the Cold War, and race relations – could not be addressed by an educational programme that limited itself to holiday reminiscences. Events that were geared towards recreating the atmosphere of foreign places remained a common and popular dimension of Rotary and WI life throughout the decade, but they were no longer seen as sufficient to meet the needs of the shrinking world. Instead, WI and Rotary encouraged members to organise educational activities that directly discussed global challenges and their practical solutions. The best resourced initiatives were those put on centrally. For example, in 1962 the WI's Denman College hosted a course on 'Africa and the new emergent countries'. Over five days attendees listened to talks on: 'The changing face of Africa' by Lord Hemingford, President of the Africa Bureau and a former headmaster in Uganda and the Gold Coast; 'Community development in Bechuanaland' by a representative of the African Development Trust; 'An economic picture of the African Countries' by the director of the Overseas Development Institute; 'Contemporary Nyasaland' by a student studying at Cambridge; 'The contribution young people can make in the African countries' by a representative for Voluntary Service Overseas; and 'Tanganyika today' by the president of the Tanganyika Council of Women, an organisation established in 1953 by colonial wives to teach domestic skills to African women.[84]

Though an important example of the range of experience and expertise that the National Federation of Women's Institutes (NFWI) was able to draw on – and also of the tendency to focus on countries within the declining or former Empire – Denman courses were only attended by a very small proportion of WI members. They are not, therefore, representative of educative international engagement across the movement as a whole.

For most members of the WI and Rotary, education in 'global challenges' at the level of the local club or institute tended to be organised in relation to specific philanthropic initiatives. From their establishment in Britain in the early twentieth century, Rotary and WI groups have always shown considerable support for local charitable causes, committing time and money to provide resources and services for their own communities.[85] In the post-war period, the geographical scope of this 'service' activity expanded significantly; support for international causes became an increasingly expected dimension of civic responsibility and a routine element of local club/institute life. This development was driven not only by WI and Rotary's own institutional responses to the 'shrinking world' but also by the growing number of humanitarian and development organisations that directly courted Rotary and WI support (see Chapter 4). For example, both organisations were major supporters of World Refugee Year in 1959–60 and of its successor, the UN-sponsored Freedom from Hunger Campaign from 1962–1970; from 1967 to the early 1970s the WI contributed to a Save the Children initiative to send clothes and fabric to the Windward Isles; and from 1966 to the present day Rotary Clubs across Britain have been key contributors to the Ranfurly Library Service, a scheme to send English-language books to developing countries.[86]

As far as their civic responsibilities were concerned, Rotary and WI members were expected not only to *feel* and *act on* sympathy towards those in need, but also to be *well informed* about the conditions of their lives. In addition to learning the specific details of the initiatives to which they contributed, members were also encouraged to use philanthropic activity as an opportunity to learn more widely about the climate, social structure, geographical conditions, economic situation, cultural traditions, and everyday life of foreign places. A small proportion of this information was gathered directly from the people that they sought to support. For example, Women's Institutes exchanged letters with the Windward Islanders to whom they sent tea chests of clothing and fabric, sharing details of everyday life in England and the Caribbean.[87] The vast majority, however, was sourced either from the NGOs and state-affiliated organisations coordinating the schemes to which they contributed or from other British organisations. The WI used the Barclays Bank booklet *Windward Islands: An economic survey*, for example, while Rotary recommended that clubs make use of Concord Films Council, a non-profit that distributed films produced by organisations such as the Freedom from Hunger Campaign, the United Nations Association, Oxfam, and War on Want to those interested in working for peace 'in all its many aspects'.[88] The emphasis on British voices and information was in part a matter of access – these experiences were more readily available to Rotary and the WI than those of recipients of aid – nevertheless it served to reinforce existing assumptions about the distribution of expertise.[89]

As part of this broader educational endeavour, NGO employees and volunteers with experience living and working overseas became particularly attractive sources of international knowledge, courted for their ability to talk about specific projects and the broader contextual issues that affected them. While, in principle, Rotary and the WI were interested in the problems faced by newly emergent states across the global South, most of the projects that they supported took place within the declining and former Empire and most of the individuals who spoke to their members about development issues did so on the basis of prior experience living and/or working within the Empire. The significance of the uneven geographic distribution of aid and development is discussed in greater detail in relation to the Freedom from Hunger Campaign and Christian Aid in Chapters 4 and 5, but I introduce it here because it also serves as an important example of the ways that new discourses of international knowledge and understanding continued to be defined within the boundaries of existing imperial experiences.

To understand how these imperial experiences came to circulate in associational life, we first need to understand the practices of late-colonial development and the impact of decolonisation on British opportunities for overseas employment. The disappearance and reconfiguration of colonial positions, Craggs and Neate remind us, resulted in the mobility of thousands of professionals in the 1950s and 1960s.[90] The scale and makeup of this post-imperial workforce was shaped by trends that had been developing since the start of the twentieth century. As Joseph Hodge summarises, over the first half of the century British colonists showed 'growing confidence ... in the use of science and expertise ... to develop the natural and human resources of the Empire and manage the perceived problems and disorder generated by colonial rule'.[91] In the fifteen years following the Second World War the British state, as Nicholas Owen puts it, 'took control of colonial development and attempted to force a programme of rapid modernization on the economies of the dependent Empire, in part through investment in agricultural production'.[92] While they did aim to increase the economic value of Britain's remaining colonies, these projects also served to 'morally rearm the imperial mission in the late colonial epoch'.[93] The formal process of decolonisation did not draw a line under these practices or the assumptions underlying them.

A growing field of research seeks to uncover the post-imperial trajectories of the individuals involved in projects of colonial expertise, the models of intervention that they endorsed, and the narratives of benevolent imperialism that they sustained. While much of this work has focused on the threads of continuity that run between colonial and post-colonial development and governance in the global South, there is also a comparatively smaller strand of research that seeks to assess the impact of imperial expertise on metropolitan Britain.[94] As Bailkin has illustrated, in the 1950s and 1960s multiple forms of expertise forged in the 'colonial laboratory' jostled for influence in domestic Britain.[95] As African and Caribbean territories gained independence in the late 1950s and 1960s many state-employed experts returned to Britain to begin 'second careers' in related 'service' fields such as government, university and hospital management, and urban reconstruction.[96] Others found work within the rapidly expanding cohort of international organisations, British development agencies, and humanitarian NGOs working in Britain's former colonies, continuing transitory lives that took them back and forth between Britain and the developing world.[97] Because these development organisations actively courted public support – in financial terms, and in order to build political pressure for the expansion of government aid programmes – they became important conduits between those with imperial experiences and participants in associational life.

As shown in Chapter 1, the Royal Commonwealth Society (RCS) was a closed loop in that it struggled to find an audience beyond those who were already committed to the Commonwealth as an idea. But humanitarian and development organisations, which appeared to universalise moral causes, offered a way for imperial experiences to be repackaged in order to maintain their relevance in the post-imperial context. By moving outside the established structures of Commonwealth societies, these actors were thus better able to shape popular understandings of who best represented Britain overseas and who was most likely to affect positive change in the post-imperial era.

The very idea of imperial expertise and experience was being called into question during this period. As Kothari has shown, the 1960s saw significant changes in the field as colonial administrators were gradually replaced by a new generation of development 'experts', the embodiment of a broader process of professionalisation and technicalisation of the

UK development industry.[98] There were significant continuities between the old and new guard: both groups shared the assumption that 'some people and places are more developed than others and therefore those who are "developed" have the knowledge and expertise to help those who are not'.[99] But there was also, Kothari explains, a shift 'from the more ideologically overt "civilising mission" of colonial rule and the valorisation of regional specialism, to the increasing importance of the universalised technical expertise of the development professional'.[100] Yet, while generalised technocrats rose to positions of authority in the field, they were notably less visible as the public face of development work in Britain in the same period.

In the 1960s 'interpreters' of development work for public audiences tended to come from one of two groups, both of which valued practical knowledge and direct experience over theoretical generalities. These were an older cadre of former Colonial Service employees and a new generation of British youth recruited into overseas voluntary schemes from the late 1950s onwards. Both groups shared their emphasis on 'know how' with many of the associations they spoke to in Britain. 'Common sense' was very much the watchword of both Rotary and the WI. Rotary described its work as built on a 'common sense and sympathetic approach';[101] the WI saw itself as having 'expanded [its] international work' in 'practical commonsense ways'.[102] As Rotarian author J. E. Parry argued, 'what we need in Rotary is not so much specialists and experts but a multiplicity of educated men with minds free and uninhibited'.[103] Indeed, Rotary was proud of the 'transcendent spirit of enthusiastic amateurism' that they brought to development initiatives.[104] Neither the WI nor Rotary denied the relevance or utility of expertise – Rotary coverage of the Freedom from Hunger Campaign stressed the importance of trends identified by experts in nutrition and population, for example.[105] They did, however, argue forcibly for the continued need for amateur enthusiasm in development efforts. This was in large part an attempt to justify their own continued significance. Hence, Rotary celebrated Lady Ranfurly's defence of the Ranfurly Library Scheme against 'murmurs that this is work which professionals and governments should be doing rather than "inexperienced amateurs.... This is a battle for everyone', Ranfurly argued, 'where the professionals and governments have not done it ... the amateurs have.'[106]

The vision of development that was most often presented to Rotary and the WI in this period was determined not by the shifts in professional practice that took place over the course of the 1960s, therefore, but by three earlier changes in the field of development. These were, broadly, the changes in the ethos of the Colonial Service from the late

1940s; increased recruitment of women into the service over the same period; and, in the late 1950s, the establishment of large-scale overseas volunteering schemes, which brought British youth into development initiatives for the first time. The first of these changes concerned a concerted attempt within the Colonial Service to reimagine colonial rule, away from authoritarian control and towards partnership, collaboration, and preparation for independence. Some administrators from the earlier generation of Colonial Service, with its emphasis on paternalistic rule, did move into development work and spoke to public audiences. One prominent example was Noel Paterson. Born in 1905, Paterson had entered the Indian Civil Service in 1929 and served as District Officer in the Andaman and Nicobar Islands in the 1940s. This imperial experience allowed him to transition into a prominent development role as Projects Officer for the UK Freedom from Hunger Campaign Committee, in which capacity he spoke at the WI Middlesex International Area Conference in 1967.[107]

But the bulk of the former service employees who engaged directly with the WI and Rotary on matters of development had been recruited in the 1940s and 1950s in the context of late colonial development. They included, for example, Peter Kuenstler, born in 1919, who toured meetings of the WI and United Nations Association in 1967. He had started his career in domestic youth work, was Secretary of the African Development Trust from 1955 to 1964, and from 1964 worked for the UN on youth and community work.[108] For Kuenstler's generation, 'progress towards the Commonwealth', rather than perpetual empire, 'was now the fundamental objective of colonial rule'.[109] These values, grounded in debates about colonial rule in the 1950s, transmitted in the 1960s within the framework of humanitarianism and development, and combined with 'common sense' notions of practical experience, formed the basis of associational access to imperial experiences.

The second major shift to impact on associational interactions with development in the 1960s was the increased representation of women within the administration of colonial development and welfare initiatives that had occurred in the post-war period. There is a large body of work detailing the attempts made by British women throughout the nineteenth and early twentieth centuries to shape and improve colonised women's lives. Throughout this period, gendered expectations of international work determined what kinds of intervention were seen as suitable: women were assumed to be naturally more sympathetic than men and, therefore, particularly suited to voluntary rather than professional work in education, children's health, and domestic care.[110] These expectations endured into the 1960s; women were more likely to work in education and social welfare than in other areas of development work. But, while these nominally feminine areas of social welfare and education were originally sectioned off from masculinised colonial administration, from the late 1940s, the increased interest in develop-ment as a guiding framework for colonial rule brought these issues into conversation with comparatively masculinised projects of technocratic agricultural development. This increasing professionalisation meant that by the 1960s a significant number of women were employed as experts in the fields of international development. Moreover, they were willing and able to speak to the public about their experiences. For example, Freda Gwilliam, born in 1907, who had been recruited by the Colonial Office in 1947 to work in girls' education across the British Empire, spoke regularly to the public in the 1960s as a representative of the Ministry of Overseas Development.[111] After a talk to the WI, Isabel Curry, the NFWI's International Secretary, praised Gwilliam for her 'masterly appraisal of the way in which women, by their perseverance, are making their mark in the welfare of the people of the world'.[112]

The significance of this shift in the makeup of international actors was that it changed conceptions of who was able to speak on these issues, whose experiences were valuable in understanding the post-imperial world, and who could effect meaningful change in that world. In this context, the NFWI came to conceive of itself as both a consumer of expert knowledge, much of it provided by women, and as an active purveyor of forms of expertise particularly suited to the needs of developing and 'emergent' countries. The WI's contributions to the broad field of development largely confirmed the long-standing gender split in international activity. At the request of the Colonial Office and British Council they advised on the establishment of women's movements overseas – in Jamaica and Southern Rhodesia in the 1940s, in Malaya, Goa, Nigeria and the Philippines in the 1950s.[113] But the WI's particular emphasis on agricultural development also illustrates the expanded role that rural women had created for themselves in this international field by the 1960s.[114] The rural makeup of the WI and its earlier focus on increasing agricultural production during the First World War meant that it was readily able to align its broader aims to improve the lives of rural women with the more technocratic vision of agricultural development that campaigns such as the Freedom from Hunger Campaign adopted. From the late 1950s, the WI's international parent body the Associated Country Women of the World played an important consultative role in UN work on rural communities and women's productive role in agriculture.[115] Though most of the overseas projects that the WI supported in this decade were focused on women as beneficiaries of the aid, these projects were not purely 'domestic' or 'home-based' in nature. The WI bought cows for young women in Jamaica, set up a 35-acre farm in Trinidad, and supported a tractor hire scheme to encourage crop rotation in Dominica.[116]

While the NFWI celebrated these activities as a collective achievement for the WI movement, it is important to note that most members were still excluded from this field of international mobility and expertise and some were frustrated by this exclusion. One member wrote to *Home and Country* to ask 'why are practically all WI trips abroad undertaken by NFWI members, for example to the Uganda Farm Institute to which all members subscribed? ... The WI movement was created for all WI members and everyone should have the chance.' The NFWI responded that members of the executive committee who went abroad were 'people who through hard work over many years have made themselves expert in their particular field [...] A WI member selected from a list sent in could hardly be expected to have the necessary knowledge or experience to discuss with leaders in other countries matters of mutual concern.'[117]

The third major shift to impact on associational interactions with development and humanitarianism in the 1960s was the emergence of a new generation of young overseas volunteers able to speak with international 'know how' and encouraged to engage with members of the public on these issues. Overseas voluntary schemes aimed at school leavers and recent graduates started with small numbers of volunteers in the late 1950s and expanded rapidly in the first half of the 1960s. A wide range of organisations were involved in this work – including the Catholic Institute for International Relations, the International Voluntary Service, the National Union of Students, the United Nations Association, and the African Development Trust – the largest and most senior of which was Voluntary Service Overseas (VSO). As Bailkin has shown, VSO was a product of decolonisation. When Alec and Mora Dickson founded VSO in 1958 to send school leavers to underdeveloped countries their aims were threefold: first, to help British youth by replacing the decreasing opportunities for international service created by the winding down of National Service and Colonial Service; second, to build friendships with indigenous elites in developing countries; and third, and relatedly, to cultivate goodwill towards Britain across the developing world through support for various education and building projects.[118] VSO's emphasis on partnership between coloniser and colonised, developed and developing, overlapped neatly with the ethos introduced into the Colonial Service in the late 1940s, an ethos which had in turn been incorporated into Rotary and WI visions of international engagement.

As Honeck and Rosenberg discuss, the faith placed in the young in this period underwrote a wide range of 'narratives of national and international progress'.[119] VSO claimed that their young volunteers, unconstrained by the imperial mind-sets of older generations, would help to establish the new affective relationships with emerging countries that were needed in the post-imperial era as they were seen as uniquely capable of gaining insight into the needs and desires of populations of former colonies. Yet, as well as endorsing this 'break' with the past, VSO also sought to preserve long-standing traditions of imperial adventure and service as a safety valve for the energetic idealism of British youth.[120] To support both objectives – the establishment of affective bonds and the useful redirection of youthful energy – they pushed back against the increasing professionalisation of development work and echoed the traditional recruitment strategies of the Colonial Service in arguing that the inherent qualities of British upper- and middle-class youth would be sufficient to ensure a meaningful contribution to developing countries.[121]

From their inception, overseas voluntary schemes were intended to shape domestic Britain as well as the developing world, affecting not just the volunteers but also the communities that they returned to. Public fundraising for volunteer schemes was typically organised through a system of sponsorship; instead of paying money into an anonymous pool, companies, charitable trusts, and local organisations such as Rotary and the WI sponsored individual volunteers. This financial arrangement encouraged clubs and institutes to maintain close contact with their sponsored volunteers. Louth Rotary Club arranged for their VSO volunteer to spend the Christmas holidays with the Rotary Club of Broken Hill in Zambia, for example, while Berkshire WI members sent over thirty parcels to Sierra Leone when a Harwell member's volunteering daughter appealed for scrap material for a craft club she was running there.[122] Through these material and logistical contributions, members of the public invested emotionally in the endeavours of young members of their own communities. Once back in Britain, volunteers were expected to share their experiences and, over the course of the decade, they gave talks to hundreds of individual clubs and institutes. Alongside increased touristic opportunities, the increasing number of overseas volunteers circulating in associational life over the course of the 1960s worked to normalise the idea of international travel in the global South.

How did these volunteers interpret development work for audiences back home in Britain? We know that volunteers responded in diverse ways to the transitional colonial administrative infrastructures that they encountered on their placements. Some emphasised their generational difference and offered appraisals of Britain's philanthropic mission and mandate that were critical of colonialism. One particular student, supported by the WI as a graduate volunteer for the African Development Trust in Tanganyika, wrote of the gulf between the paternalism of old colonialists and the newer approaches of a younger generation of volunteers in Africa. 'Can youth achieve what our parents have failed to do', he asked, 'and unite the world with the common purpose of victory over poverty?'[123] The extent to which this view jarred with older conceptions of trusteeship is evident in external reports of this student's time in Tanganyika. A project supervisor and contact of the WI described him as a troublemaker, writing that a newsletter the student published was very badly received by the white population there, that 'he did not fit in at all', and that he 'rubbed everybody's back up'.[124] Yet in a clear example of the generational divide, the same supervisor's son defended the volunteer, saying that 'he went down very well with the Africans'.[125]

It is important, however, not to overestimate the radicalism of volunteer voices in the 1960s. Many also endorsed the narratives of British exceptionalism promoted by VSO and shared their experiences in ways that reinforced hierarchical concepts of non-western societies as 'young', 'learning' civilisations in need of British guidance. One volunteer in British Guiana wrote that 'the Amerindians are very responsive when one is on the spot: but completely unreliable when you're not ... This poses a bit of a dilemma as it means one has to be permanently leading them: whereas I feel the real purpose of anything I do is to teach them to lead themselves'.[126] This appraisal echoed the trusteeship model endorsed by the post-war Colonial Service.

Through the framework of development and humanitarianism, the range of people trusted to share knowledge and interpret the wider world broadened, offering appealing alternatives to the previously lauded qualities of individual masculine heroism. Collectively, this expanding body of humanitarian and development speakers – Colonial Service employees recruited in the post-war period, newly professionalised female experts, and young volunteers – emphasised qualities of service, a pragmatic desire to make a difference, and an interest in partnership and understanding with the populations in the developing world. Yet, in celebrating this kind of action, this particular form of knowledge sharing also reinforced certain colonial habits of mind. While the WI, in particular, made some efforts to learn directly from the women they supported, these exchanges were designed to supplement and not replace the reports from NGO practitioners. The sense that developing nations were not yet ready to go it alone was particularly apparent in the interest that the WI and Rotary took in monitoring the effectiveness of their donations. Rather than relying on direct feedback from recipients, they entrusted to British experts the job of assessing, recording, and reporting on the outcomes of their efforts. Further emphasising the hierarchical nature of these practices, institutes were encouraged to follow the progress of the projects that they financed, 'just as a good godmother will keep in touch with the progress of her god-child'.[127]

In the 1960s those claiming experience and/or expertise within these networks of associational life tended to share the same two underlying assumptions: that the British were capable of understanding the needs of populations in developing countries and of determining the most effective strategies to meet those needs and that the forms of 'know how' developed as a result of Britain's imperial rule remained not only useful, but vital, in the era of decolonisation. This attitude is represented by Alan Catterick, an agricultural engineer who was recruited by International Voluntary Services to work at Malkers Research Station in Swaziland in 1963, shortly after graduating from university. At the time, Catterick wrote to the NFWI to thank them for their support and describe his work there:

> The European, through technical knowhow, initiative and financial backing are reaping a rich harvest in sugar cane, rice, citrus, cotton and pineapples, where the majority of the Swazi through lack of these abilities are reduced to subsistence farming. [...] Although it is not at first apparent to these people the benefit of these schemes, in the long term development they will benefit greatly. You may think that they are not grateful for the work being done for them, but at the moment they are unable to show their feelings except for resentment for the Europeans who they feel are exploiting them.

Catterick was critical of an unbalanced economy from which Swazi benefited little and understanding of Swazi hostility towards Europeans; he took it upon himself in his letter to explain and justify that hostility to those in Britain. Yet he was unwavering in his faith in the work of the British to improve the quality of Swazi lives through education in European techniques. As he concluded, 'I have found it a very thrilling and moving experience to have worked on these two projects and I hope that the people working on the site feel as proud as I do of the British people.'[128]

Difference, agency, and the cultural value of foreign representatives

Thus far this chapter has focused on the influence of white British citizens' experiences of post-war mobility on associational efforts to promote international knowledge and understanding. The examples have shown that, excepting their voiced concerns about the superficiality of some touristic practices, the WI and Rotary placed considerable faith in the ability of white Britons to not only understand the foreign countries that they lived in, travelled to, or worked in, but also to prescribe and coordinate British-led solutions to any problems that they diagnosed. Yet post-war mobility did not just move white British citizens around the globe, it also brought increasing numbers to Britain from around the world: as tourists, students, and both short- and long-term economic migrants. While black people had been present in Britain for centuries, post-war initiatives to increase immigration from the Commonwealth meant that the numbers of West Indian and South Asian people living in Britain increased significantly in the 1950s and 1960s.[129] For participants in associational life – and particularly for those living outside large cities, like most members of the WI and Rotary – this presented new and increasing opportunities to interact with people whose skin colour was different from their own.

Both organisations saw these encounters as a crucial and exciting component of their work towards greater international understanding, actively seeking out opportunities to meet with people from overseas. In the 1960s Women's Institutes and Rotary Clubs across Britain hosted visitors from all over the world. These included significant numbers from the Empire and Commonwealth, among them students studying at British institutions and guests of the British Government and British Council. Members of the WI's Yorkshire International Subcommittee invited Indian students from the universities of Hull and Leeds to attend their International Day on India;[130] the Cheddar Valley WI entertained five visitors from British Guiana, Nigeria, and Trinidad, all teachers on a home economics course at Bath College of Education;[131] Barnsley Rotary arranged an international meeting attended by a panel of speakers from Nigeria, Thailand, Cyprus, India, and Britain; and the Matlock club listened to Rotary Foundation Fellow Jaswant Chaudhari speak about India and 'the cause of international understanding' at an event attended by over 120 Rotarians and their wives.[132]

Chapter 3 considers the affective dimensions of encounters like these, but here I want to focus on what Rotary and the WI's pursuit of international knowledge through foreign visitors tells us about changing attitudes towards formerly colonised populations. Did the WI and Rotary treat foreign visitors as sources of authoritative international knowledge in the same way that they did mobile white Britons? That is, did they recognise the agency of foreign people to describe their own experiences and seek to learn not simply *about* foreign people but also *from* them? With these interactions, as with other international talks, there are no detailed records of either the content of discussions or members' reactions to them. From the fragmentary descriptions that appear in the publications of both organisations, it is clear that Rotary and WI attitudes to foreign 'representatives' were neither straightforward nor consistent, but there are some discernible patterns.

In a minority of cases, WI and Rotary described foreign visitors from the developing world in similar terms to those they used to describe white British speakers who had spent time overseas: as reliable sources of expertise and as partners in the search for solutions to global challenges. For example, in a *Rotary* report on an International Service weekend in Nottingham attended by 90 Rotarians and Rotary wives as well as students from twelve countries (Australia, Canada, Ceylon, France, India, Japan, Kenya, Malaysia, Mauritius, the Solomon Islands, Spain, and the USA), the author concluded that the international students' participation had shown that Rotarians must 'learn to look through the eyes of the younger generation, and to make our contribution to international service not for them, but with them'.[133] In 1967 Aroti Dutt the Indian President of the ACWW addressed WI audiences at six International Area Conferences, setting out the work that the organisation was doing to raise the standard of living around the world.[134] In 1968 the WI described an ACWW conference as a valuable opportunity to exchange information with women from around the world, concluding that 'women of older nations could learn something from the emergent nations where, in spite of great handicaps, the women were taking over positions of high authority often denied to their western sisters'.[135] This language of partnership, agency, and the shared production of knowledge became a much more significant feature of the WI's international work in the 1970s and 1980s.[136] In those decades associational discourses around global challenges became much more centred on the empowerment of populations in the global South and the recognition of local expertise. This transition was guided in part by the more politicised strategies of humanitarian NGOs, but also by newer movements for ethical consumerism.[137]

In the 1960s, however, this was still a minority view. In a majority of cases, expertise was treated as an exclusive status, achievable only by western observers. Visitors from the developing world were rarely spoken about as experts, even of their own circumstances. This distinction is illustrated by an article about the Oversea Service College published in *Rotary* in 1965 that promoted the training received by those preparing to work overseas: 'They have heard up-to-date talks by first-class lecturers and by well-informed men and women recently returned; they have met some of the nationals of the region and learnt at first hand some of their views and attitudes.'[138]

While 'well-informed' white speakers who had lived overseas were valued as reliable sources of objective information about economic problems and political systems, non-white speakers' usefulness was limited to their subjective 'views and attitudes'. This emphasised the agency of the (white, British) audience who were assumed to be capable of interpreting foreign people's subjectivities. In doing so, it echoed colonial assumptions about Britain's ability to understand the needs of societies under its rule. There were important exceptions to this trend elsewhere; the Royal Commonwealth Society invited an increasing number of speakers from colonies and former colonies to address its lunchtime audiences in the 1960s, while the Commonwealth Institute employed speakers from the Commonwealth to deliver their educational programme to visiting schoolchildren. But these did not necessarily filter through into the wider networks of associational life.

While their collective efforts at international education show that the WI and Rotary turned away from an insular/provincial gaze in this period, they did not so easily shed the 'exotic gaze of the coloniser'.[139] Instead of imagining themselves as an audience to black and Asian visitors as sources of first-hand or expert knowledge – as they tended to do with white British speakers – WI and Rotary were more likely to establish themselves as observers of examples of a foreign culture. Members from both organisations tended to place greater emphasis on cultural difference when discussing people with a different skin colour to their own, treating cross-racial interactions as opportunities for ethnographic information-gathering and entertaining spectacle. The brief descriptions of these events printed in *Rotary* and *Home and Country* suggest that foreign visitors were more likely to be asked to perform than to describe their cultural difference. Three guests from Nigeria, the Caribbean, and Vietnam who attended Greysouthern WI's meeting 'delighted their audience with some of their native songs'.[140] Along similar lines, both organisations were much more likely to comment on the dress of their visitors than any knowledge they may have shared about their home country. For example, at Carnoustie Rotary Club's International Exhibition the black students who manned the Nigerian stand were described as being 'clad in native costume', while La Moye WI welcomed 'an Indian visitor whose yellow sari made a bright splash of colour on a grey day'.[141] Based on the brief descriptions available, these events look to have recreated elements of cultural display typical of the grand-scale imperial exhibitions of the late nineteenth and early twentieth centuries, but on a smaller scale and in a wider range of local settings.[142]

The WI and Rotary's promotion of a celebratory approach to cultural difference as a key component of international understanding also shares a particular affinity with the ideas that emerged around Commonwealth multiculturalism at this time. As Radhika Natarajan suggests, 'Commonwealth multiculturalism depended on the legibility of distinct national cultures', not on their hybridity.[143] Natarajan uses the 1965 Commonwealth Arts Festival to illustrate this process, showing how organisers promoted difference, contrast, and diversity 'in the service of "breaking down ... ignorance and scepticism" among British audiences'.[144] Through their celebration of cultural difference, organisers of the Arts Festival sought to improve not only Britain's reputation with other Commonwealth nations but also the British public's attitude towards Commonwealth people living in Britain.[145] As Lord Taylor explained, the Festival would 'illustrate in dramatic fashion the varied backgrounds of these immigrants and may help to give their neighbours here a new understanding of them'.[146] There is considerable need for further research into the relationships between apolitical associations – like the WI and Rotary – and Britain's immigrant communities in this period, but it seems likely that, along similar lines to their educational practices, both organisations would have been more likely to celebrate 'cultural diversity' than 'cultural homogeneity'.[147]

The WI and Rotary's focus on the performance of cultural difference also illustrates the particular patterns of imperial nostalgia and amnesia that developed in the 1960s. As Natarajan has shown through her analysis of the Commonwealth Arts Festival, 'the embrace of difference' was not just a statement about multiculturalism, it was also closely 'entwined with imperial nostalgia' for lost, primitive cultures.[148] Displaying 'the distinctiveness and purity of folk forms and crafts that were not *westernised*', Low argues, was a key priority for festival organisers and seems also to have been a priority at WI and Rotary events attended by foreign visitors.[149] This was not a nostalgic celebration of imperial rule of the kind that was seen in the 1980s with the boom of Raj costume dramas.[150] Rather it was a particular form of historical amnesia that overlooked the role of empire in 'destroying' the cultural differences that it celebrated. As Elizabeth Buettner reminds us, calling attention to the work of Fredric Jameson, Renato Rosaldo, and Raphael Samuel, 'in deracinated postmodern circumstances the allure of disappearing worlds, environments "at risk," and nostalgia for what has been destroyed can readily become enhanced'.[151] In the 1960s this form of nostalgia was uncritically sustained by those who celebrated cultural difference, embraced the modern Commonwealth, and supported self-consciously 'progressive' discourses of development and self-determination.

Finally, Rotary and the WI's focus on the performance of dehistoricised and decontextualised cultural difference also served to obscure and deny the political concerns of the people that they sought to 'understand'. Once again, this is reminiscent of the discourses surrounding other initiatives, such as the Commonwealth Arts Festival. Writing before its launch, Lord Balfour, a Festival patron, suggested that the arts were the ideal form through which to foster international cooperation and understanding because they were 'unaffected by political, economic and military considerations'.[152] Balfour's pronouncement overlooked the political concerns of participating artists and failed to predict the ways in which the Festival came to act as a lightning rod for questions about Commonwealth equality and immigration.[153] Yet it is indicative of broader tendencies to regard arts and culture as 'safe' sites for exchange in a complicated political climate. The work of the British Council in this period, for example, exemplifies this belief.[154] Although there is very little detail available about the smaller scale events that took place for members at local Rotary and WI branches, the brief mentions that these events did get in *Rotary* and *Home and Country* suggest that they emphasised cultural differences and everyday life over political concerns. As the WI described, members should be aiming to learn about other nations' 'culture – their music and art – their handicrafts, the foods they grow, their cooking and other pastimes'.[155] Rotary and the WI's emphasis on cultural rather than political differences in their educational pursuits aligns with their approach to international friendship. These decisions, though rarely explicitly discussed, were entirely typical of both organisations' broader attempts to establish and preserve depoliticised forms of people-to-people international engagement in this decade.

In conclusion, the WI and Rotary's pursuit of international knowledge exposed members to multiple and often partial (in both senses of the word) interpretations of the declining empire. Dependent on the speakers that addressed individual institutes and clubs, members' education in international affairs could be accompanied by a combination of nostalgia, regret, anxiety, optimism, pragmatism, idealism, and enjoyment. The common ground shared by these different perspectives was that they all fed into a narrative about Britain as a *caring* nation, one populated by people who were both *interested* in the outside world and felt a sense of *responsibility* to act to ensure its wellbeing. The broad discourses of informed international understanding described in this chapter did not exist in isolation; they provided important support to the narratives of British benevolence and post-imperial responsibility. Although there were occasions when the discourse of 'understanding' was used to justify inaction – a process I discuss in relation to Rotary and South

Africa in Chapter 3 – knowledge-based understanding was more commonly seen as a necessary foundation to the kind of caring, responsible, active citizenship that, it was hoped, would sustain Britain's global role in the post-imperial world.

Notes

1 *The Times* (6 April 1962).
2 Craggs, 'Commonwealth geographies', p. 177.
3 M.L.J Dierikx, *Clipping the Clouds: How Air Travel Changed the World* (Westport, CT: Greenwood, 2008).
4 Advertisement for flights to Mexico, 1960s, www.britishairways.com/en-gb/information/about-ba/history-and-heritage/posters/posters-1960–1973.
5 'International service', *Rotary* (February 1964), p. ii.
6 *Ibid.*
7 May Mackintosh, 'The winds of all the world', *Rotary* (August 1960), p. 250.
8 Victor Middleton and Leonard John Lickorish, *British Tourism: The Remarkable Story of Growth* (Oxford: Butterworth-Heinemann, 2007), pp. 22–26.
9 Linda Ambrose, *A Great Rural Sisterhood: Madge Robertson Watt and the ACWW* (Toronto: Toronto University Press, 2015), p. 126.
10 Ewa Mazierska and John K. Walton, 'Tourism and the moving image', *Tourist Studies*, 6:1 (2006), 7.
11 WL, NFWI, 5/FWI/G/1/3/2/9, 'World wise with the W.I.s', NFWI (January 1964).
12 Barbara Kaye, *International Countrywomen: The Many Aspects of International Work Undertaken in the Women's Institutes* (London: NWFI, 1967). Also quoted in *Home and Country* (March 1967).
13 WL, NFWI, 5/FWI/G/1/3/2/9, 'World wise with the W.I.s', NFWI (January 1964).
14 See David Arnold (ed.), *Imperial Medicine and Indigenous Societies* (Manchester: Manchester University Press, 1988); Shula Marks, 'What is colonial about colonial medicine? And what has happened to imperialism and health?', *Social History of Medicine*, 10:2 (1997), 205–219.
15 See James R. Ryan, *Picturing Empire: Photography and the Visualization of the British Empire* (London: Reaktion Books, 2013); Felix Driver, 'Geography's empire: histories of geographical knowledge', *Environment and Planning D: Society and Space*, 10:1 (1992), 23–40.
16 Cited in J.A. Mangan, 'The grit of our forefathers', in John MacKenzie (ed.), *Imperialism and Popular Culture* (Manchester: Manchester University Press, 1986), p. 131.
17 See, for example, Bernard Porter, *The Absent-Minded Imperialists: Empire, Society, and Culture in Britain* (Oxford: Oxford University Press, 2006).
18 Bailkin, *Afterlife of Empire*, p. 7.
19 Beaumont, *Housewives and Citizens*, p. 23.
20 *Ibid.*, p. 25.
21 WL, NFWI, 5/FWI/G/1/3/2/9, 'International work of the Women's Institutes', NFWI (May 1955).
22 Brendan Goff, 'The Heartland Abroad', p. 50.
23 Goff, 'The heartland abroad', pp. 33–48; Roger Levy, *Rotary International in Great Britain and Northern Ireland* (Plymouth, 1978).
24 Daniel Gorman, 'Empire, internationalism, and the campaign against the traffic in women and children in the 1920s', *Twentieth Century British History*, 19 (2008), 189.
25 Daniel Gorman, 'Ecumenical internationalism: Willoughby Dickinson, the League of Nations and the World Alliance for Promoting International Friendship through the Churches', *Journal of Contemporary History*, 45 (2010), 63–4.

26 Andrew Arsan, Su Lin Lewis, and Anne-Isabelle Richard, 'Editorial – the roots of global civil society and the interwar moment', *Journal of Global History*, 7:2 (2012), 164.

27 Goff, 'The heartland abroad', p. 13.

28 Helen McCarthy, 'The League of Nations, public ritual and national identity in Britain, c.1919–56', *History Workshop Journal*, 70:1 (2010), 120.

29 WL, NFWI, 5/FWI/G/1/3/2/9, 'Working internationally', NFWI (no date, c.1960).

30 Barbara Bush, 'Britain's conscience on Africa: White women, race and imperial politics in inter-war Britain,' in Clare Midgley (ed.), *Feminism and Empire: Women Activists in Imperial Britain* (London: Routledge, 2007), p. 201; Clare Midgley, 'Bringing the Empire home: Women activists in imperial Britain, 1790–1930', in Hall and Rose (eds), *At Home with Empire*, p. 246.

31 *Western Daily Press* (6 May 1925); *Derby Daily Telegraph* (10 March 1933). For Rotary see Stephen Constantine, 'The Buy British campaign of 1931', *European Journal of Marketing*, 21:4 (1987), 44–59.

32 'International work of the Women's Institutes'.

33 'International service', *Rotary* (February 1964), p. iii.

34 Anderson, *The Acceptable Face of Feminism*, pp. 123–144.

35 *Ibid.*, p. 143; WL, NFWI, 5/FWI/D/2/2/20, 'Course 41: Africa and the New Emergent Countries'.

36 'Please, God, open our eyes', *Rotary* (April 1968) p. 93.

37 WL, NFWI, 5/FWI/G/1/3/2/9, 'International work of the Women's Institutes', NFWI (May 1955).

38 Interview with John Little, *Rotary* (April 1965), p. 106.

39 WL, NFWI, 5/FWI/G/1/3/2/9, 'World wise with the W.I.s', NFWI (January 1964).

40 *Ibid.*

41 'A noble benefit and a gracious gift', *Rotary* (June 1968), p. 163.

42 WL, NFWI, 5/FWI/D/ 2/2/20, 'International work of the WI', Agenda for National Conference, 1961.

43 'International service', *Rotarian* (June 1959), p. 683.

44 *1959 Proceedings: Fiftieth Annual Convention of Rotary International* (Rotary International, 1959), p. 56; WL, NFWI, 5/FWI/G/1/3/2/9, 'World wise with the W.I.s', NFWI (January 1964).

45 McCarthy, 'Public ritual and national identity', 127.

46 J. Coatman, review of Zimmern, *The Third British Empire*, 3d edn (1934), *International Affairs*, 14:3 (1935), 419–20.

47 McCarthy, 'Public ritual and national identity', 127.

48 David Cannadine, 'Introduction: Independence Day ceremonials in historical perspective', *The Round Table*, 97:398 (2008), 2.

49 J. E. Parry, 'Think of the world', *Rotary* (September 1960), p. 298.

50 See, for example, Wm Roger Louis and Ronald Robinson, 'The imperialism of decolonisation', *The Journal of Imperial and Commonwealth History*, 22:3 (1994), 462–511; Gordon Cumming, *Aid to Africa: French and British Policies from the Cold War to the New Millennium* (Abingdon: Routledge, 2017); Charlotte Lydia Riley, '"Tropical Allsorts": the transnational flavor of British development policies in Africa', *Journal of World History*, 26:4 (2016), 839–864.

51 Parry, 'Think of the world'.

52 J. M. Lee, 'British cultural diplomacy and the cold war: 1946–61', *Diplomacy and Statecraft*, 9:1 (1998), 112–134; Liping Bu, 'Educational exchange and cultural diplomacy in the Cold War', *Journal of American Studies*, 33:3 (1999), 393–415; Yale Richmond, *Cultural Exchange and the Cold War: Raising the Iron Curtain* (Pennsylvania: Penn State Press, 2010).

53 TNA, CAB/129/47, Memorandum by Secretaries of State for Foreign Affairs, Colonies and Commonwealth Relations on 'Future of the British Council', 26 July 1951, p. 6.

54 *Working With Women Worldwide: Highlights of 75 Years of ACWW* (London: Associated Country Women of the World, 2004), pp. 21–24.

55 Alison Blunt, *Travel, Gender and Imperialism; Mary Kingsley and West Africa* (New York: Guilford Press, 1994); Mary Louise Pratt, *Imperial Eyes: Travel Writing and Transculturation* (London: Routledge, 1992); David Spurr, *Rhetoric of Empire: Colonial Discourse in Journalism, Travel Writing and Imperial Administration* (Durham, NC: Duke University Press, 1993); C. J. Christie, 'British literary travellers in Southeast Asia in an era of colonial retreat', *Modern Asian Studies*, 28:4 (1994), 673–737; R. Phillips, 'Decolonizing geographies of travel: reading James/Jan Morris', *Social &Cultural Geography*, 2:1 (2001), 5–24. An important exception is the work of Hsu Ming Teo, 'Wandering in the wake of Empire: British travel and tourism in the post-imperial world', in Ward (ed.), *British Culture and the End of Empire*, pp. 163–189.

56 WL, NFWI, 5/FWI/G/1/3/2/9, 'International work of the Women's Institutes', NFWI (October 1957).

57 Kaye, *International Countrywomen*, p. 14.

58 *Home and Country* (May 1966, October 1966, February 1966, January 1968).

59 The Yorkshire Film Archive, York [hereafter YFA] Charles Joseph Chislett Collection [hereafter CJCC] and Rotherham Archives and Local Studies Service, Rotherham [hereafter RALSS], 358/F Boxes 1–5.

60 Details of these trips are available in YFA, CJCC and RALSS.

61 Teo, 'Wandering in the Wake', p. 164.

62 *Ibid.*, p. 166.

63 YFA, CJCC, 329, Charles Chislett, 'Africa old and new', c.1965.

64 H. G. Hutchinson (1926) cited in W. R. Katz, *Rider Haggard and the Fiction of Empire* (Cambridge: Cambridge University Press, 1987), p. 1.

65 Webster, *Englishness and Empire*, pp. 182–218; Jeffrey Richards, 'Imperial heroes for a post-imperial age: films and the end of empire', in Ward (ed.), *British Culture and the End of Empire*, pp. 129–144.

66 James Buzard, *The Beaten Track: European Tourism, Literature and the Ways to Culture* (Oxford: Oxford University Press, 1993); Culler, 'The semiotics of tourism', *The American Journal of Semiotics*, 1:1 (2007), 127–140; Paul Fussel, *Abroad: British Literary Travelling Between the Wars* (Oxford: Oxford University Press, 1980); Teo, 'Wandering in the Wake', p. 172.

67 R. English and M. Kenny (eds), *Rethinking British Decline* (London: Macmillan, 2000).

68 The scope of Chislett's affiliations is evident from the papers in RALSS, 358/F.

69 YFA, CJCC, 331, 'All for Good Causes', newspaper clipping, 21 February 1959 and 'General Notes from Charles. J. Chislett', no date.

70 Heather Norris Nicholson, 'Through the Balkan States: home movies as travel texts and tourism histories in the Mediterranean, c.1923–1939', *Tourist Studies*, 6:12 (2006), 15. See also Barber 'The roots of travel cinema. John L. Stoddard, E. Burton Holmes and the nineteenth century illustrated travel lecture', *Film History*, 5 (1993), 68–84.

71 YFA, CJCC, 331, 'General Notes From Charles J. Chislett', no date.

72 For further analysis see Anna Bocking-Welch, 'Ghost hunting: amateur film and travel at the end of empire', in Martin Farr and Xavier Guegan (eds), *The British Abroad Since the Eighteenth Century, Volume 2* (Basingstoke: Palgrave Macmillan, 2013), pp. 214–231.

73 YFA, CJCC, Charles Chislett, 'Air Cruise to the Lebanon, Syria and Jordan', *Rotary in the Ridings* (c.1964), p. 15.

74 Jacinta Matos, 'Old journeys re-visited: aspects of post-war English travel writing', in Michael Kowalewski (ed.), *Temperamental Journeys: Essays on the Modern Literature of Travel* (Athens, GA: University of Georgia Press, 1992), p. 216.

75 Renato Rosaldo, 'Imperialist nostalgia', *Representations*, 26 (1989), 107–122.

76 YFA, CJCC, C. Chislett, 'Two Million Days Ago', *Rotary in the Ridings*, 33:5 (1963), 18.

77 A. L. Stoler, 'Imperial debris: reflections on ruin and ruination', *Cultural Anthropology*, 3:1 (2008), 328.

78 YFA, CJJC, 333, 'Africa Old and New', c. 1965.
79 Thompson, *Empire Strikes Back?*, p. 241.
80 'The Non-Specialist', *Guardian* (23 October 1961).
81 WL, NFWI, 5/FWI/G/1/3/2/9, 'International work of the Women's Institutes', NFWI (October 1957).
82 WL, NFWI, 5/FWI/D/2/2/18, 'National Federation Circular', 6 March 1969; WL, NFWI, 5/FWI/D/2/2/20, 'Travel talks and short tours – are they enough?', Conference of International Sub-Committee, 2 October 1969.
83 WL, NFWI, 5/FWI/G/1/3/2/9, 'International work of the Women's Institutes', NFWI (May 1955).
84 WL, NFWI, 5/FWI/D/2/2/20, Denman International Courses, 'The International work of the WI', Description for Course 41, 'Africa and the new emergent countries' 1961; 'Collection level description: Papers of Dennis George Ruddock Herbert, Lord Hemingford' www.bodley.ox.ac.uk/dept/scwmss/wmss/online/blcas/herbert-dgr.html, (accessed 21 July 2017).
85 Andrews, *Acceptable Face of Feminism*; Levy, *Rotary International in Great Britain and Ireland.*
86 'Lady Ranfurly's love', *Rotarian* (July 1972), pp. 29–31.
87 WL, NFWI, 5/FWI/D/2/2/18, Isobel Curry to Beryl Rose, Save the Children, 23 May 1969.
88 'Notebook for January' *Rotary* (January 1965), p. 21; WL, NFWI, 5/FWI/D/2/2/18, Isobel Curry to Barclays Bank, 14 August 1969.
89 Uma Kothari, 'Authority and expertise: The professionalisation of international development and the ordering of dissent', *Antipode*, 37:3 (2005), 428–9.
90 Ruth Craggs and Hannah Neate, 'Post-colonial careering and urban policy mobility between Britain and Nigeria, 1945–1990', *Transactions of the Institute of British Geographers*, 42:1 (2017), 45.
91 Joseph Hodge, *Triumph of the Expert: Agrarian Doctrines of Development and the Legacies of British Colonialism* (Athens, OH: Ohio University Press, 2007), p. 8.
92 Nicholas Owen, 'Critics of Empire in Britain', in Judith Browne and Wm Roger Louis (eds), *The Oxford History of the British Empire* vol. 4 (Oxford: Oxford University Press, 1999), p. 203.
93 Hodge, *Triumph of the Expert*, p. 8.
94 On development see Uma Kothari, 'From colonialism to development: reflections of former colonial officers', *Commonwealth & Comparative Politics*, 44:1 (2006), 118–136; Hodge, *Triumph of the Expert*. On Britain see: Kirke-Greene, 'Decolonisation: the ultimate diaspora'; Bailkin, *Afterlife of Empire*; Craggs and Neate, 'Postcolonial careering'.
95 Bailkin, *Afterlife of Empire*, pp. 7–9.
96 Kirke-Greene, 'The ultimate diaspora', pp. 136, 150.
97 Hodge, *Triumph of the Expert*, p. 20.
98 Kothari, 'Authority and expertise'.
99 Jane L. Parpart, 'Deconstructing the development "expert": Gender, development and the "vulnerable groups"', in Jane L. Parpart and Marianne H. Marchand (eds), *Feminism/Postmodernism/Development* (Abingdon: Routledge, 1995), p. 221.
100 Kothari, 'Authority and expertise', p. 435.
101 John Little, *Rotary* (April 1965), p. 107.
102 WL, NFWI, 5/FWI/G/1/3/2/9, 'Working internationally', NFWI (no date, c.1960).
103 Parry, 'Think of the world', p. 298.
104 'Please, God, open our eyes', *Rotary*, p. 93.
105 'World hunger', *Rotary* (September 1961), p. 285.
106 'Lady Ranfurly's love', *Rotarian* (July 1972) p. 30.
107 'World within reach', *Home and Country* (September 1967), p. 305; 'Paterson, Noel Kennedy', *Who Was Who*, www.ukwhoswho.com/view/article/oupww/whowaswho/U167908 (accessed 26 July 2017).
108 Peter Kuenstler obituary, *Guardian* (9 January 2011).

INTERNATIONAL MOBILITY AND INFORMED UNDERSTANDING

109 Chris Jeppesen, '"A worthwhile career for a man who is not entirely self-seeking": service, duty and the Colonial Service during decolonisation', in Andrew W. M. Smith and Chris Jeppesen (eds), *Britain, France and the Decolonisation of Africa: Future Imperfect?* (London: UCL Press, 2017), p. 134.

110 These are broad generalisations of dominant trends. A rich literature details the nuanced beliefs and practices of women in this field. See, for example, Clare Midgley (ed.), *Feminism and Empire: Women Activists in Imperial Britain* (London: Routledge, 2007); Clare Midgley, 'Bringing the Empire home: women activists in imperial Britain, 1790–1930', in Hall and Rose (eds), *At Home with Empire*; Antoinette M. Burton, *Burdens of History: British Feminists, Indian Women, and Imperial Culture, 1865–1915* (London: University of North Carolina Press, 1994); Susan Pedersen, 'The maternalist moment in British colonial policy: the controversy over 'child slavery' in Hong Kong', *Past and Present*, 171 (2001), 161–202.

111 Clive Whitehead, 'Miss Freda Gwilliam (1907–1987): a portrait of the 'great aunt' of British colonial education', *Journal of Educational Administration and History*, 24:2 (1992), 145–163. Gwilliam spoke at the Middlesex and Devon International Area Conferences in 1967, 'World within reach', *Home and Country* (September 1967), p. 305.

112 'Learning to live', *Home and Country* (November 1968), p. 418.

113 Skelton, 'From peace to development', p. 174.

114 For discussion of other women's organisations involved in development in this period, see Skelton, 'From peace to development'.

115 Skelton, 'From peace to development', p. 147.

116 *Home and Country* (June 1967).

117 *Ibid.* (December 1966).

118 Bailkin, *Afterlife of Empire*, pp. 56–58.

119 Mischa Honeck and Gabriel Rosenberg, 'Transnational generations: organizing youth in the Cold War', *Diplomatic History*, 38:2 (2014), 235.

120 Lee, 'British cultural diplomacy', 125. Adams, *Voluntary Service Overseas*, pp. 23–4. For further discussion of youth see Anna Bocking-Welch, 'Youth against hunger: service, activism and the mobilisation of young humanitarians in 1960s Britain', *European Review of History*, 23:1–2 (2016), 154–170.

121 Bailkin, *Afterlife of Empire*, p. 75; Jeppesen, 'A worthwhile career', pp. 148–53.

122 *Home and Country* (July 1967); 'Rotarians at work', *Rotary* (March 1965), p. 93.

123 WL, NFWI 5/FWI/D/2/2/33, Jonathan Power to Isobel Curry, 1 November 1964.

124 WL, NFWI 5/FWI/D/2/2/95, Notes from Mrs Landell Mill's interview about funded graduate volunteers, c.1964.

125 *Ibid.*

126 Mora Dickson, *A World Elsewhere: Voluntary Service Overseas* (London: Dennis Dobson, 1964), p. 90.

127 Kaye, *International Countrywomen*, p. 9.

128 WL, NFWI 165/2/2/95, Alan Catterick to NFWI, 16 October 1964.

129 Randall Hansen, *Citizenship and Immigration in Post-war Britain* (Oxford: Oxford University Press, 2000); Paul, *Whitewashing Britain*.

130 Borthwick Institute for Archives, York, WI/Int. 1, Yorkshire International Subcommittee Minutes, 13 April 1961.

131 'News from Overseas', *Home and Country* (May 1966).

132 'Rotarians at work', *Rotary* (January 1961), pp. 208–209.

133 'A noble benefit and a gracious gift', *Rotary* (June 1968), p. 163.

134 'World within reach', *Home and Country* (September 1967), p. 305.

135 'Learning to live', *Home and Country* (November 1968), p. 417.

136 See Skelton 'From peace to development', pp. 197–254.

137 Lent, *British Social Movements*; Matthew Hilton, *Consumerism in Twentieth-Century Britain: The Search for a Historical Movement* (Cambridge: Cambridge University Press, 2003).

138 'It's so different over there!', *Rotary* (August 1965), p. 226.

139 This distinction is discussed in Goran Therborn, 'At the birth of second century sociology: times of reflexivity, spaces of identity, and nodes of knowledge', *The British Journal of Sociology*, 51:1 (2000), 51.

140 ''News from Overseas', *Home and Country* (October 1966).

141 'A Rotary miracle at Carnoustie', *Rotary* (July 1965), p. 211; 'News from Overseas', *Home and Country* (May 1966).

142 Peter Hoffenberg, *An Empire on Display: English, Indian, and Australian Exhibitions from the Crystal Palace to the Great War* (Berkeley, CA: University of California Press, 2001).

143 Natarajan, 'Performing multiculturalism', 732.

144 *Ibid.*, 715.

145 Craggs, 'The Commonwealth Institute', 258.

146 Cited in Craggs, 'The Commonwealth Institute', 258.

147 Bailkin, *Afterlife of Empire*, 239.

148 Natarajan, 'Performing multiculturalism', 732.

149 Low, 'At home?', 103.

150 Buettner, 'Cemeteries, public memory and Raj nostalgia'; Elena Oliete-Aldea, *Hybrid Heritage on Screen: The 'Raj Revival' in the Thatcher Era* (London: Springer, 2015).

151 Buettner, 'Cemeteries, public memory and Raj nostalgia', 14.

152 Cited in Low, 'At home?', 101.

153 See Low, 'At home?'; Natarajan, 'Performing multiculturalism'; Craggs,'The Commonwealth Institute'.

154 Ali Fisher, 'A story of engagement: the British Council 1934–2009' (London: Counterpoint, 2009).

155 WL, NFWI, 5/FWI/G/1/3/2/9, 'World wise with the W.I.s', NFWI (January 1964).

CHAPTER THREE

Friendship, hospitality, and the hierarchies of affective international relationships

Instrumentalising affect

In the summer of 1964 Rotary's International Service Committee organised an international rally at Butlin's Holiday Camp in Clacton-on-Sea. More than 1500 Rotarians (including wives and families) attended the rally. Having travelled from clubs across Britain to the seaside resort, Rotarians entered what the organisers called the 'Hall of Nations'. Here delegates were encouraged to 'get to know' representatives from more than twenty-two countries (including Chile, Iceland, the USSR, and Pakistan). The Butlin's Hall of Nations replicated, on a much smaller scale, the Houses of Friendship that had been a feature of Rotary International conventions since 1924. These were the social heart of Rotary conventions and were designed to be inviting spaces 'conducive to congeniality and to the furtherance of friendship'.[1] Although Rotary's international magazine boasted about Rotarians' natural disposition for situations like this – describing them as 'the most gregarious of social animals'[2] – for its organisers, the Butlin's international rally was not primarily about the enjoyment of those attending. Instead, organisers saw the informal conversation and exchange that the rally facilitated as an important contribution to Rotary's international service work.

To prove the value of the rally on these terms, *Rotary* cited the Nigerian delegate who reported that the spirit of the gathering had restored her rapidly dwindling faith in the possibility of cooperation between nations of different colours and creeds.[3] By celebrating this renewed faith as a significant outcome, and by framing the international connections that its members made within the loftier discourses of 'world fellowship' and 'international service', Rotary turned the cultivation of friendship into a civic act.[4]

This chapter is about the instrumentalisation of friendship within associational life. Using Rotary and the Women's Institute (WI), it shows how associations structured the bonds of friendship, shaping not only the practical possibilities of their members' international friendships but also the wider meaning of these encounters in the context of decolonisation and globalisation. In using the language of utility, I do not mean to characterise these relationships as coldly functional. Both organisations recognised the emotional significance of friendship to the individuals involved, describing personal relationships as warm, tender, exciting, and enjoyable. Indeed, the emotionality and individuality that members of the WI and Rotary brought to these relationships is precisely what made them so useful to their institutions' pursuit of international understanding. The relationships discussed in this chapter may have been given public value by the institutional frameworks within which they took place, but they were only made possible by the actions and emotional labour of the individual members involved. As Rotary explained, 'the group alone can do nothing. The individual is the answer because the individual alone has human qualities.'[5]

In the 1960s, Rotary and the WI saw the formation of international friendships as serving two distinct yet overlapping public functions. First, friendships were used as a means to support internationalist objectives of knowledge-exchange, collaboration, and international understanding. Both organisations saw personal contact as an important and rewarding counterpart to their educational work in this area. The WI told its members that 'personal contact is obviously the most satisfying way of learning to understand overseas peoples'.[6] Closely echoing this sentiment, the Chairman of RIBI's International Committee explained that 'informal contact between people was the only satisfactory way in which to attain understanding and respect between individuals'.[7] In addition, international friendships were seen to serve national interests; they were used as a tool of soft diplomacy in order to improve Britain's international reputation and with the aim of securing or maintaining the loyalty of foreign populations. To know us, the logic went, was to love us.

The pursuit of international friendship was not a new idea. International and imperial organisations had actively promoted the development of personal connections since the end of the nineteenth century. When Rotary's first international clubs were established in the 1910s the movement was already committed to building international networks of 'acquaintances'; by 1918 they had embraced Woodrow Wilson's claim that 'the only cement that will hold this world together will be the cement of friendship'.[8] In the inter-war period, the WI joined Rotary and an increasing number of organisations carrying out this work, vowing in 1927 to 'further close relations with similar Associations of women overseas by correspondence, and where possible by interchanging visits with a view to mutual assistance and understanding'.[9] In the 1950s and 1960s, both organisations' efforts to promote international friendship increased in line with the broader expansion of their international activity. Personal relationships were deemed a crucial mechanism for capitalising on, and managing, the 'entirely new sense of oneness in mankind' that had emerged in the decades following the Second World War.[10] 'Dramatically – suddenly – our world has been compressed into a neighbourhood,' explained the President of Rotary International in 1960, 'but a neighbourhood in desperate need of wisdom and human warmth; in equally desperate need of more and ever more bridges of friendship so that good men can meet and become good neighbours'.[11]'The most important development of the age', he concluded, was 'to be found among the intangibles.'[12]

What is distinctive about friendship schemes in the post-war period is not simply the expansion of these approaches, but their increasing alignment with the international objectives and diplomatic strategies of the British state. From the late 1940s, Britain's diplomatic strategy began to move away from 'selling Britain' and towards softer forms of cultural diplomacy that prioritised the development of informal, friendly ties.[13] Two key factors drove this transformation. First, the apparent inadequacies of traditional diplomatic methods (in the lead up to the Second World War, in the escalating Cold War, and in the deterioration of imperial and Commonwealth relations) encouraged the use of alternative strategies. By the 1950s, cultural diplomacy was recognised as an 'indispensable weapon in the armoury of foreign policy'.[14] Non-state organisations sought to position themselves in order to capitalise on this development. The East and West Friendship Council, one of the longest standing organisations to offer hospitality to African, Caribbean, and Asian students, wrote to *The Times* in 1946 to remind readers of the importance of their work: 'while our politicians seem to be finding international agreement more difficult than many had hoped, may we draw attention to an opportunity on our very doorstep, by which the least of us can begin to build up those personal contacts which must precede the wider international understanding and friendship'.[15] By the 1960s, the apparent gulf between state and inter-personal relations was particularly concerning in relation to the Commonwealth: 'personal bonds', hoped *The Times*'s Commonwealth correspondent, could underpin, or substitute, 'the disintegrating political and official structure of the Commonwealth association'.[16]

The second and overlapping factor driving the shift in diplomatic strategy was the impending collapse of the British Empire and the need to develop and maintain good relations with nations gaining independence. As Richard Seymour, controller of the British Council's Commonwealth Division explained in 1957, 'we want the colonial peoples ... to be our friends when they do become nations'.[17] In the context of growing nationalist movements – and, in particular, their critiques of Britain's assumed superiority – it would be damaging to appear to be 'trying to convert the world to the "British way of life."'[18] Yet there was a widespread belief that something should be done to combat the encroachment of Communism, build loyalty, and rehabilitate Britain's international image after the disastrous Suez crisis.[19] Friendship and interpersonal relationships seemed to offer a way of developing a 'better understanding and appreciation' of British cultural achievements without the appearance of explicit propaganda. The close alignment between this approach and Rotary and the WI's own developing principles of international understanding meant that government schemes could easily co-opt associational efforts to their own ends.

As well as acting as a foundation for international understanding and a mechanism of cultural diplomacy, friendly encounters also played an important role in the establishment and maintenance of institutional, national, transnational, and Commonwealth identities. Who the WI and Rotary chose to make friends with, and the terms in which they described these relationships, reveal how these organisations saw their members in relation to the wider world. Scholars have convincingly shown that in order to understand colonial relations we have to attend to the discourses and experiences of affect, intimacy, and emotion. Ann Laura Stoler's ground-breaking work on colonial intimacy has revealed that the management of sexual arrangements and affective attachments was critical to the production of colonial categories.[20] Research on non-sexual interactions, such as friendships, has shed further light on how different groups within the Empire related to each other. Work on the British diaspora, for example, shows that pro-imperial organisations such as the Victoria League saw the maintenance of affective ties between settlers and the metropole as an essential component of imperial unity.[21] In her work on anti-imperialism and 'crosscultural collaboration between oppressors and oppressed' in the fin-de-siècle period, Leela Gandhi shows how affective, friendly relationships also acted as the foundation for 'solidarity with foreigners, outsiders, [and] alleged inferiors'; friendship also worked in ways that undermined rather than underpinned the stability of the imperial project.[22] Alongside the 'lived experience' of affective relationships, scholars have also recognised the important role that the language of sentiment played in shaping imperial identities in Britain and overseas. Discourses of friendship were used to legitimate colonial expansion and palliate the violence of Empire.[23]

Despite the visible fruits of this mode of inquiry, affect has been 'largely left out of the history of decolonisation'.[24] Yet, as Bailkin rightly argues, the conditions created by the end of empire required Britons to reappraise their affective relationships with the outside world.[25] Bailkin's own research into decolonisation and welfare provision has given us a rich picture of some of the individual and familial dramas that developed in relation to these interlinked processes, but there is considerable scope for further research. In this chapter I contribute to this wider literature of affect by focusing on how associational organisations reimagined their affective relationships with the outside world and mobilised international friendship as the ideal tool for the post-colonial period. I will show that the discourse and practice of international friendship offered members of associational life a way to counterbalance the power struggles and violence of colonial rule while sustaining ties with existing allies.

In order to illustrate the different ways in which friendships were instrumentalised and understood, I discuss two specific types of friendly act: first, club-to-club connections developed with Rotary and WI members living overseas and, second, the hospitality offered to overseas students within Britain. Through these case studies I hope to contribute not only to discussions about affect and imperialism, but also to debates about the tensions between cosmopolitanism and isolationism in post-imperial Britain. Scholarship on race relations and national identity has tended to characterise the 1950s and 1960s as a period of intense hostility towards migrants and outsiders, one in which narratives of British identity centred on themes of invasion, embattlement, and insularity.[26] This is not to suggest that hostility did not exist but rather to show that there was more heterogeneity in the social mood than is usually recognised. As Mica Nava has shown, 'throughout the [twentieth] century empathy, hospitality, inclusivity, conviviality and the allure of difference in England have *always* co-existed with the most hostile manifestations of racialization'.[27] Recent research has shown that anti-racism became a prominent (though often complicated) feature of left-wing social movements over the course of the 1960s.[28] Using the WI and Rotary as case studies, I show that principles of cosmopolitanism were not the sole property of the politically active left wing. Studying the formation of friendships in different settings reveals that celebrations of cultural difference were also a central feature of Rotary and WI projects of international understanding.

That said, as the examples discussed make clear, not all friendships were equal. While friendships formed with white counterparts overseas were typically imagined as reciprocal – based on the equal exchange of knowledge, experience, and intimacy – those formed with black and Asian counterparts, whether in an overseas club or as a guest in one's home, were more likely to blur the line between friendship and philanthropy. British Rotary and WI members often saw themselves as the 'senior partner' in these relationships, with more to give than to gain. As the final section of this chapter explores, the hierarchical nature of international friendships reveals the enduring influence of imperial ideas and networks on the pursuit of international understanding within civic society.

Kith, kin, and commerce: making friends overseas

Rotary and the WI encouraged their members to see themselves as part of international communities connected by shared values and goals. At Rotary's international convention in Detroit in 1950, Carlos Romulo, the organisation's president, told the gathered audience that 'Rotarians are not ordinary people; they have a broader outlook than most men; they are not tethered by provincialism; nothing human is without interest to them, devoted as they are to international brotherhood.'[29] Framed in these terms, membership of Rotary inspired what Victoria de Grazia pithily describes as 'the half narcissistic, half-altruistic belief in the omnipresence of like-minded people'.[30]

By the 1960s, the movement represented a considerable and still growing cohort. In 1960, the total membership of Rotary Clubs worldwide was approximately 493,000; by 1965 this had increased to 572,750 (of which 312,960 belonged to clubs in North America).[31] As Brendan Goff explains, Rotary International 'presented itself as a kind of Esperanto for an emerging transnational class of businessmen and professionals'.[32] Its international magazine, the *Rotarian*, described itself as 'a forum, a mirror, sometimes perhaps a torch; it is a market, a job, a communication link'.[33] Emphasising the roles played by individual members, the magazine described how it 'links a man to his big organization and to the other men in it. It links their families. It starts with Mrs Smith of Tennessee writing to Mrs Jones of England; soon they'll be exchanging recipes, later on children.'[34] The British publication *Rotary* adopted a similar approach, encouraging its readers to 'experience the thrill of knowing that you are marching in splendid company – the world fellowship of Rotarians united in the idea of service'.[35] As an RIBI booklet on International Service proudly boasted, 'membership of a world movement provid[ed] a ready-made link, and from that assumption of fellowship everything should follow without barrier or hindrance'.[36]

The international rural women's movement was much larger than Rotary International, but its affiliations were also much looser. Members of the British WI were automatically affiliated to the Associated Country Women of the World (ACWW), which had been established in 1933 to promote international goodwill, friendship, and understanding between countrywomen and homemakers around the world. Aroti Dutt, an Indian woman and ACWW's president from 1965 to 1971, described how the organisation represented 'an unseen bond of friendship among women of the world whose skin, colour, religion, social customs, and way of living are different'.[37] By 1974, ACWW represented 8 million members belonging to 290 different women's societies from 74 different countries.[38] Representatives met at triennial conferences to share experiences and reflect on how to live in the changing world.[39] But despite the size of ACWW's membership, only a small proportion of this rural community were active participants in its internationalist work.

As Rotary recognised, 'the fact that a movement exists in over a hundred countries is no guarantee of its internationalism'.[40] By the 1960s, Rotary and the WI actively encouraged their members to pursue friendships in order to build up strong connections between clubs and institutes around the world. It is difficult to judge precisely how many clubs took up these opportunities. The 'News from Overseas' section of *Home and Country* was often dominated by references to link societies and pen friends, suggesting that these relationships formed a substantial portion of the 'everyday' international activities of WIs across the country.[41] But county-level international subcommittees also complained that their local WIs did not fully appreciate the importance of the movement's affiliation to international bodies such as the ACWW.[42] Every issue of *Rotary* discussed the international connections of specific clubs, but the magazine also acknowledged that some Rotary Clubs struggled in this field. Sowerby Bridge Club in Yorkshire, for example, recognised that they were not particularly well situated for international friendship. They enticed few foreign visitors to the club, their efforts to connect with a matched district in Japan failed completely, and their letters to clubs in France went unanswered.[43]

What vision of international friendship did these organisations seek to promote? While Rotary and the WI recognised that the establishment and maintenance of friendly connections relied on the initiative of local clubs and institutes, both organisations took an active interest in the types of friendship that their members were forming. Rotary was particularly concerned that new opportunities for international travel and communication had led some of its members to prioritise breadth over depth. 'It's all too easy to become a nationality collector', they warned, reminding members that, 'True International Service [lay] deeper than a tally of hands shaken and names exchanged.'[44] The WI provided similar warnings to their members: 'travel does not broaden the mind if it involves no more than looking at scenery; minds broaden minds'.[45] Wary of the weakness of shallow connections, Rotary and the WI taught their members how to do institutional friendship properly through the repeated promotion and celebration of a specific set of behaviours.[46]

Whatever the geographical divide that they bridged, the essential building blocks of friendships described in *Rotary* and *Home and Country* remained roughly the same. The central feature was the ritualised exchange of gifts, echoing patterns of state diplomacy. Many Rotary Clubs had special banners and flags made in order to exchange with clubs overseas, for example, while the WI often exchanged craftwork such as embroidery. In functioning as a symbol of mutual goodwill, these gift exchanges laid the foundations for international understanding. To build on these foundations and achieve understanding, Rotary and WI magazines also encouraged their members to exchange information with overseas clubs. This often included the exchange of club programmes, town histories, recipes, and photographs, all items intended to provide insight into the day-to-day experiences of associational life in a different country. In Yorkshire, the Barnsley branch of Rotary made a film to show in other countries, the Bingley branch arranged for transparencies of Bingley to be shown at Rotary Clubs in Australia, and Chislett's Rotherham Club entered into a stamp-collecting agreement with the Kuala Lumpur Club.[47] The homogeneity of these ritualised performances of friendship may seem to indicate the widespread adoption of internationalist principles of partnership, but it obscures significant variations in the way that the WI and Rotary imagined these relationships. Hierarchies, preferences, and more exclusive identities start to emerge when we look beyond the ritualised and performative aspects of 'Link' and 'Contact' friendships to consider their geographic distribution and the different kinds of value that were ascribed to them. Significant variations between Rotary and WI friendships reveal the different ways in which their members imagined themselves in relation to the wider world as well as the uneven influence of empire and globalisation on post-war civic society. The considerable differences in the origins and development of each organisation help us to understand why, despite similar international remits, the profiles of their international friendships look so different.

Based on the examples discussed in the 'News from Overseas' section of *Home and Country*, the overwhelming majority of the 'Links' that WIs formed were with white counterparts living in the Old

Commonwealth. One month's news, for instance, detailed institutes sending a year's supply of *Home and Country* to their Canadian Link, the receipt of a letter from a Link correspondent in British Columbia, a gift of oranges by a former WI president now living in Australia, and a gift of embroidery sewn by 'native women' from an ex-member's Rhodesian Institute.[48] Another 'News from Overseas' item described the Link-minded Burgh Heath WI, which, acting on a belief that Link contact would help foster the feeling of 'world-wideness' in the WI movement, nurtured connections with groups within the Commonwealth: in Ontario, Australia, and New Zealand.[49] In contrast to this show of Old Commonwealth loyalty, 'News from Overseas' made almost no reference to Link societies in New Commonwealth countries in Asia, Africa, or the Caribbean and very few to Links in Europe.

The WI's interactions with the Old Commonwealth were made practicable by what Jean Smith describes as 'the long life of imperial organisations and the networks they created'.[50] Since the aftermath of the Anglo-Boer South African War (1899–1902), when imperial activists determined that British settlement in the dominions was the best 'safeguard' of colonial loyalty, women had played a central role in imperial settlement schemes. Female emigration societies argued that women were particularly suited to pass on British values to the next generation.[51] The pattern of the WI's friendly connections in the 1960s was shaped not only by this long tradition of female emigration but also, more specifically, by the revival of imperial settlement schemes in the post-war period. Australia and New Zealand introduced assisted passage schemes in 1947, contributing to a temporary surge in emigration figures. In the late 1940s and 1950s, driven by the desire to correct a perceived gender imbalance in settler populations, the British state actively promoted women's migration to the Dominions, particularly South Africa and Southern Rhodesia.[52] Anecdotal evidence in 'News from Overseas' suggests that many of the WI's Old Commonwealth Links had been established either through the post-war emigration of existing acquaintances, many of whom were once WI members in Britain, or through the return to Britain of women who had lived in a dominion and maintained contacts there.[53]

There is more to this distorted distribution than simple practicability, however. Many New Commonwealth countries also had rural women's movements of their own that British WIs *could* have chosen to correspond with. As I described in the previous chapter, in the 1940s and 50s, the British WI had helped to set up rural women's movements in Malaya, Jamaica, Goa, Nigeria, and the Philippines.[54] ACWW and NFWI publications encouraged WI members to connect with rural women around the world. An article in *Home and Country* describes a 'Journey to the Caribbean' that saw Lady Anglesey, then chair of the WI, visiting a number of projects that the movement had raised money for as part of the Freedom from Hunger Campaign. The article discusses the Jamaica Federation of Women – which hosted Lady Anglesey during her visit – as 'virtually the WI of the country'; it describes how four hundred members of the Trinidad WI met Lady Anglesey for tea in 'the magnificent Trinidad Hilton Hotel'; and it details a stop in St Kitts to sing *Jerusalem* with the island's WI group.[55] This account of a series of warm encounters makes clear that WI members would not have been oblivious to the potential of forming friendship Links with women in the New Commonwealth, yet this was clearly not sufficient grounds to initiate correspondence.

To make sense of why limited patterns of friendship persisted in spite of increased opportunities for racial and geographical diversity we need to address the value and meaning that the WI ascribed to their Links. Though rarely stated explicitly, it is clear that reciprocal bonds of friendship with 'kith and kin' offered a way for WI members to preserve the significance of the Old Commonwealth. This fits within a longer history of imperial networks formed between women in Britain and the self-governing dominions.[56] For many at the turn of the century, Riedi argues, the Empire meant above all 'Greater Britain', that is, 'the colonies of white settlement which shared a language and culture with the "mother country."'[57] In its early years, British women were told that joining the WI meant 'becoming a member of a great rural sister-hood, not only here, but all over the Empire'.[58] Moreover, the ACWW had always made it possible for members to nurture the more exclusive bonds of Empire alongside their claims to internationalism. In 1950, for example, the WI arranged an Empire 'get together' for countrywomen from Canada, Australia, South Africa, Ceylon, and Northern Ireland; representatives from these countries met first at Denman College before they travelled to join about seven hundred other members of the ACWW in Copenhagen for the organisation's triennial meeting.[59]

The idea of 'Greater Britain' may have been shrinking by 1960 – a process driven in large part by the greater economic and political independence of the old dominions – but 'News from Overseas' makes clear that Women's Institutes continued to place a high value on friend-ships within the Old Commonwealth.[60] 'Amid the prevailing gloom of Commonwealth problems', read the section in January 1966, 'it is a pleasure to report the sending by Effingham of a portrait of the late Sir Winston Churchill as a Christmas present to their New Zealand Link knowing how much it will be treasured.'[61] Though the WI voiced no direct objections to the New Commonwealth, the redemption that seemed to be offered by the New Zealand Link group's predicted

[98]

enthusiasm for Churchill – that is, by its anticipated affirmation of British values – emphasised that for the WI the Old Commonwealth remained a source of easy friendship and comfortable cooperation. When the WI sought to build relationships with white Commonwealth compatriots they were doing what Zelinsky describes as 'questing after one's own kind'.[62] Old Commonwealth friendships were rarely described as directly contributing to the WI's objectives of international under-standing, presumably because participants felt that they already understood each other. In contrast, when links were formed with women in 'emerging nations' they were conceived of in much more practical terms. Where the former was done entirely for pleasure, the latter was done also out of duty. Discussions emphasised how participants would 'learn' from each other and help each other to improve women's lives and rural conditions.[63] The greater use of this language of utility suggests links with non-settler communities were more likely to be formalised as productive – as being for the good of the wider world.

The geographical distribution of RIBI friendships was markedly different from that of the WI. Rotary's own networks were not only much broader than those of the WI, individual Rotarians were also much more likely to visit clubs in other countries. A charitable scheme to drive a lorry of medical supplies 7,600 miles from Whitney Rotary Club to the Shining Hospital at Pokhra in Nepal gives some sense of this breadth: on their way to Nepal, the lorry and its drivers stopped to receive hospitality and assistance from Rotary Clubs in Belgium, Germany, Switzerland, Italy, Austria, Greece, Turkey, Iran, Afghanistan, Pakistan, and India.[64] As this ambitious journey illustrates, while imperial networks influenced some of RIBI's international friendships, they were proportionally much less significant to Rotary than they were to the WI. This is partly because the international expansion of Rotary was much more closely tied to American cultural imperialism than to British imperialism. US members played a prominent role in the spread of new clubs overseas, particularly in the inter-war era.[65]

Rotary's American origins had a significant impact not only on the patterns of British Clubs' international friendships but also on the meanings that they gave to them. Rotary was a crucial component of what de Grazia describes as the 'irresistible' advance of American consumerism into Europe in the twentieth century.[66] As Goff has shown, Rotary also exported a distinctively American form of inter-nationalism: the 'democracy of business'.[67] Within this vision, Rotary saw the accommodation of differences across national cultures as crucial to the spirit of 'consumer-oriented corporate capitalism'.[68] Did British participation in Rotary internationalism indicate the Americanisation of British practices of international engagement? The rhetoric of business-informed internationalism is easily apparent in *Rotary* magazine, which frequently characterised friendships as productive relationships. Speaking at RIBI's annual conference in 1961, for example, Lord Kilmuir, the Lord High Chancellor, discussed the value of personal meetings with foreigners. 'In a life which has contained much international negotiation,' he concluded, 'I rate a good personal contact at 20 per cent of the way to success. If they do not exist, you may never get in sight of understanding.'[69]

That said, British clubs did more than just plug in to American networks. Rotary connections were much more multi-directional than this narrative of Americanisation would suggest. By 1930, as Goff describes, 'it was perfectly normal for Japanese Rotarians to visit Australian Rotarians in their factories, for Mexican Rotarians to wine and dine Italian Rotarians on business trips, for Polish Rotarians to attend conferences hosted by Cuban Rotarians, and so on – all without direct reference to or guidance from U.S. Rotarians'.[70] As scholarship on other transnational organisations has suggested, distinctive national and regional cultures often shape the practices of local branches.[71] Rotary was no different. Su Lin Lewis's work on Rotary in Malaysia illustrates that Rotary's rapid international diffusion was at least as much testament to its flexible institutional form as it was to the efforts of its American promoters.[72] In the British context, Rotary's American influences did not overwrite British clubs' other allegiances. For British Rotarians two distinctive patterns of international friendship are apparent in the 1960s, the first shaped by the country's proximity to mainland Europe, and the second by the enduring influence of imperial networks.

Based on reports given in *Rotary*, European links made up the majority of Rotary Clubs' friendly connections in the 1960s. Rotary had been well established in Europe since the inter-war period, with clubs in most major cities. The high proportion of British-European friendships was certainly shaped by geographical proximity; it was much easier for Rotarians to visit contact clubs in Europe than those further afield. But RIBI clubs' European friendships were also influenced by post-war projects of peace and unity. In 1961, for example, members of Northampton Rotary Club chartered a coach for a goodwill tour of Continental Rotary Clubs, visiting Brussels, Bastogne, Luxembourg, Baden Baden, Lucerne, and Dijon.[73] By profiling a different European club in each issue, the regular *Rotary* feature 'Rotary across the channel' reinforced the sense of familiarity that individual clubs were seeking to develop.

Rotary's growing European connections indicate Britain's reorientation towards Europe in the 1960s: if not necessarily in cultural terms, then as a matter of geopolitical and economic expediency. Though the British state was struggling to gain admission to the EEC, Rotary's non-state activities fit a broader pattern of European integration projects taking place in this period. Their friendship work most closely paralleled the geographic distribution and rhetoric of contemporaneous municipal town-twinning efforts. In the 1960s, British municipalities participated in town-twinning schemes that sought to bind together western Europeans as well as those that, more controversially, sought to bridge Cold War divides.[74] The ritualised traditions of town twinning – the exchange of gifts and ceremonies centred on food and dance – were similar to Rotary's own rituals of international friendship in that they simultaneously celebrated cultural differences and shared humanity.[75] The principles of economic exchange that often underpinned municipal internationalism in this period also correspond with Rotarians' commitments to serve their own business communities. For Rotarians, European friendships brought peace *and* prosperity.

Even as Rotary's European connections increased in the post-war period, a significant proportion of RIBI friendships remained with clubs in the declining empire. Unlike British Rotary Clubs' European connections, which tended to be a post-war development, relationships with clubs in dominions, colonies, and former colonies were more likely to date from before the war. In the first half of the twentieth century, RIBI had developed 'thick relationships' with clubs popping up all over the Empire.[76] In many cases, the Rotary Clubs that British Rotarians connected with in the 1960s would have been established by British Rotarians working in imperial outposts. As with the WI, many of these were also linked to settlement schemes in the dominions, a pattern that continued into the post-war period. Over four months in 1956, for example, 14,000 emigrants left Britain for Australia under an assisted passage scheme. Many of them did so as 'Rotary to Rotary' families, chosen and vetted by Rotary Clubs in England before travelling to sponsored homes and jobs found for them by Rotary Clubs in Australia.[77] In comparison to the WI, RIBI maintained connections to a much broader network of Rotary Clubs, extending beyond the dominions and settler colonies and into other parts of the Empire. Indeed, the discussion of international connections in *Rotary* differs significantly from that in *Home and Country* in that it reveals neither an explicit nor implicit preference for the Old Commonwealth and its comforting familiarity.

The comparatively wider geographic reach is not the only factor distinguishing Rotary's imperial connections from those of the WI. The Clubs that British Rotarians connected with were also more likely to be racially diverse than those in the WI's network. Rotary Clubs were often distinctive within imperial settings because, in contrast to the racial exclusivity of imperial clubhouses and the overseas branches of the Royal Commonwealth Society (RCS), many provided a way of breaking the colour bar in colonial society. The Cairo Rotary Club, for example, had active members from fourteen nationalities and seven religions.[78] In the inter-war period, new clubs' racial diversity had destabilised the 'tacit whiteness of Rotary International's civic inter-nationalism' and acted as an 'acid test' for Rotary International's fourth object: 'advancing international understanding, goodwill and peace'.[79] By the 1960s, British Rotarians spoke in praise of racially diverse overseas clubs while critiquing those who failed to represent their communities. As a Jersey member wrote to *Rotary* magazine in 1964,

> I recall joining the Club of Bombay in 1930, when Europeans started most movements, and then there were only one or two Indian members so far as I remember. But very soon it was realised this was very wrong, and in a few years we were very representative of the varied races in Bombay. [...] On looking at the Bombay Roster of a few years ago [...] I gather that Indians are in the large majority, which is as it should be.[80]

The celebration of friendship and fellowship across a racially diverse international membership worked to confirm British Rotarians' sense of their own cosmopolitanism and modernity. Even if British clubs were rarely cosmopolitan in their makeup – Rotary membership in Britain was almost exclusively white in the 1960s – they could at least claim to be cosmopolitan in their outlook. As I discuss in the next section, the immigration patterns of the 1960s made it increasingly possible for both Rotary and the WI to pursue international friendship and perform cosmopolitan identities without recourse to their own international networks.

Hospitality as state-approved friendship

Rotary and the WI's pursuit of international friendships was not limited to overseas connections; members were also encouraged to take oppor-tunities to interact with those from overseas within Britain. This happened not only through the educational events, but also through offers of hospitality to those visiting or temporarily resident in Britain. In histories of decolonisation and immigration it has been more common to study sites of exclusion and hostility than inclusion and sympathy. As Nava observes, cultural historians have tended to focus on the activities and ideas of those belonging to a hostile tradition of xenophobia and racism that was 'embedded in a legacy of Empire, national chauvin-ism and racial supremacy'.[81] These attitudes certainly existed, but it is important to recognise that this was not the only reaction either to immigration or to global race relations. While responses to the new waves of immigrants after the Second World War were often antagonistic, they could also be, as Nava has argued, 'ardently sympathetic'.[82] As well as recognising politicised claims to cosmopolitanism that developed in the 1960s, we also need to recognise that non-activist members of the public, such as Rotarians and the WI, also pursued encounters with cultural difference and challenged the assumptions of racist rhetoric. In this section I address this gap in the literature by using the provision of hospitality for foreign students as an example of the non-activist acts of inclusion that existed within associational life and their association with discourses of international responsibility. The hospitality that members of Rotary and the WI offered to foreign students not only tells us about the cosmopolitan roles that members of associational life imagined for themselves, it also illustrates the significant influence of state priorities on associational practices of international engagement.

In the context of decolonisation, hospitableness became an important and yet fraught feature of British national identity.[83] Speaking at the House of Commons debate on the Commonwealth Scholarship Bill in 1959, Labour MP Hector Hughes complained that the 'the world does not give sufficient credit to Britain's magnificent services to human progress by her acceptance and absorption of refugees from other lands'.[84] Setting aside the fact that Britain's track record for hospitality was considerably more patchy than Hughes implied, why should this lack of recognition matter? In the 1950s and early 1960s, the protection and projection of a reputation for generous hospitality stopped being simply a matter of national pride and became an issue of increasing geopolitical significance. As the pace of decolonisation accelerated, narratives about British hospitality were mobilised to provide evidence of the country's commitment to Commonwealth ideals of cooperation, tolerance, and partnership. As Craggs has shown, cooperative Commonwealth relations were often 'performed through hospitable acts'. This included the welcome given to the Queen on her Commonwealth tours, the hospitality provided in the RCS's bars and restaurants, and the invitations to tea extended to Commonwealth students studying in Britain.[85] In providing a performance of an 'optimistic and friendly Commonwealth', hospitality became a mechanism through which to 'counteract more problematic narratives of decline, discord and disharmony'.[86]

Not everyone was convinced by this narrative, however. When Anthony Sampson asked in the *Observer*, 'We pride ourselves on being the centre of a multiracial Commonwealth. But do we really deserve the title?' the article's headline – 'The dead hand of hospitality' – had already given away his answer.[87] Attempts to paint Britain as a hospitable and welcoming nation ran up against stereotypes of its population as cold, uptight, and unfriendly. To some black visitors, this 'impervious coldness' came across as 'a relic of white supremacy that [was] dying hard'.[88] The emotional detachment of the cold shoulder was often matched by the physical barrier of the closed door. The operation of an informal colour bar denied many Asian, African, and Caribbean visitors and immigrants access to sites of hospitality, while the 1962 Commonwealth Immigrants Act put up a legal barrier to migration.[89]

Though, by the start of the 1960s, the British state appeared to have given up on appearing hospitable to permanent economic migrants from the Commonwealth, they continued to maintain a close interest in the experiences of overseas students.[90] This is because the provision of education had become a crucial part of Britain's wider efforts in the post-war competition for global influence.[91] In 1950 there were approximately 12,500 overseas students in Britain. A decade later, this figure had more than quadrupled to 55,087. By 1964 there were an estimated 64,169 overseas students undergoing full-time training, with the most significant increases in those attending technical colleges and nursing training.[92] Of these, roughly two-thirds were from the Commonwealth and British Dependencies.[93] The hospitality extended to these students became increasingly important over the course of the 1950s as recognition of the increasing pace of decolonisation marked them as the successor generation: 'the hereditary elite of the colonies and the leaders of tomorrow'.[94] As A. J. Stockwell points out, 'the presence of unprecedented numbers of colonial students in post-war Britain placed the Colonial Office in a novel position. It was now obliged to deal at first hand, rather than at arm's length, with the grievances and ambitions of colonial peoples'.[95]

Done well, the education of colonial and Commonwealth students in Britain could prove the nation's commitment to these Commonwealth ideals.[96] At the reading of the Commonwealth Scholarship Bill in 1959, Hughes was confident about the work being done in this field and implored Parliament to see this as

> a time when it is fitting for us notionally to take our stand on a little hill and survey our country in which we live and our Commonwealth in which we live and realise what is its glory, its freedom and its activities which have attracted people from many lands and made it one of the strongest forces for culture and peace in the world.[97]

Conservative MP Brian Harrison echoed Hughes's naive combination of pride and optimism, predicting that those who came to Britain under the scholarship scheme would 'experience what all young men experience when they come from the Commonwealth: the joy of utter political equality; and having experienced it they will not go back to any part of the Commonwealth without the determination that they will take political equality with them'.[98] Students' positive experiences in Britain were expected to instil a respect for British 'ways of life' that would provide the foundation for cooperative post-colonial relations.[99]

Done badly, however, it was feared that the provision of education at British universities would do more harm than good to Commonwealth relations. The Colonial Office had already recognised this possibility in the 1930s. As the governor of Nigeria observed, 'the harm that can be done, on his return to his own country, by one African student who has managed to accumulate a store of real or fancied grievances during his stay in England far outweighs the good done by a dozen students who come back successful and satisfied'.[100] By the mid-1950s there was growing concern that Britain was not getting it right and increasing anxiety about the implications this could have for the handover of power and post-colonial relations. The first systematic surveys introduced to record the experiences of colonial students 'revealed ignorance and prejudice across British society and charted the disillusionment of Britain's "disappointed guests."'[101] Difficulties securing accommodation were commonly cited as a key factor, but commentators also recognised that there were wider issues that prevented students from interacting with their British peers. Far from experiencing Britain's mythic hospitableness, many students went home feeling 'lonely, unwanted and without friends'.[102] As the *Surrey Comet* reported in 1961, 'our apparent rejection of [students] now is a personal problem; it could be a national calamity for us if others in Europe provide, as seems likely, what we are reluctant to offer'.[103]

These concerns created the broad context in which the WI and Rotary involved themselves in student hospitality and imagined this work as international service, but they were not the only significant factor. Associational participation became an increasingly important part of state-led hospitality initiatives as a result of changes introduced throughout the 1950s and 1960s. In 1950, when the British Council took over responsibility from the Colonial Office for the welfare of colonial students, they adopted a set of strategies that emphasised personal contact.[104] By the 1960s, the Central Office of Information's (COI) approach to entertaining official state guests had come under increasing scrutiny. The Institute of Race Relations complained that the COI provided no opportunities for their guests to interact with 'ordinary citizens'. Far from inspiring an appreciation of the British way of life, the typical experience was 'a glum meal in the uninspiring company of his escort' and a long evening 'spent moping around a friendless hotel'.[105] Why were visitors put through a silent lunch at the old-fashioned Simpsons in the Strand, asked Sampson 'when they could have enjoyed a lively meal at the LSE canteen'?[106] In contrast, the British Council worked hard to humanise hospitality and in doing so made voluntary associations an increasingly important part of diplomatic work. As they recognised, this 'field of work' lent itself to the 'voluntary pattern'.[107]

With rapidly growing student numbers, the British Council was increasingly reliant on the labour of volunteers to meet this demand. Luckily, a wide range of associations were interested in participating in hospitality work. Alongside Rotary and the WI, this voluntary field included the Victoria League, the British Council of Churches (BCC), the English Speaking Union, the YMCA and YMWA, the United Nations Association, Toc H, and the Royal African Society.[108] A significant part of British Council work was the coordination of more than 70 voluntary bodies to provide accommodation and hospitality and to assist students 'to merge so far as possible into the life of the community'.[109] In 1958, for example, the Council's London department for Student Welfare coordinated hospitality for 2,212 students (of which 1,246 were from the Empire and Commonwealth).[110] The late 1950s and early 1960s were characterised by the expansion and consolidation of this work across the country. In 1963–64 organisations and individuals made 12,958 invitations through the British Council.[111] By the mid-1960s, reports from area officers reveal the strain of increasing workloads and the difficulty the British Council faced in maintaining contacts suitable for hospitality work.[112]

The increasing demand for homely and personal hospitality coincided with Rotary and the WI's growing sense of international responsibility. From the mid-1950s onwards the welfare of overseas students was at the fore of Rotary's service work in the UK.[113] In 1956, the Conference of Voluntary Societies on the Welfare of Overseas Students in London described how 'Rotarians and their wives provide a great deal of both group and individual hospitality for overseas students'. The 'range of occupations' represented within Rotary put them in an ideal position 'to establish friendly relations with their student guests on the basis of a shared professional interest'.[114] From the mid-1950s the Colonial Office and British Council also regularly asked the NFWI to arrange for overseas students to 'see something of [the] movement'.[115]

Though the British Council remained a key 'source' of overseas guests throughout the 1960s, many WI County Federations also took the initiative to bypass the British Council and contact local colleges and universities directly. As a pamphlet described, the foreign and colonial students studying in these institutions represented 'a piece of international work lying ready to hand'.[116] Both the WI's and Rotary's work in this field remained steady throughout the 1960s. In 1964, the Institute for Race Relations praised Rotary for their 'untiring' work arranging evening, day, and weekend functions where their members could get to know individual students, and the WI for inviting students to stay in their homes while they carried out their studies.[117] The frequent references in *Rotary* and *Home and Country* to the hospitality provided by clubs, institutes, and individual members suggests that both organisations were proud of their work with Commonwealth visitors.[118] From the NFWI's point of view, their members were 'doing splendidly' in this project: a 1967 *Home and Country* reported that stories came in from all over the country of

> delighted students going on tours arranged by County Federations and individuals being welcomed into homes, shown round farms, hop fields, schools; taken into dances, dressmaking classes, WI meetings; fetched in cars, put on to buses and trains and generally cherished by WI members at every step.[119]

The scope of the international responsibility that WI and Rotary members felt was not restricted to the Commonwealth and declining empire, and nor were their offers of hospitality. In 1960, for example, Wisbech Rotary Club provided hospitality to student 'representatives' from Norway, Yugoslavia, Italy, Israel, Pakistan, Vietnam, Sweden, Spain, Finland, Kenya, Ghana, Nigeria, Russia, Germany, France, Denmark, India, 'Persia', and Tanganyika, all working on the Cambridgeshire summer fruit harvest.[120] A Buckinghamshire WI member hosted various visitors, including 'an African chief over here to study youth organisations, a young Australian magistrate who studied Local Government ... a Dutch girl journalist who was shown various newspaper offices, Canadian farmers, and students from Thailand'.[121] Nevertheless, through their interaction with the British Council, Rotary and the WI became agents in state projects of soft diplomacy that sought to improve relations with the Commonwealth. The specific, individual acts of hospitality offered by the WI and Rotary gained significance from broader discourses about national compassion and diplomacy. As *Home and Country* informed their readers, the guests of the WI 'on returning home, most of them to responsible posts, give a good account of us to their families and, in due course, to their children'.[122] In the same vein, Rotarians read that their hospitality 'help[ed] to create a favourable opinion of Britain in the future leaders of the world'.[123] Black students were more likely than white students to feature in the photographs accompanying *Home and Country* and *Rotary* articles on hospitality, and were also more likely to be discussed in articles giving members advice on how to make the most of hospitality.[124] This seems to indicate that the organisations felt there was more at stake in hospitality offered to black and Asian guests from the Commonwealth than to white students from elsewhere in the world.

As well as allowing WI and Rotary members to fulfil their commitment to international service, hospitality also offered ways of thinking about the boundaries of national identity within the domestic sphere. Whereas club-to-club friendships formed by Rotary and the WI were usually discussed as an exchange between public spaces, hospitality was more likely to occur within the private sphere of the home. Commentators on state diplomacy and overseas students worried that many visitors did not get to see the inside of a British home.[125] The Institute of Race Relations, for example, suggested that the most valuable part of arranging home-stays for community development trainees was the 'private conversation' they had with their hosts in the evenings.[126] This view was echoed by a Buckinghamshire member of the WI, who stressed that 'it's only by coming into our homes that they can really get to know us'.[127] By linking the private sphere to authenticity, and by stressing the importance of authenticity to effective diplomatic relations, commentators made the threshold of the home a significant diplomatic boundary.

The home has often been an important site of national identity. Chris Waters, Alison Light, and Raphael Samuel have argued that in the inter-war period 'hearth and home' rather than 'sceptre and sword' became the key symbols of national existence.[128] As Light describes, 'the 1920s and '30s saw a move away from formerly heroic and officially masculine public rhetorics of national identity [...] to an Englishness at once less imperial and more inward-looking, more domestic and more private – and, in terms of pre-war standards, more "feminine"'.[129] Wendy Webster has extended this 'narrative of nation' into the post-war period by characterising the 'home' as the key symbol of Englishness in 1950s and 1960s narratives of immigrant 'invasion'. Webster argues that Commonwealth immigrants were disassociated from domestic life, that they were portrayed as violating English domestic boundaries, and that they were configured as transient and rootless against an England that stood for order and homeliness.[130] Employing similar rhetoric, Bill Schwarz ties post-war immigration to Britain's imperial past by conceiving it as a restaging of the primal colonial encounter in reverse. With immigration, he argues, the colonial frontier came 'home'.[131] Within this literature, the threshold of the home is often depicted as a politicised site of racial tension.[132] While these ideas of invasion clearly had considerable purchase in national discourses of race and immigration, they are not readily applicable to the associational provision of hospitality for students. In the case of student hospitality, the home still figures as a key location in the interaction between 'insiders' and 'outsiders'. Yet rather than a violated sanctuary it acted instead as a site in which familial and friendly bonds could be formed. Many WI members and Rotary wives opened their doors and enthusiastically invited 'strangers' across the threshold and into this inner sanctum of Englishness. In doing so, they opened up the private and domestic home of tea and jam, knitting, and sewing – in many ways the most traditional, safe, and insular location of identity available to them – and made it public.

The interest of the WI and Rotary in these students provides an important counterbalance to the popular cultural trope that only 'outsiders' in the white population *chose* to socialise with immigrants.[133] It was a show of support for an ideal of cosmopolitan openness (one that ran counter to the isolationism gaining momentum on the far right) and for the members of a marginalised community. WI and Rotary may have conceived of their support for overseas students as an act of international service – an international good on the same terms as their philanthropy and pursuit of knowledge – but it also intersected with their domestic efforts to improve race relations, discourage prejudice in the white population, and offer services to permanent as well as temporary migrants. At an organisational level both the WI and Rotary were committed to challenging racial discrimination within Britain. In 1967 *Home and Country* reminded readers that the long-term aim was 'to create conditions in which young immigrants may settle happily and without prejudice in close relationship with the indigenous population'.[134] Although it is fair to assume that some Rotary and WI members would have disagreed with their organisations' official stance on race relations, there is considerable evidence that these objectives were acted on at a local level. For example, Rotary Clubs in Barking and Southwark set up groups to investigate problems facing the black population, address the concerns of those who 'suspect[ed] discrimination against them', and 'foster better relationships'.[135]

Offers of student hospitality are an important indicator of openness towards outsiders, particularly when considered alongside both organisations' wider work with migrants, but the fact that these interactions were a choice remains significant. Hospitality is conditional on the guest's implicit acceptance of the host's rules. Since the WI and Rotary were always the hosts to and never the guests of overseas students, the interactions always occurred on their terms. Take, for example, the 'kind' but firm manner in which a WI member explained to a male African guest that his advances towards her daughter were not welcomed:

'while her daughter enjoyed his company, she did not, in fact, like the idea of sex before marriage'.[136] The matter-of-fact manner in which this incident was reported in *Home and Country* in 1967 lacked the panic and hyperbole that some scholars have characterised as typical of discussions of inter-racial sexual relationships in the late 1950s and early 1960s, suggesting that attitudes were gradually changing. Nevertheless, it still served as a clear reminder of the host's authority to set the terms of the encounter.[137] The *offer* of hospitality – the invitation to temporarily cross the threshold – means that these should not be read as examples of the breakdown of national boundaries, but rather of their gentle reinforcement and careful management.

By the mid-1960s, the government's interest in the Commonwealth was waning. The tied narratives of generous hospitality and Commonwealth cooperation that had been belied by the restrictive Commonwealth Immigration Act of 1962 were further undermined by the introduction of overseas student fees for Commonwealth students in 1966. As J. M. Lee describes, cost–benefit analysis of educational assistance led some to conclude that it would be 'cheaper to send out training missions than to receive candidates for training'.[138] In later years, Lee suggests, the decision on fees was seen as '"the end of innocence", the point at which Britain shed the role of being a mother country'.[139] From the end of the Second World War until 1966/67, Commonwealth students had represented more than half of overseas full-time university enrolments. By 1971 that figure dropped to 41 per cent.[140] Yet despite these structural shifts in state provision, the patterns of associational hospitality that were established in the 1950s and early 1960s remained largely the same. Such was their demand for Commonwealth students to host that by 1970 the WI were struggling to find enough guests to entertain.[141]

Transformative affect? Difference, reciprocity, and responsibility in international friendship

What do associational friendships tell us about changing attitudes towards international relations at the end of empire? In the realm of personal relationships, a healthy friendship is typically understood to be mutual and reciprocal; each party respects the other and each contributes to, and benefits from, the exchange. Although the WI and Rotary employed the language of friendship to describe a wide range of individual and institutional relationships with people from overseas, their members did not imagine all of these relationships as between equals. J. M. Lee characterises the tactics of cultural diplomacy that developed in the post-war period as a new form of post-imperial 'outreach' through which 'imperialism gave way to cooperation, and cultural hegemony to cultural exchange'.[142] Examples of cooperation and cultural exchange are evident in many aspects of the international work of Rotary and the WI, but they are not evenly distributed. Superficially, the language of international friendship imagined members of the WI and Rotary as part of a cooperative international community bound by ties of affection and understanding. In practice, it was also used to delineate institutional, national, and Commonwealth identities, variously granting and denying access to more exclusive communities. To illustrate how friendship worked to demarcate the identities of WI and Rotary members, I discuss three intersecting issues: the identification and fetishisation of cultural difference (particularly along racial lines); the different expectations about the transformative effect that friendship could or should have on those taking part; and, finally, the distinction between philanthropic and reciprocal models of friendship.

While friendships with other members of the white middle class were imagined as an opportunity to bond together people with pre-existing shared characteristics, friendships formed with black and Asian counterparts, whether in an overseas club or as a guest in one's home, were typically understood to act as a bridge between culturally distinct groups.[143] As discussed in Chapter 2, WI and Rotary efforts to enhance international knowledge showed a shared fascination with cultural difference. The same was true of their hospitality work. As with invited speakers at educational events, student guests were frequently asked to 'perform' their difference. When Stepney Rotary Club held an event for nurses from overseas working in local hospitals, they requested that they attend dressed in national costumes. The result was a 'wonderfully colourful occasion'.[144] Foreign guests at a Nottingham International Service weekend were described as 'charming and decorative'.[145] As with the educational events, institutional offers of friendship and hospitality were used as opportunities for ethnographic information-gathering and entertaining spectacle.[146] In circumstances such as these, friends and guests were not treated as individuals, but as symbols of foreign culture.

How did the WI and Rotary's preoccupation with the cultural difference of non-white visitors fit within broader debates about race and post-imperial British identity in the 1960s? Maggie Andrews has argued that the WI was radical in its rejection of definitions of black as other in this period. While the movement was, as a whole, welcoming towards immigrant populations and open towards contact with foreigners, I disagree with Andrews's suggestion that the WI did not still see these groups as other. Andrews cites the following extract from an article titled 'Black Beauty' in *Home and Country* as an example of these radical rejections:

> Coming down the corridor towards them was a nurse. She was black … and she was wonderfully beautiful, radiantly alive. Her white uniform emphasised her colour vividly. Oh dear, thought Mrs Martin nervously. Supposing Andrew says something awkward. But Andrew gazed with awe. 'Oh Mummy', he breathed ecstatically at last, 'Isn't she beautiful'.[147]

What Andrews sees as a radical shift was rather a relocation of long-standing discourses of blackness to an 'everyday' British setting. While it certainly offers a positive description of blackness, this extract does not escape the vocabulary of race. The WI and Rotary's attempts to be accepting and welcoming were still bounded and structured by long-standing discourses about skin colour. Whether positively or negatively expressed, identifying difference continued to be an important part of how members of these associations processed their increased interaction with black people in this period.

In this context it is unsurprising that many black students learnt to be wary about the intentions of those offering hospitality. In an article explaining the conditional nature of much hospitality, Sheila Kitzinger set out a common dilemma:

> Mr Smith writes a note to John inviting him for coffee the following evening. The note looks all right and it is certainly very kind – but since they have never met, what does Mr Smith want to get out of him? – John asks himself. Is he just curious about colored people? Is he retired from the Colonial Service and nostalgic for Nigeria? Or is it religion that he is going to drag him into? With these suspicions in mind John goes to the coffee party and sees that most of the other guests are also colored. … Obviously Mr Smith is not interested in him as a person, and this is only one better … than the sort of party at which he often finds himself where he is presented as a freak, where there is someone who plays the flute, someone who stands on his head – and a colored man.[148]

These concerns were not universal – many students reported that the British Council had arranged warm and enjoyable experiences for them – but they do illustrate the ways in which foreign friends and guests could become what Sara Ahmed describes as 'a commodity fetish', 'circulated and exchanged in order to determine the borders and boundaries of given communities'.[149] In these circumstances, the celebration of difference and the performance of cosmopolitanism had the effect of reinforcing rather than breaking down boundaries. The institutional discourses of Rotary and the WI did not represent friendship and hospitality as a route to cultural hybridity, but rather emphasised the value of maintaining cultural diversity. Individuals were obligated to learn *about* others, not to become like them.

It is very difficult to determine with any precision how individual members of Rotary and the WI *were* shaped by their cross-cultural encounters, though it is certain that they were. We can, however, analyse the expectations each organisation had about the *likelihood* that international friendships would be transformative for those taking part. As both organisations repeatedly insisted, the changing international picture of the 1950s and 1960s made it increasingly necessary for their members to 'learn to live' in a shrinking, crowded, and complex world.[150] Rotary and the WI did occasionally describe the specific information or skills that their members stood to gain from international friends.[151] But more often they lauded the general transformative effects of their friendship schemes: the whole business of cross-cultural encounters, from the 'homework beforehand' to the exchange of letters, club visits, and hospitality, would teach participants how to be understanding.[152] Conceived in this way, the lessons learned by members *before* the initial encounter or exchange took place were as important to the project of international understanding as the relationship itself. The steps that Rotary and the WI took to guide their members through this process were shaped by their assumptions about the utility of friendship as a diplomatic tool. Whether the emphasis was on preserving global peace or improving Britain's international standing, for friendship to be effective, both parties needed to feel that the relationship was based on mutual respect. While friendships with Europeans, Americans, and white settlers across the Commonwealth were expected to fall into this pattern naturally, Rotary and WI provided explicit advice to members who were planning to form friendships with blacks and Asians. In doing so, they treated the ability to show respect to those who were culturally different as a learned behaviour that all members could develop.

To support this process of self-improvement, the WI warned its members against patronising their guests – telling them that the fact that Africans are 'over here … proves them to be intelligent and used to an extremely civilized society'.[153] They also advised against generalisation, reminding members of the diversity of the African continent: 'Nigerians are not likely to know any more about the languages and customs of Ghana', readers of *Home and Country* were told, 'than we know about the languages and customs of China.'[154] Rotary took a similar tack, explaining to its members that:

If the host's mind is not full of notions about making this poor, half-savage fellow feel 'at home', he will not launch into an eulogy of the tribal

[113]

African way of life; for he will realise that the poor half-savage fellow is possibly an ardent young nationalist, impatient for the modernization of his country, with clear political and economic ideas that might put his host's to shame.[155]

Implicit within this advice is a recognition that Britain's relationship with its former colonies needed to change and that attitudes forged in the crucible of imperial power were no longer appropriate in an era of decolonisation, self-determination, and collaboration. Dependent on the degree of cynicism with which we approach the matter, decolonisation either demanded or facilitated greater self-reflexivity from the British public. At a state level, the loss of global power made it increasingly necessary to think about how Britain's actions and attitudes were perceived overseas and what could be done to improve that perception. But the advice given by Rotary and the WI indicates that the responsibility for self-appraisal and self-improvement was also taken up in civic society. Rotary suggested that Britain needed the trust of newly independent peoples and that 'the only way to engender trust is to earn it: by banishing preconceived notions and pointless worry so that the stranger himself may be seen, and not some falsified image'.[156] In 1970, WI members asserted that it was necessary to 'see ourselves through others eyes' and change one's behaviour to minimise the 'British characteristics distasteful to overseas visitors'.[157] Just as attitudes of racial superiority had been learned through centuries of imperial rule, they could and should be unlearned in an era of decolonisation.

This was, however, a process of fits, starts, and startling contradictions. The movements' published materials indicate that increased contact and exposure did not automatically lead to increased cultural sensitivity. Articles in *Home and Country* frequently exoticised foreign countries and encouraged WI members to participate in forms of engagement that were centred on novelty and difference. For example, when the Beatles visited Japan, *Home and Country* held a competition for the best verse of a new song for the Beatles 'with a suitable oriental slant'. Entrants included the lines 'she's a cutie, my slant-eyed girl' and the unexpectedly racy 'baby be my little geisha, be my fragrant lotus bloom, it's so hard babe to release ya, you're so groovy let's get zoom'.[158] As part of the evening entertainment at Carnoustie Rotary Club's International Weekend in 1965, at which Nigerian guests from the Dundee College of Education did 'native dances', a local troupe of Black and White Minstrels gave a performance that 'brought the house down'.[159] WI and Rotary's advice to members thinking about hosting guests also illustrates that both organisations struggled to talk about cultural difference without recourse to imperial hierarchies of

[114]

civilisation.[160] For every warning they gave against generalisation they made one of their own. 'Life for the inhabitants of the Asian and African countries is leisurely,' prospective WI hosts were told, 'all time belongs to them.'[161] When giving advice to members about how to approach interaction with Caribbean and African immigrants, *Rotary* told readers that 'the nearer people are – in terms of generations and race memory – to a simple or primitive way of life, the more instinctively alert they will be (especially the women) not only to the deliberate slight, but also to the unspoken reticence, the half-formed thought'.[162] The terms in which Rotary and the WI encouraged their members to accommodate difference illustrates the endurance of racialised thinking, even among those who sought to break down barriers of understanding. But it also shows that both organisations saw the 1960s as a transformational moment in which Britain and its public could redefine their relationships with former colonies.

As well as assessing the modifications that members of Rotary and the WI made to their own behaviour, it is also useful to think about whether the codes of international friendship, service, and understanding obligated them to seek to alter the behaviour of others. How did friendship feed into broader ideas of international responsibility? While Rotary's Fourth Objective required that its members seek to understand their counterparts overseas, the organisation also discouraged them from trying to change each other's behaviour. Travelling Rotarians were told not to attempt to advise on how to improve another country, they should particularly avoid advocating the adoption of any of their own country's methods.[163] The WI's account of their hospitality work suggests that they adopted a similar approach: 'we are a listening family', they explained, one which, 'having made people from other countries feel at ease, prefer[s] them to do the talking'.[164] These recommended practices of non-intervention fit the increasingly accepted model of cultural diplomacy: it was better to change others' behaviour by example than by telling them what to do. They offer further evidence that the British public acknowledged and sought to adapt to the changing international dynamics of decolonisation. But they also illustrate some of the important distinctions between different manifestations of post-war internationalism. For internationalists on the radical left, friendship was intrinsically tied to solidarity. In the Anti-Apartheid Movement, as in the anti-Vietnam War movement and the CND, the language of friendship was used to discuss international solidarity and the obligation to take political action.[165] The same was not true of discourses of friendship within 'apolitical' associational life.

British Rotary's interaction with clubs in apartheid South Africa offers a useful test case, revealing the possibilities and limitations of

Rotarian principles of friendship and international understanding when applied across racial lines. Should 'real' friends call each other out on their inappropriate behaviour? And in what circumstances did another club's misbehaviour require you to break off your friendship with them? As Goff has discussed, Rotary's civic internationalism claimed to 'rise above the political'.[166] As a general rule, Rotarians were advised to avoid politics and religion as topics of conversation when making new friends.[167] In practice, however, Rotary did not exist in a political vacuum and the networks of Rotarian 'friendship' were frequently exploited as a conduit for politicised information. As one member observed, 'whenever there is a political crisis somewhere in the world it is almost certain that some Rotary Club in that area will circularise all Clubs the world over to explain why one side of the controversy is right and the other wrong'.[168]

For British Rotarians, the most contentious issue of the 1960s was apartheid South Africa. In 1965 a South African Rotary Club distributed a pamphlet titled 'The Goodwood Handshake' to Rotary Clubs around the world. The pamphlet, its authors claimed, sought to counter some of the 'sensationalist' images of apartheid in the international press and to encourage Rotarians to visit South Africa to see the situation for themselves.[169] British Rotarians' responses to the letter reveal their different interpretations of the responsibilities demanded by Rotary's Fourth Objective. Was the letter a gesture of friendship, as the title suggested? Or did it exploit Rotary's principles of goodwill? Some British Rotarians argued that the authors of the 'Goodwood Handshake' were not interested in the advancement of international understanding, but rather the defence of apartheid. One member, for example, dismissed the pamphlet as a piece of 'blatant political propaganda' in which 'the smallest hint of criticism of the [apartheid] regime has been suppressed'.[170] Not all were so critical, however, and others celebrated the pamphlet on the grounds that direct communication was a necessary component of international understanding. Without 'full knowledge of all sides of any question', one member argued, Rotarians could not claim to have achieved international understanding.[171] Which was the truer demonstration of Rotarian values: 'fraternal fidelity' with South African Rotarians or the disavowal of racial segregation and all associated with it?[172]

Rotarian responses to apartheid were caught between two conflicting principles: the organisation's commitment to political neutrality, and its aspiration to improve international understanding and cooperation. As the debates that played out over three months in the letter pages of *Rotary* reveal, the issue was not easily reconciled. As one member explained in relation to the 'Goodwood Handshake': 'I do not feel that

I am entitled to sit in a chair, thousands of miles from the scene of its operation, lacking personal knowledge of South Africa and the South Africans, and either condone or condemn it out of hand.'[173] As well as excusing the inaction of British Rotarians, the principles of non-intervention were easily manipulated by white South Africans who wanted to avoid international scrutiny of 'local' issues. In 1964 for example, a Rotary member from Johannesburg wrote in to *Rotary* in response to criticism that the South African Rotary movement was not doing enough for racial equality. The central point of his complaint – which also asserted that black Africans did not yet have the skills and abilities to be granted 'human rights' – was that Rotarians 'the world over' should mind their own business and trust that 'whatever the problems existing in various countries, these are being dealt with by Rotarians of that country to the best of their ability'.[174]

Formulated in this way, in order to fulfil their commitment to international understanding, Rotarians were required to observe, cata-logue, and accept cultural differences; they were actively discouraged from questioning or intervening to change the behaviour of others. Rotary may have had dreams of saving the world through international service, yet as Brendan Goff describes, for the most part clubs met social needs that were personal and local rather than political and systemic.[175] While the movement as a whole was committed to equality, the responsibility to bring that equality into being remained a local matter entrusted to local Rotary Clubs. This fairly passive model of friendship as understanding and acceptance may stand in sharp contrast to the activities of left-wing social movements in this period, but it does at least indicate a willingness on Rotary's part to acknowledge and reflect on the dilemmas posed by international friendships. The WI, in contrast, did not publicly acknowledge that their friendships with members of Rhodesian and South African Women's Institutes could be interpreted as a political act, even within the context of increased calls for sanctions against apartheid regimes. Rather than seeing an awkward aberration of post-colonial values, they continued to treat their settler contacts as part of an uncomplicated community of Commonwealth friendship. Though *Home and Country* did not endorse these views, key aspects of local WI friendship practices were compatible with the more extreme arguments put forward by those who sought to preserve the whiteness of 'Greater Britain'. H. B. Isherwood wrote to *The Times* in 1964 to argue that 'recognising the accelerated trend towards racial divergence we should without delay associate ourselves with our own brethren, men of our own breed and Christian heritage, men in whom in the last resort we could trust – in Canada, Australia, New Zealand, Southern Rhodesia and – yes, ultimately in South Africa'.[176] The WI's support for black and Asian immigrants and visitors was unlikely to have pleased Isherwood, but the enduring imperial patterns of their international friendships may well have done.

Further inconsistencies in the way that the WI and Rotary adhered to the ideals of partnership, equality, and collaboration help us to build a picture of their hierarchical understanding of their place within the world, and of their responsibilities towards it. The most striking inconsistency is the ease with which both organisations tended to blur the line between caring *about* others and assuming responsibility *for* them. This type of transformation was typical of friendships formed with black and Asian members of the New Commonwealth, but not of those between white Europeans or members of the Old Commonwealth. Philanthropic work was a key component of both organisations' international remits. As the WI set out, members should be committed to 'reaching, understanding and helping the rest of the world'.[177] Rotary went one step further and explicitly set out the causal connections between these three responsibilities. 'If there can be widespread understanding of the people of other nations and their problems', the President of Rotary International explained in 1967, 'the impulse to help these people help themselves will be a natural consequence.'[178] Friendship, alongside the educational efforts, became a tool in these organisations' broader projects to extend care to distant strangers.[179] Rather than providing a foundation for solidarity, friendship was folded into a care-giving relationship, denuded of its political potential while simultaneously being used to describe relationships based on uneven power.

In the case studies discussed in this chapter, this stance is most obvious in relation to hospitality. Although Rotary and the WI described contact with overseas students as 'enormously rewarding' and as having what the WI described as 'a real two-way result', both organisations also saw their role as hosts as a fundamentally philanthropic one.[180] Within the schema of their international work, the WI categorised hospitality to non-white colonial and Commonwealth students as 'help given to other countries'.[181] By conceiving of their work as philanthropic, Rotary and WI established the terms for a hierarchical form of friendship. Hospitable acts simultaneously performed benevolence and projected power. As Kitzinger described in 1961, 'the friendship which is proffered in these cases is based upon condescension and pitying interest, and is conditional upon the acceptance of inferior status by the colored man'.[182] The power dynamics of hospitality also served to determine and preserve boundaries. In these circumstances, a friend or guest was not always treated as an individual 'but as a "thing" towards which attitudes of friendship and toleration are directed, on principle, by kindly and well-meaning people'.[183]

Just how easily the lines between international friendship and a more hierarchical philanthropic relationship could be blurred is also evident in the WI's frequent deployment of family metaphors to describe them. The literary and artistic iconography of empire has long drawn upon familial images. These range from the brotherly – in the abolitionist slogan 'Am I not a man and a brother?' and the 'great Masonic doctrine of the universal brotherhood of man'[184] – to the parental – in configurations of childlike 'natives' in need of the support and guidance of a white imperial power. As Lynn Hunt has discussed in relation to the discourse of the French Revolution, family models reflect how 'people collectively imagine – that is, think unconsciously about – the operation of power'.[185] Discussing colonial India, Elizabeth Buettner shows how recurring terms such as love, trust, worship, reverence, and gratitude were used to depict coloniser/colonised interactions as 'at once harmonious and hierarchical'.[186] As Marcus Power argues of Commonwealth discourses, the use of gendered and generational metaphors in conjunction with the multiracial family metaphor 'gives the impression of a voluntary union for mutual good whilst at the same time maintaining the notion of hierarchy and placing white Commonwealth nations at the head of the family'.[187]

While the WI understood the relationship between themselves and women in old white dominions and settler populations as sisterly, they were more likely to employ a mother–daughter metaphor to describe their relationship with non-white women in the New Commonwealth nations. A circular on hospitality for Commonwealth nurses commented that 'there is nothing they like better than to stay in an English home and to be made to feel part of the family'.[188] This sentiment was echoed in a captioned photo in *Home and Country* of a host and their Lesotho guests describing 'Shropshire WI member, Mrs Williamson, with her own family and the "additions" to her family'.[189] One member, describing a young Nigerian who decided to call her 'Mamma', explained that 'this love was the very thing [she] wanted' from her guests'.[190] Yet although these comments brought the New Commonwealth within the family circle, the frameworks of hospitality also subtly figured these students in the role of the child to the WI's beneficent mother. A Preston WI member – who offered help and friendship to a Hull midwifery student from Lesotho – was described by the Yorkshire County Secretary as having 'more or less adopted Mrs Taoana and her family'.[191] Tapping into long-standing maternal discourses, these distinctions divided the wider family of the Commonwealth into the sororal white dominions and the childlike 'emerging nation'.

These familial and philanthropic discourses are an example of what Ruth Glass characterised in 1960 as 'benevolent prejudice'.[192] They may have encouraged understanding, tolerance, and interaction but they also assumed that friends from the developing world needed assistance. As Frank Trentmann reminds us, unless the moral obligations are reciprocal, caring is not a relationship between equals.[193] That friendship and international understanding were so easily reframed as philanthropy – as an unequal relationship in which Britain had more to give than to gain – tells us something important about how middle-class Britons imagined their responsibilities to the decolonising world. Chapters 4 and 5 examine the imperial legacies that shaped this humanitarian impulse and the types of philanthropic international engagement in which members of associational life participated.

Notes

1 *Proceedings: Thirtieth Annual Convention of Rotary International, 1939* (Rotary International, 1939), p. 6.
2 'The hosting habit', *Rotarian* (March 1967), p. 43.
3 *Rotary* (July 1964), p. 205.
4 Levy, *Rotary International*, p. xi; *Rotary Club of Workington 1929–1979: 50 years of Rotary*, p. 7.
5 *Rotary* (February 1964), p. 41.
6 WL, NFWI, 5/FWI/G/1/3/2/9, 'International work of the Women's Institutes', NFWI (October 1957).
7 *Rotary* (July 1964), p. 205.
8 Goff, 'The heartland abroad', p. 30.
9 WL, NFWI, 5/FWI/G/1/3/2/9, 'Working internationally', NFWI (no date, c.1960). For other friendship and understanding schemes see: Harper, '"Personal contact is worth a ton of text-books'; Bu, 'Cultural understanding and world peace'.
10 Harold Thomas, *Rotarian* (January 1960), p. 10.
11 Harold Thomas, cited in *Rotarian* (June 1980), p. 27.
12 Thomas, *Rotarian* (January 1960), p. 10.
13 Lee, 'British cultural diplomacy'.
14 TNA, CAB/129/80, Memorandum by Secretary of State for Foreign Affairs, 'The permanent establishment of the British Council', 23 March 1956.
15 Letter, HM Grace and Maurice Cole of East and West Friendship Council, *The Times* (5 December 1946).
16 'Are Commonwealth societies fulfilling their purpose?', *The Times* (10 June 1966).
17 Richard Seymour, 'The British Council and the Commonwealth', *Journal of the Royal Society of the Arts*, 105:5010 (1957), 782.
18 Seymour, 'British Council and the Commonwealth', 782–3.
19 J. M. Lee, 'Commonwealth students in the United Kingdom, 1940–1960: Student welfare and world status', *Minerva*, 44 (2006), 17.
20 Ann Laura Stoler, *Carnal Knowledge and Imperial Power: Race and the Intimate in Colonial Rule* (London: University of California Press, 2002).
21 Katie Pickles, 'A link in the "great chain of Empire friendship": the Victoria League in New Zealand', *Journal of Imperial and Commonwealth History*, 33:1 (2005), 29–50.
22 Leela Gandhi, *Affective Communities: Anticolonial Thought, Fin-de-siècle Radicalism, and the Politics of Friendship* (London: Duke University Press, 2005), pp. 2, 6.

23 Vanessa Smith, *Intimate Strangers: Friendship, Exchange and Pacific Encounters* (Cambridge: Cambridge University Press, 2010), p. 10.

24 Bailkin, *Afterlife of Empire*, p. 93.

25 *Ibid.*, p. 93.

26 Wendy Webster, '"There'll always be an England": Representations of colonial wars and immigration, 1948–1968', *Journal of British Studies*, 40:4 (2001), 557–584; Marcus Collins, 'Pride and prejudice: West Indian men in mid-twentieth century Britain', *Journal of British Studies*, 40 (2001), 391–418; Chris Waters, 'Dark strangers' in our midst: Discourses of race and nation in Britain, 1947–1963', *Journal of British Studies*, 36 (1997), 207–38.

27 Mica Nava, *Visceral Cosmopolitanism: Gender, Culture and the Normalisation of Difference* (Oxford: Berg, 2007), p. 7; Mica Nava, 'Sometimes antagonistic, sometimes ardently sympathetic: Contradictory responses to migrants in post-war Britain', *Ethnicities*, 14:3 (2014), 458–80.

28 On the presence *and* silence of race in left-wing activism see Burkett, *Constructing Post-Imperial Britain*, pp. 174–91.

29 Cited in 'Think of the world', *Rotary* (September, 1960), p. 298.

30 Victoria de Grazia, *Irresistible Empire: America's Advance through Twentieth Century Europe* (London: Belknap Press), p. 50.

31 *1965 Proceedings: Fifty-sixth Annual convention of Rotary International* (Rotary International, 1965), p. 214.

32 Goff, 'The Heartland abroad', p. 4.

33 *Rotarian* (January 1965), p. 7.

34 *Ibid.*

35 *Rotary* (March 1964), p. vi.

36 *International Service* (London: Rotary International, c.1960), p. 6.

37 *Working With Women Worldwide*, p. 23.

38 *The Associated Country Women of the World, History* (London: Associated Country Women of the World, 1974).

39 Isabel Curry, 'Learning to Live', *Home and Country* (November 1968), p. 417.

40 *International Service* (London: Rotary International, c.1960), p. 3.

41 See, for example the 'News from overseas' section in *Home and Country* over a 6 month period from February–July 1967.

42 Borthwick, WI/Int 1, Yorkshire Federation International Committee Minutes, 18 November 1965.

43 *Rotary* (February 1965), p. 44.

44 *International Service* (London: Rotary International, c.1960), p. 9.

45 WL, NFWI, 5/FWI/G/1/3/2/9, 'World wise with the W.I.s', NFWI (January 1964).

46 For further discussion of how institutions structure friendships see Antoine Vion, 'The institutionalization of international friendship', *Critical Review of International Social and Political Philosophy*, 10:2 (2007), 281–97.

47 *Rotary in the Ridings* 33, 5 (March/April 1963); RALSS, 358/F, Box 2, Charles Chislett to Alan Welstenhelm, British High Commission KL, 30 May 1968.

48 'News from overseas', *Home and Country* (February 1967).

49 *Ibid.* (September 1968).

50 Jean P. Smith, 'The Women's branch of the Commonwealth Relations Office': The Society for the Overseas Settlement of British Women and the long life of empire migration', *Women's History Review*, 25:4 (2016), 530.

51 Riedi, 'Women, gender and the promotion of empire', 584.

52 Smith, 'The Women's Branch', 522.

53 See, for example, 'News from overseas', *Home and Country* (February 1967).

54 Skelton, 'From peace to development', p. 174.

55 Lady Anglesey, 'Journey to the Caribbean', *Home and Country* (June 1967), pp. 212–13.

56 Eliza Riedi, Ian C. Fletcher, Laura E. Nym Mayhall, and Philippa Levine (eds), *Women's Suffrage in the British Empire: Citizenship, Nation and Race* (London:

Routledge, 2000); Angela Woollacott, *To Try Her Fortune in London: Australian Women, Colonialism and Modernity* (Oxford: Oxford University Press, 2001).

57 Eliza Riedi, 'Women, gender, and the promotion of Empire: The Victoria League, 1901–1914', *The Historical Journal*, 45:3 (2002), 571.
58 Madge Robertson Watt, 1918, quoted in Linda M. Ambrose, *A Great Rural Sisterhood: Madge Robertson Watt and the ACWW* (London: University of Toronto Press, 2015), p. 19.
59 'Empire get together', *Cheltenham Chronicle* (9 September 1950).
60 A. J. Hopkins, 'Rethinking decolonisation', *Past & Present*, 200 (2008), 211–47.
61 'News from overseas', *Home and Country* (January 1966).
62 Wilbur Zelinsky, 'The twinning of the world: sister cities in geographic and historical perspective', *Annals of the Association of American Geographers*, 81:1 (1991). Also discussed in Nick Clarke, 'Globalising care? Town twinning in Britain since 1945', *Geoforum*, 42 (2011), 115.
63 WL, NFWI, 5/FWI/G/1/3/2/9, 'World wise with the W.I.s', NFWI (January 1964).
64 'Nothing is impossible if one wants to', *Rotary* (October 1967), pp. 261–5.
65 See de Grazia, *Irresistible Empire*; Goff, 'Heartland abroad'.
66 De Grazia, *Irresistible Empire.*
67 Goff, 'Heartland abroad', pp. 1–18.
68 De Grazia, *Irresistible Empire*, p. 26.
69 *Guardian* (17 April 1961).
70 Goff, 'Heartland abroad', p. 19.
71 Holger Nehring, 'National internationalists: British and West German protests against nuclear weapons, the politics of transnational communications and the social history of the Cold War, 1957–1964', *Contemporary European History*, 14:4 (2005), 559–82.
72 Su Lin Lewis, 'Rotary International's 'acid test': multi-ethnic associational life in 1930s Southeast Asia', *Journal of Global History*, 7:2 (2012), 305.
73 'Rotarians at work', *Rotary* (October 1961), p. 346.
74 Clarke, 'Town twinning'.
75 Vion, 'The institutionalization of international friendship'.
76 De Grazia, *Irresistible Empire*, p. 54.
77 'Rotarians at work', *Rotary* (October 1968), pp. 283–4; *Manchester Guardian* (22 December 1956).
78 RALSS, 358/F, Box 3, Letter from Cairo Rotary Club to Rotherham Rotary Club, 12 October 1956.
79 Goff, 'Heartland abroad', p. 83; Lewis, 'Rotary International's "acid test"', 305.
80 S. Jepson Letter to the Editor, *Rotary* (February 1964), p. 55.
81 Nava, 'Sometimes antagonistic', 461.
82 *Ibid.*
83 For discussion of the ongoing influence of this narrative see Sarah Gibson, '"Abusing our hospitality": inhospitableness and the politics of deterrence', in Jennie Germann Molz and Sarah Gibson (eds), *Mobilizing Hospitality: The Ethics of Social Relations in a Mobile World* (London: Routledge, 2016), pp. 159–76.
84 Hector Hughes, *Hansard*, HC 25 November 1959 Fifth series vol. 614 c. 420.
85 Ruth Craggs, 'Hospitality in geopolitics and the making of Commonwealth international relations', *Geoforum*, 52 (2014), 93.
86 Craggs, 'Geopolitics of hospitality', 98.
87 *Observer* (26 July 1964).
88 TNA, BW3/53GK, G. Animashawun 'African students in Britain', *Race*, 5:1 (July 1963), 45.
89 For discussion of earlier issues with hospitality see Daniel Whittal, '"In this metropolis of the world we must have a building worthy of our great people"': race, empire and hospitality in imperial London, 1931–48', in Eve Rosenhaft and Robbie Aitken (eds), *Africa in Europe: Studies in Transnational Practice in the Long Twentieth Century* (Liverpool: Liverpool University Press, 2013), pp. 76–98.
90 Paul, *Whitewashing Britain*, pp. 131–69.

91 J. M. Lee, 'Overseas students in Britain: How their presence was politicised in 1966–67', *Minerva*, 36 (1998), 311. For wider discussion of the influence of the Cold War on immigration and race relations policy see Bailkin, *Afterlife of Empire.*

92 TNA, BW3/37, Overseas Students in Britain Annual Totals 1950–1964, Appendix A Area Officers' Conference, 1965.

93 TNA, BW3/53, Institute of Race Relations Report on the Hospitality Arrangements Made for Overseas Visitors to the London Area, 1964.

94 Cited by A. J. Stockwell, 'Leaders, dissidents and the disappointed: Colonial students in Britain as empire ended', *Journal of Imperial and Commonwealth History*, 36:3 (2008), 497.

95 Stockwell, 'Leaders, dissidents and the disappointed', 493.

96 This was not a new idea. Since the late nineteenth century, educational scholarships for white settlers had been used to promote imperial citizenship and foster the 'invisible ties' of empire. See Tamson Pietsch, 'Many Rhodes: travelling scholarships and imperial citizenship in the British academic world, 1880–1940', *History of Education*, 40:6 (2011), 723–39.

97 Hector Hughes, *Hansard*, HC 25 November 1959 Fifth series vol. 614 c. 420.

98 Brian Harrison, *Hansard*, HC 25 November 1959 Fifth series vol. 614 c. 436.

99 Lee, 'Commonwealth students', 17.

100 Stockwell, 'Leaders, dissidents and the disappointed', 489.

101 *Ibid.*, 492.

102 Philip Goodheart, *Hansard*, HC 25 November 1959 Fifth series vol. 614 c. 432.

103 *Surrey Comet* (14 October 1961).

104 Lee, 'Commonwealth students', 9; TNA, BW/3/48, 'Co-operation between the British Council and voluntary and other organisations assisting in the welfare of overseas students in London', c.1955.

105 TNA, BW3/53, Institute of Race Relations report, 1964.

106 *Observer* (26 July 1964).

107 TNA, BW3/48, Memo: The British Council Welfare of Overseas Students and Trainees in the United Kingdom c.1961.

108 TNA, BW3/48, 'Conference of voluntary societies on the welfare of overseas students in London', Appendix A, March 1956.

109 TNA, BW3/48, Memo: The British Council Welfare of Overseas Students and Trainees in the United Kingdom c.1961.

110 TNA, BW/3/42 'Assistance given to overseas students in London, Report for year 1.2.58–31.1.59', 1959.

111 TNA, BW3/53, Institute of Race Relations Report, 1964.

112 TNA, BW3/37, Area Officer Conference paper on Problems of area organization and deployment of staff, no date.

113 TNA, BW3/57, Report on British Council Centres c.1968.

114 TNA, BW3/48, Conference of Voluntary Societies on the Welfare of Overseas Students in London, Appendix B, 1956.

115 WL, NFWI, 5/FWI/G/1/3/2/9, 'International work of the Women's Institutes', NFWI pamphlet, May 1955.

116 *Ibid.*

117 TNA, BW3/53, Institute of Race Relations Report, 1964.

118 'The longest guest list in the world', *Home and Country* (February 1967), p. 46; 'At number 39', *Home and Country* (October 1967), p. 357; 'News from overseas' *Home and Country* (July 1967); 'News from overseas' *Home and Country* (April 1967); 'News from overseas' *Home and Country* (May 1966).

119 'Longest guest list', *Home and Country* (February 1967), p. 46.

120 'Fruit Picking Fellows', *Rotary* (May 1961), p. 167.

121 'Longest guest list', *Home and Country* (February 1967), p. 46.

122 *Ibid.*

123 *Rotary* (March 1964), p. 87.

124 See, for example, 'Student adoption', *Rotary* (April 1960), pp. 118–19; 'Longest guest list', *Home and Country* (February 1967), p. 47.

125 'The dead hand of hospitality', *Observer* (26 July 1964).
126 TNA, BW3/53, Institute of Race Relations Report, 1964.
127 *Home and Country* (February 1967), p. 46.
128 Waters, 'Dark strangers', 212; Raphael Samuel (ed.), *Patriotism: The Making and Unmaking of British National Identity*, vol. 1, *History and Politics* (London: Routledge, 1989), p. xiv; Alison Light, *Forever England: Femininity, Literature and Conservatism Between the Wars* (London: Routledge, 1991).
129 Light, *Forever England*, p. 8.
130 Webster, *Englishness and Empire*, p. 10.
131 Schwarz, 'Re-racialisation of England', 73.
132 Matthew Whittle, 'Hosts and hostages: mass immigration and the power of hospitality in post-war British and Caribbean literature', *Comparative Critical Studies*, 11 (2014), 77–92.
133 On the 1950s, see Buettner, 'Would you let your daughter marry a negro? Race and sex in 1950s Britain', in Philippa Levine and S. Grayzel (eds), *Gender, Labour, War and Empire: Essays on Modern Britain* (London: Springer, 2008), pp. 226–7. On similar attitudes in the Second World War, see Sonya Rose, 'Sex, citizenship, and the nation in World War II Britain', *The American Historical Review*, 103:4 (1998), 1147–76. On the inter-war period, see Lucy Bland, 'White women and men of colour: miscegenation fears in Britain after the Great War', *Gender & History*, 17:1 (2005), 29–61.
134 *Home and Country* (September 1967).
135 'Rotarians at work', *Rotary* (March 1965), p. 94.
136 *Home and Country* (February 1967), p. 47.
137 Buettner, 'Would you let your daughter marry a negro?', pp. 224–31. See also the representation of this panic in *Sapphire* (1959) and *Flame in the Streets* (1961).
138 Lee, 'Overseas students in Britain', 316.
139 *Ibid.*, 320.
140 Commonwealth Students made up 54% of overseas students in 1966/7. Figures drawn from Hillary Perraton, *A History of Foreign Students in Britain* (Basingstoke: Palgrave, 2014), p. 84.
141 WL, NFWI, 5/FWI/D/2/2/20, Report of Denman College International Conference, held 10–12 July 1970.
142 Lee, 'Commonwealth students', 23.
143 For further discussion of this distinction see Clarke, 'Globalising care?', 117.
144 Herbert Ward, *The Rotary Club of Stepney: An Outline Review of its Work, 1929–1979* (London: The Rotary Club of Stepney, 1978), p. 25.
145 'A noble benefit and a gracious gift', *Rotary* (July 1968), p. 162.
146 For a discussion of the use of friendship in ethnography see Sara Ahmed, *Strange Encounters: Embodied Others in Postcoloniality* (London: Routledge, 2000), pp. 65–8.
147 Cited in Andrews, *Acceptable Face of Feminism*, p. 163.
148 Sheila Kitzinger, 'Conditional philanthropy towards colored students in Britain', *Phylon*, 21:2 (1960), 167.
149 Ahmed, *Strange Encounters*, p. 150.
150 *Home and Country* (November 1968), p. 417.
151 WL, NFWI, 5/FWI/G/1/3/2/9, 'World wise with the W.I.s', NFWI (January 1964); 'Learning to live', *Home and Country* (November 1968), p. 418.
152 'Longest guest list', *Home and Country* (February 1967), p. 47.
153 *Ibid.*
154 *Ibid.*
155 'White and coloured', *Rotary* (April 1960), p. 132.
156 *Ibid.*
157 WL, NFWI, 5/FWI/D/2/2/20, Report of international conference at Denman College 10–12 July 1970, sent with NFWI newsletter.
158 *Home and Country* (August 1966).
159 'A Carnoustie miracle', *Rotary* (July 1965), p. 212.

160 For further discussion of this problem see Natarajan, 'Performing multiculturalism'.
161 'Longest guest list', *Home and Country* (February 1967), p. 47.
162 'White and coloured', *Rotary* (April 1960), p. 132.
163 *International Service* (Rotary International, London), p. 23.
164 'Longest guest list', *Home and Country* (February 1967), p. 46.
165 Rob Skinner, *The Foundations of Anti-Apartheid: Liberal Humanitarians and Transnational Activists in Britain and the United States, c.1919–64* (London: Springer, 2010); Sylvia A. Ellis, 'Promoting solidarity at home and abroad: the goals and tactics of the anti-Vietnam War movement in Britain', *European Review of History*, 21:4 (2014), 557–76; David Hostetter, 'House guest of the AEC: Dorothy Hutchinson, the 1958 fast at the Atomic Energy Commission, and the domestication of protest', *Peace & Change*, 34:2 (2009), 133–47; Håkan Thörn, 'Solidarity across borders: The transnational anti-apartheid movement', *Voluntas: International Journal of Voluntary and Nonprofit Organizations*, 17:4 (2006), 285–301.
166 Goff, 'Heartland abroad', p. 4.
167 *International Service* (London: Rotary International, c.1960), p. 7.
168 R.A. Grange-Bennet, *Rotary* (December 1965), p. 358.
169 Gary Garrood, *Rotary* (December 1965), pp. 358–59.
170 Grange-Bennet, *Rotary* (December 1965), p. 358.
171 Garfield Daniel, *Rotary* (November 1965), p. 334.
172 Jonathan Wiesen has asked a very similar question of Rotary's approach to German clubs' associations with National Socialism. Jonathan S. Wiesen, 'Service above self? Rotary Clubs, National Socialism, and transnational memory in the 1960s and 1970s', *Holocaust and Genocide Studies*, 23:1 (2009), 7.
173 Garfield Daniel, *Rotary* (November 1965), p. 334.
174 H. S. Read, *Rotary* (January 1964), p. 27.
175 Brendan Goff, 'Philanthropy and the "perfect democracy" of Rotary International', in David Hammack and Steven Heydemann (eds), *Globalization, Philanthropy, and Civil Society: Projecting Institutional Logics Abroad* (Bloomington: Indiana University Press, 2009), pp. 55–6.
176 Letter to Editor H. B Isherwood, *The Times* (8 April 1964).
177 'World within reach', *Home and Country* (September 1967), p. 305.
178 'Let international service open a window to the world for people of your town', *Rotarian* (March 1968), p. 14.
179 For the wider literature on geographies of care see: David Conradson, 'Geographies of care: spaces, practices, experiences,' *Social & Cultural Geography*, 4:4 (2003), 451–4; Clive Barnett and David Land, 'Geographies of generosity: Beyond the "moral turn"', *Geoforum*, 38:6 (2007), 1065–75. For a historical explanation of these processes see Thomas Haskell, 'Capitalism and the origins of the humanitarian sensibility, Part 1', *The American Historical Review*, 90:2 (1985), 339–61.
180 WL, NFWI, 5/FWI/G/1/3/2/9, 'International work of the Women's Institutes', NFWI (October 1957).
181 *Ibid.* (May 1955).
182 Kitzinger, 'Conditional philanthropy', 171.
183 *Ibid.*, 172.
184 Jessica Harland-Jacobs, 'All in the family: Freemasonry and the British Empire in the mid-nineteenth century', *The Journal of British Studies*, 42, 4 (2003), 448–82.
185 Lynn Hunt, *The Family Romance of the French Revolution* (Berkeley, CA: University of California Press, 1992), pp. 8, 199.
186 Buettner, *Empire Families*, p. 262.
187 Marcus Power, 'The Commonwealth, "development" and post-colonial responsibility', *Geoforum*, 40 (2009), 16.
188 WL, NFWI, 5/FWI/D/2/2/90, Circular: Holiday Hospitality for Commonwealth Nurses, 3 July 1969.
189 'Longest guest list', *Home and Country* (February 1967).
190 *Ibid.*

191 Borthwick, WI/ Int. 1, Women's Institute Yorkshire Federation International Committee Minutes, 11 June 1964.
192 Ruth Glass, *Newcomers: The West-Indians in London* (London: Centre for Urban Studies, 1960), p. 218.
193 Frank Trentmann, 'Before "fair trade": empire, free trade and the moral economies of food in the modern world', Environment and Planning D: Society and Space, 25 (2007), 1086.

CHAPTER FOUR

Philanthropic connections and Britain's 'lost vocation'

The Freedom from Hunger Campaign and the new humanitarian order

This chapter[1] and the next are about humanitarianism as a guiding principle of international engagement. Where Chapters 2 and 3 discuss how the British public were encouraged to care *about* people in other countries, Chapters 4 and 5 focus on how they were encouraged to care *for* them. Concern for the welfare of distant strangers was not new in the 1960s, but the public's experiences of it were significantly altered by the rapid growth of the non-state humanitarian sector. While giving aid and assistance to those overseas was not universally supported, this was the field of civic international engagement that expanded most rapidly in the 1960s, largely because it was able to attract the most diverse participation. The growth of the humanitarian sector was driven, in large part, by the end of empire. The events of decolonisation not only focused government and public attention on the needs of populations in the global South, they also stimulated debates about Britain's global purpose. As Michael Barnett has observed, humanitarianism often flourishes at the very moment that nations begin to worry about losing a sense of mission.[2] This chapter and the next illustrate that the processes of decolonisation and the legacies of Britain's imperial past determined both the imagined and material networks of humanitarian aid and development in the 1960s. Caring for others came to occupy a central role in debates about Britain's global moral authority.

In order to explore these issues, this chapter focuses on British participation in the United Nations Freedom from Hunger Campaign (FFHC), an international initiative to 'help the hungry to help themselves'.[3] The Food and Agricultural Organisation (FAO) launched the campaign in 1960 to raise funds from NGOs, communities and individuals in UN member states in order to finance agricultural development

[127]

projects across the underdeveloped world. Following in the footsteps of World Refugee Year, which had raised money to help relocate refugees from Europe and the Middle East in the aftermath of the Second World War, the FFHC was the second international fundraising campaign to come under the UN umbrella.[4] With the involvement of more than one hundred countries it was, by a considerable margin, the largest humanitarian effort of its time. The networks, practices and discourses that it established were at the foundation of the modern international development movement.[5] As well as helping to raise their public profile and fundraising capabilities, for participating NGOs such as Oxfam and Christian Aid, which started out as relief organisations in the aftermath of the Second World War, the FFHC also stimulated a move towards a developmental, preventative model of international aid.

Britain's participation in this campaign reveals the close relationship between humanitarian aid and the politics of empire in the post-war period. Although the FFHC was a global movement, it also informed, and was informed by, specific national experiences. Participants in Madagascar, for example, brought what the FAO described as 'the concrete experience of dealing with the serious problems that inevitably surround the development of a newly liberated country'.[6] Britain's own participation was shaped by the legacies of imperial and humanitarian intervention as well as the contemporary context of decolonisation. From the humanitarian 'discovery' of hunger in the late nineteenth century to the Colonial Welfare and Development Act of 1940, imperial Britain played a central role in describing the modern meaning of hunger and determining the systems for redressing it.[7] It was in Britain, James Vernon argues, that hunger first came to be acknowledged as an imperial and later a global problem, and, concomitantly, where political movements and forms of statecraft developed to combat it, intending, ultimately, to free the world from its 'scourge' altogether.[8] Over the course of a century, a wide array of British actors, including politicians, economists, social scientists, journalists and philanthropists, participated in efforts to govern and eradicate hunger.

In the aftermath of the Second World War, however, Britain began to lose its monopoly on the concern with hunger.[9] By the time the FFHC was launched in 1960, hunger and development had become global issues of concern, championed not only by wealthy nations, but also by newly independent states and an ever-expanding set of humanitarian organisations, including Oxfam, CARE, World Vision, Christian Aid and War on Want. As Frederick Cooper describes, disintegrating colonial empires were rapidly internationalised in this period. Newly independent states were 'still at the bottom of a development hierarchy, but now the object of concern of all "advanced" nations', not least the

United States'.[10] Moreover, by the time the FFHC was launched, its sponsor, the UN, was felt to be a particularly important and threatening part of this process. Discussing the campaign in 1963, the Cabinet Committee on Development Policy expressed concerns about the increasingly expansionist tendencies of the FAO, criticising the unwelcome influence that it sought to exert on British aid policy.[11] By the 1960s, Britain was just one country among more than a hundred taking part in the FFHC and this inevitably raised questions about its changing status within a rapidly growing field. As Earl De La Warr, former Chairman of the Royal Commonwealth Society (RCS) and Chairman of the UK National FFHC Committee warned, 'it is up to us in the United Kingdom to see to it that we play a worthy part in what has now become a great new international attack on hunger'.[12]

This chapter uses the British public's support for the campaign as a window on to the changing experience of British humanitarianism during an era of decolonisation. Although a substantial body of work now addresses the relationship between practices of colonialism and development in the post-war period, less attention has been paid to the humanitarian or public dimension of this relationship. The typical narrative of post-war development is one of professionalisation – what Joseph Hodge describes as the 'triumph of the expert'. As the experienced colonial district administrator who 'knew his native' was replaced by the educated specialist who 'knew his science', so too was the enthusiastic amateur volunteer marginalised from the increasingly professionalised ranks of non-governmental development employees.[13] In many respects the FFHC is the perfect illustration of these trends; in order to develop solutions to undernourishment and low agricultural production, cadres of experts were sent out into the field to carry out research, their findings were recorded in technical publications and these were then picked over at international conferences. But there was another side to the FFHC, one that propelled development work into the public sphere. While the earlier work of the FAO had dealt almost exclusively with technocrats and governments – focused on the science of nutrition and the logistics of food supplies – the FFHC emphasised the collective agency of humanitarian organisations and the fundraising public.

Through Freedom from Hunger, the FAO aimed 'to awaken the conscience of the world to the continuing problem of hunger and malnutrition in many lands' and, using study and publicity, to create 'a body of aroused and informed public opinion ready to demand and support the measures needed to speed up the at present unsatisfactory rate of progress'.[14] Rather than excluding the public from the 'triumph of expertise', the FFHC's educational imperative worked to include them within it, providing the public with an unprecedented opportunity to participate in international development. Between 1960 and 1965, when the majority of the educational and publicity work took place, the British public raised almost seven million pounds in support of the FFHC.[15] To reach this figure, contributions were sought from 'every town, city, village and hamlet', bringing together members from over one hundred affiliated organisations, including the RCS, Christian Aid, Oxfam, the Rotary Club, the WI, War on Want, and the United Nations Association.[16] Women's groups held whist drives and coffee mornings, primary schools organised jumble sales, teenagers went on sponsored walks, businessmen attended 'hunger lunches', community associations put on concerts, and churches organised 'hot dog suppers'; Members of Parliament donated an hour's pay to the cause; and Cerebos Meat and Fish Spreads rather perplexingly donated 800,000 jars of fish paste that they would have otherwise dumped in the sea.[17] Away from the performance of public fundraising, people also made private contributions: an anonymous widow gifted her late husband's coin collection to the campaign and a mother, grateful that her own children 'never had to go short of food', posted a small donation to her local campaign treasurer.[18]

The diverse base of support that Freedom from Hunger was able to mobilise is reflected in the records kept by Rotherham's committee treasurer (the same Charles Chislett discussed in Chapter 2).[19] Donations came in from across the community to fund the provision of tools and equipment for an agricultural engineering workshop at the University College of Rhodesia and Nyasaland. The committee received money from primary and secondary schools; from local businesses such as Steel, Peech and Tozer, Glen Quarries, and the Baker Electric Company; from sports and social organisations such as the Rotherham Harriers, the Phoenix Golf Club Ladies Section, the County Police Office Sports and Social Club, the Greaseborough flower arrangement class, the Rotherham and District Allotments and Gardens Council, and the Lambretta scooter club; and from women's organisations such as the Women's Cooperative Guild, the Rotherham Conservative Women's Association, the Rotherham Ladies Circle, the Electrical Association for Women, the Mothers' Union, the Women's Voluntary Service for Civil Defence and the Women's Gas Federation.[20] This long list of Rotherham associations illustrates how Freedom from Hunger was able to mobilise and draw on pre-existing networks of associational life. It also suggests that many of those who contributed to the campaign did so not as individuals but as part of a group, reinforcing ideas of collective civic responsibility.

The broad base of support that Freedom from Hunger attracted is not just indicative of the widespread influence of humanitarian campaigning in this period; it also had important implications for the multiple narratives that developed around the campaign. Because Freedom from Hunger was such a multi-faceted project – drawing together national governments, colonial administrations, international UN agencies, humanitarian NGOs and a diverse fundraising public – its meaning was neither singular nor fixed. The FFHC's ability to sustain contradictory narratives about its value and purpose was key to its broad appeal. In order to ensure productive contributions from a wide participation base, those supporting the Campaign were encouraged to see FFHC in the perspective of their own community of interest. 'Business men's groups', the FAO suggested, 'may give special emphasis to what private enterprise can do to stimulate production', while 'religious groups may wish to emphasise the opportunities for sharing problems or duties'.[21]

Beyond the objectives and expectations of FAO campaign material, the FFHC provided a canvas onto which members of the British government and public could project their own narratives of humanitarianism, development, and Britain's changing global role. The different narratives that coalesced around the campaign in Britain raise important questions about how the public experienced Britain's imperial decline. Did their moral geography change as they lost their empire? Was there a role for the empire/Commonwealth within the framework of international humanitarianism? Which imperial legacies remained intact in the FFHC, which were adapted, and which discarded? To answer these questions, this chapter focuses on three key conceptualisations of the FFHC: the first foregrounded continuity with an imperial tradition; the second sought to replace imperial traditions with an internationalist model of geopolitics; and the third obscured the imperial past, instead emphasising internationalism on a person-to-person scale.

Benevolent Britain and the imperial tradition

The imperial legacies of the FFHC were reflected in a public narrative that situated the campaign as the next stage in a long trajectory of British imperial benevolence. It is now well documented that the history of international humanitarianism is closely intertwined with the history of imperialism. Thomas Haskell's work on the eighteenth and nineteenth centuries shows how the economic and political ties to overseas that were formed through imperial expansion were not only crucial in making philanthropy in some places more practical than in others, they also provided the foundations of benevolent and humanitarian sentiment back home in Britain. Looking at what he calls the 'unprecedented wave of humanitarian reform sentiment' that swept through Europe in the hundred years following 1750, Haskell argues that empire expanded 'the range of opportunities available to [the public] for shaping the future and intervening in other lives'. It was this expansion, he claims, that pushed Britain over the threshold and into humanitarian action.[22]

Since the late eighteenth century a significant part of Britain's imperial identity has been bound up with ideas of benevolent leadership and public philanthropy that constructed an image of the British Empire as an uplifting force.[23] As Lambert and Lester have argued, so enduring and widespread was a 'proselytised association between Britishness and benign rather than malignant intervention, that it still characterises popular and indeed some academic thinking about the distinctions between European empires'.[24] Britain's self-identification as a benevolent nation did not disappear at the end of the empire. If anything, discourses of benevolence grew stronger rather than weaker as the British Empire lurched towards dissolution. The inter-war and immediate post-war period is commonly characterised as a 'moment of intense and anxious engagement with empire' in which local and national groups involved themselves in the affairs of the colonies across a wide range of issues.[25] Not only were Britain's material interests in empire renewed by its increased reliance on the sterling area, but related discourses of trusteeship and development also worked to reinvigorate an ideological engagement with empire.

In the late colonial epoch, as well as continuing to draw heavily on older philanthropic motifs such as abolitionism, missionary work and famine relief, Britain's sense of imperial mission was rearmed by the beliefs and practices embodied in the 1940 Colonial Development and Welfare Act, which allocated metropolitan resources to programmes aimed at raising colonised populations' productivity and standard of living.[26] As explored in Chapter 2, these discourses of trusteeship and development made it possible to think about the end of empire as a positive, constructive act rather than a passive, enforced dissolution. Since the inter-war period, decolonisation had been widely conceptualised as the ultimate goal of imperialism and as a final affirmation of British imperial benevolence.[27] Recent scholarship may have undermined interpretations of decolonisation as a carefully orchestrated fulfilment of Britain's long-standing commitment to self-government, but this narrative was still meaningful in the 1960s.[28] As the Duke of Edinburgh, Prince Philip, told the public in 1966, British service overseas had '*resulted* in the independence of almost all the old colonial protected territories [my emphasis]'.[29] What this interpretation did not solve, however, was the question of 'what next?' What happened to this narrative of national purpose in the wake of decolonisation? And what would happen to imperial benevolence without an empire upon which to bestow it?

By emphasising continuity rather than change, Freedom from Hunger could be understood as the latest in a long line of British interventions in global hunger. Earl De La Warr claimed that 'no country in the world has had greater experience than has our own in working in underdeveloped countries'.[30] This narrative was repeated almost verbatim two years later by the campaign patron, the Duke of Edinburgh, who described how 'the British, perhaps more than most people, have a long tradition of successful service overseas'.[31] And it resurfaced again and again in statements that drew on the motifs of British administrative expertise, benevolent paternalism and charitable practice. Speaking about the campaign in the House of Lords, the Bishop of Coventry argued that Freedom from Hunger could be 'one of our finest hours if, having trained many countries for self-government and freedom, we train them and other nations for industrial self-development'.[32] At the launch party for the fundraising stage of the campaign in June 1962, Harold Macmillan gave a speech in which he celebrated the nation's aptitude for humanitarian intervention. 'Work of this kind', he suggested, 'is particularly suited to the British genius for voluntary effort and coordination.'[33]

The narratives of British exceptionalism that coalesced around the FFHC reveal underlying concerns about declining status and international reputation. The statesmen and campaign representatives who emphasised Britain's particular strengths in humanitarianism were also aiming to assert British authority in an increasingly international field.[34] By presenting the FFHC as an opportunity to continue the 'worthy British tradition of governmental voluntary assistance', commentators established the continuing relevance of Britain's imperial experience in the post-imperial period. As the Duke of Edinburgh explained, 'Today newly independent and developing countries are facing the most critical years of their existence and they need a very particular kind of help. People are still needed to fill the gaps in the developing fabric of the public, educational and agricultural services.'[35] Such claims were well suited to the model of development promoted by the FFHC. The campaign was at the vanguard of those arguing the need to move away from existing models of humanitarian relief (provided in response to particular crises or needs) towards a preventative model for development that would address the causes of poverty. This made it possible to tie the welfare and development initiatives of late colonial administrations to the longer history of imperial benevolent action by the British public.

Within these discourses, taking a lead in international projects such as the FFHC also became a way for Britain to reclaim some of the moral authority that had been lost during the Suez crisis. For the beleaguered Foreign Office the FFHC was a chance 'to demonstrate our interest at the United Nations in the economic and social field and dispel the reputation for reluctance we have unfortunately acquired in this field'.[36] Putting a more positive spin on these motivations for benevolence, the Duke of Edinburgh proclaimed that 'with the whole-hearted support of the entire nation, the British Freedom from Hunger Campaign can become an example to the rest of the world'.[37] That this particular statement was widely used as a 'tag line' in FFHC newspaper advertisements suggests that organisers expected the appeal to national pride to be an effective way to rouse public support.[38]

These narratives of exceptionalism also implicitly sought to make the British Empire and Commonwealth a shining example of moral intervention, highlighting the ways in which NGO activity might intersect with governmental interests. When asking the RCS to spare a contribution for 'this tremendous worldwide crusade', for instance, advertisements from the FFHC described how it was 'helping strengthen the British Commonwealth' by setting under-privileged countries and people on their feet.[39] In order to ensure the realignment of British imperialism with a distinct humanitarian ethos, most commentators were wilfully blind to the oppressive methods by which colonial authority was maintained, overlooking the political struggles of national-ist movements taking place over the course of the FFHC. While issues of non-compliance had dogged a number of late colonial development initiatives, for instance, they rarely entered into public discourses of humanitarian aid.

When conceptualised as a continuation of imperial benevolence, the FFHC served a dual purpose. As discussed, when projecting outwards it was a way to save face and legitimate the leading role that many in Britain hoped to take in this new international field of development. But for many commentators at the time, there was more than pride and status at stake. Looking inwards, this narrative was also capable of smoothing over some of the disruption rendered by decolonisation on metropolitan identities and, in particular, on ideas about national purpose. By framing the FFHC as a seamless and satisfying substitute to the imperial burden – one that called on the particular administrative and organisational skill set that Britain had developed as an imperial power – some commentators found an alternative vocation. In a speech on the floor of the House of Lords in which he responded to Dean

Acheson's claim that Britain had lost an empire but not yet found a role, Dr Bardsley, the Bishop of Coventry, shared his belief that 'part of that mission is to be found in our contribution to this vast world problem of famine relief'.[40] If, as Anthony Hartley diagnosed, the British public were nostalgic for a wider field of action, philanthropic campaigns such as the FFHC could provide it for them.[41] Despite the global outlook promoted by the FAO, this narrative makes clear that it was still possible to reconcile Britain's membership of an international humanitarian community with the special bond of empire, even at the point of imperial collapse.

Situating the FFHC within narratives of imperial benevolence may have been largely about seeking 'emotional' reassurance in a time of considerable flux, but it was not entirely an act of fiction. Colonial advisers of the 1940s had already established a precedent for the overwhelmingly agrarian vision that the FFHC projected for the future of developing countries.[42] As Uma Kothari describes, 'there has not been a unilateral trajectory from a colonial to a development moment but rather an intertwining of these fields wherein heterogeneous and shifting ideologies and practices were imbricated in each other'.[43] Freedom from Hunger encouraged the overlap of charitable enthusiasm, colonial administrative experience, and the technocratic expertise of development experts. Such imbrications are apparent in a number of dimensions of the FFHC. Take, for example, personnel. If, in the words of Anthony Hartley, decolonisation took away a British 'vocation' then the FFHC in a very literal sense provided some sections of society with a new one. As discussed in Chapter 2, many of those who worked for the colonial administration towards the end of empire went on to become 'experts' in the international development movement.[44] Through Freedom from Hunger, the Department for Technical Cooperation, which had been established in 1961 to bring together expertise on colonial development, helped British-funded FFHC projects to recruit members of the expatriate civil service to work as experts overseas.[45]

In addition to the many (ex)colonial 'experts' working on FFHC projects out in the field, a significant proportion of those sitting on the UK Campaign Committee also had experience in colonial administration. The chairman of the committee, Earl De La Warr, came to the post after a long career in colonial and agricultural administration and four years as chairman of the RCS. Other members included Arthur Gaitskell, a member of the Colonial and then Commonwealth Development Organisation between 1954 and 1973; Sir William Slater, chairman of the Colonial Development Corporation's panel of scientific advisers; and Leslie Farrer-Brown, who was heavily involved in the Colonial Social Science Council, the Overseas Visual Aid Centre and the

Commonwealth Trust. At a time when imperial continuities might be embarrassing, it is significant that committee minutes celebrated rather than obscured these imperial connections. When looking to replace the retiring Vice Chairman, Arthur Rucker, for instance, De La Warr was keen to find 'the right type of retired colonial governor or diplomat' to fill the role.[46] Rucker's successor, Sir Gilbert Rennie was lauded for his 'long and distinguished career in the colonial services', where he had served between 1948 and 1954 as Governor and Commander in Chief of Southern Rhodesia.[47]

Significant though this overlap in personnel was, the most striking of the continuities between FFHC and the practices of late colonial development was the geographic distribution of British-funded projects. The vast majority of these fell within the bounds of the Empire-Commonwealth. The people of Accrington raised money to finance the introduction of new varieties of rice in Fiji, for example; Wandsworth and Putney supported a project to train buffalo in Sarawak; and Morecambe financed the purchase of a 10-ton fish freezer for British Guiana.[48] At the end of the first five years of the campaign more than £3 million had been spent supporting 117 projects in Africa (amounting to more than half of the total funds raised by the British public) and a further £1.2 million on projects in Central and South East Asia. Significantly less was spent in areas where Britain had a smaller imperial influence: just £89,000 in the Far East, for example, and £322,152 in Central and South America.[49] In a number of cases FFHC funds even went into pre-existing development projects, established either by colonial governments or missionary societies and stretched beyond the end of empire by ongoing FFHC support. Britain did not have a monopoly on projects in its former colonies. Sweden sponsored a home economics centre for women in Tanzania, Canada and Denmark jointly funded a food technology training centre in India, and the German Evangelical Church Organisation supported a project on swamp rice production in Liberia.[50] In general, however, imperial powers such as France, Britain, and Spain focused their support for the FFHC within their own former colonies and protectorates. Britain's experience was therefore representative of a wider pattern of post-imperial aid giving.

Freedom from Hunger might have been a global campaign, but from Britain's perspective it did little to shake the existing geographies of imperial preference. This significant bias was not merely coincidental. The UK Campaign Committee made a conscious decision to 'concern itself mainly with the provision of assistance to the under-developed territories in the Commonwealth'.[51] On the basis of this decision they contacted colonial governments and the High Commissioners of recently independent countries to put together the portfolio of development projects that the British public would support. At the prompting of the Foreign Office in 1962, the Committee's projects group had made some efforts to improve the geographical distribution of projects, acknowledging that the vast majority of those approved thus far related to Africa, and particularly British East Africa.[52] Help was extended to some foreign countries such as Greece and Thailand, but this never really swayed the balance away from the Empire-Commonwealth. Comments made by the Committee reveal an awareness of the overlapping imperial and international geographies of the campaign. As they described, the 'campaign is world-wide and the United Kingdom Committee cannot therefore confine its attention solely to Commonwealth countries. Nevertheless the Committee will give a high degree of priority to sound schemes submitted from within the Commonwealth'.[53]

The records of the UK Campaign Committee never explicitly comment on why British support for the FFHC followed this pattern. Nostalgic narratives of benevolent imperialism were surely influential, particularly given the backgrounds of many of those involved, but it is clear that this geographical 'favouritism' did not *just* stem from a sense of extended imperial responsibility: there were also obvious practical and pragmatic advantages to working within the Empire-Commonwealth. First, the asymmetrical networks of people and information that had developed over a long imperial history made the declining empire a convenient geography in which to conduct development projects.[54] Colonial administrators had existing experience in these locations; many organisations affiliated to the FFHC already had people on the ground in a number of colonial territories; and, perhaps most importantly, the Colonial Office was able to play a key role in the execution of British FFHC projects, often acting as mediator between the FFHC and colonial governments. Second, the campaign was seen as a sensible way for the British government to reduce the financial burden of administering development projects; publicly raised FFHC money was often fed into pre-existing programmes.[55] As the Foreign Office described, 'we are cooperating fully with the campaign organisers, especially (but not exclusively) as regards the needs of the colonial territories who stand to gain considerably from the fund which is about to be raised'.[56] Third, the wider context of the Cold War generated pressure to use development as a way of shoring up newly independent countries against the threat of communist expansion.[57] Ambassadors visiting funded projects were encouraged to make sure recipients knew where the money was coming from, particularly in countries where the British government was 'doing little in the way of aid'.[58]

Through these links, the FFHC increased the public's participation in the final days of the imperial project, involving them (albeit indirectly) in projects that were once the purview of the Colonial Office. Many of the practical and pragmatic continuities that characterised Britain's participation in the FFHC would not, however, have been immediately apparent to the fundraising public. Most operational decisions relating to the Foreign and Commonwealth Office took place behind closed doors and were not widely publicised. As the next sections discuss, a sense of British imperial purpose was noticeably lacking from the more 'everyday', or practical, forms of participation that characterised how most people interacted with the campaign. Instead, supporters tended to adopt discourses of internationalism that either overlooked or overwrote the imperial continuities of the campaign.

Disrupting continuities: internationalism and the United Nations

In a reflection of events taking place within the broader UN infrastructure to which the FAO belonged, Freedom from Hunger inspired and supported models of internationalism that sought to supersede the geopolitics of imperialism. Where once the League of Nations had been envisioned as an adjunct to the British Empire, now the UN seemed to threaten its existence. The founders of the UN deliberately played down any continuities between their new world organisation and the League of Nations, and, by the time the fundraising element of FFHC was launched in Britain in 1962 the UN had acquired a global reputation as an 'aggressive, anti-colonial champion of self-determination'.[59]

In 1960 the General Assembly had passed Resolution 1514 calling for a rapid and unconditional end to colonialism and in 1961 Committee 17 was established to work towards these aims. As Wm Roger Louis describes, 'the Committee became famous in the history of the UN for its persistent, voluble and impassioned attacks on Western colonial powers, especially Britain'.[60] In 1963 alone Committee 17 discussed Southern Rhodesia, Aden, Malta, Fiji, British Guiana, Kenya, Northern Rhodesia, Nyasaland, Zanzibar, Basutoland, Bechuanaland, Swaziland, Gibraltar, and the Gambia, many of these being countries in which FFHC projects were then taking place. Even more problematically for the Colonial Office, the Committee demanded visiting missions to Aden, Fiji, and British Guiana, all of which had the potential to upset the delicate balance between indigenous inhabitants and immigrant populations with violent results.[61] David Jerrom, head of the International Relations department in the Colonial Office, complained of how the 'wretched committee ... has become a political factor of importance in all delicate colonial situations'.[62] As Mazower describes, 'every act of decolonisation swelled the size of the [UN General] assembly and diluted the strength of Europe's voice'.[63] By 1965 almost 50 of the 119 members on the General Assembly had only recently emerged from colonial rule.

Great hopes were invested in the organisational galaxy of the UN in the early 1960s. The United Nations charter, the 1948 Universal Declaration of Human Rights, and the constitution of the Food and Agricultural Organisation all expressed hope of a 'new world conscience'.[64] FAO represented what felt like a new opportunity for 'genuine international cooperation' in pursuit of development. As Director General of the FAO, B. R. Sen was the public face of this new dynamic. Born in India in 1900, Sen studied English literature at the Scottish Churches College in Calcutta before completing a PhD in history and economics at Oxford. He served a long career in the Indian Civil Service and eventually became Director General of Food for India in 1943, a post created following the Bengal famine of 1942–43.[65] His election as Director General of the FAO in 1956 made him the first individual from a developing country to become the head of a UN agency and a sympathetic advocate for the needs of newly independent countries. What was needed, Sen argued, was 'a conscious dedication to the right of man to grow to his full stature, regardless of the place of his birth, the colour of his skin, or of the faiths and beliefs he might cherish'.[66]

While FAO campaign materials never explicitly condemned the role of imperial powers, they did encourage supporters to recognise and respond to changes brought about by decolonisation. A 1962 FAO pamphlet explained that

> Since the end of the Second World War 800 million people in various parts of the world have won their independence [...] This is a major revolution of our time because nearly one third of the human race, within the span of 15 years have become masters of their own destiny [...] to secure a life of dignity and freedom from the misery and degradation of poverty.[67]

Earl De La Warr – who was the most public face of the British campaign alongside the patron the Duke of Edinburgh – also reflected on this changing dynamic.

> A little while ago constructive work in helping primitive peoples to grow more food for themselves was largely limited to the British Colonial and some other territories. Now, however, the Food and Agriculture Organization is conducting a worldwide campaign through its own and a vast number of other agencies. Everywhere we look the cry is for independence. Dependence on charity is not independence. Our movement should therefore be the corollary of "trade not aid."[68]

While De La Warr's comments rather simplistically equated his long-term aims for colonialism (to prepare countries for independence) with the aims of the contemporary development movement, they also indicate a willingness and desire to move away from colonial hierarchies.

A number of the charitable organisations affiliated to the FFHC tapped into similar discourses of global change, distancing themselves from the imperial continuity narrative of the central committee and challenging what they saw as ongoing practices of paternalism and neo-colonialism. Christian Aid, the focus of Chapter 5, was one of the more vocal organisations to do this. Stepping outside the comfortable discourses of trusteeship expressed by many on the national FFHC committee, Christian Aid described how its 'responsibility extend[ed] beyond the provision of a tractor or the equipment of a hospital', arguing that it 'must be concerned about international agreements on commodity prices'.[69] Oxfam made similar appeals, arguing at an FFHC event that 'there can be no permanent peace or security so long as the existing disparities persist'.[70]

Despite these examples of critical engagement, political advocacy did not become a consistent feature of humanitarian NGOs' remits until the 1970s. While many imagined the FFHC as an example of the new kinds of international partnership possible in the post-colonial era, as a whole, FFHC projects looked to find participatory means for coping with the present rather than encouraging the poor to seek justice for past crimes against them.[71] Public discussion of the campaign in Britain reflected this. Despite the wider context of decolonisation and readily available vocabulary of self-determination, for example, British participants in the FFHC invited far less criticism of the colonial administration than had earlier public campaigns carried out at the height of Britain's imperial power. As James Vernon suggests, hunger has long been grounds for political mobilisation and at various points in the nineteenth and early twentieth centuries hunger (and more specifically famine) was put forward as evidence of the failings of the colonial state.[72] In contrast, the dominant discourse of development framed the FFHC not in the language of emancipation or justice, but with a vocabulary of charity and technical expertise. This framing was determined by international and national factors.

Although the UN General Assembly became increasingly vocal in its condemnation of colonialism, not all UN agencies followed in its footsteps. The technical and administrative development discourses embraced by the FAO in the 1960s tended to exclude political agency. Joseph Hodge has shown how poverty had already begun to be depoliticised and dehistoricised in colonial development discourses of the

1940s and 1950s, which recast the social and economic problems of British dependencies as technical ones that could be fixed by rational planning and expert knowledge.[73] By the early 1960s these assumptions dominated development discourse and the underdeveloped world that the FFHC sought to support was rarely seen as something actively produced in the course of colonisation.[74] This vision of intervention was much more conservative than the ideas discussed at the FAO in the 1940s and early 1950s.

The FAO's first director was Sir John Boyd Orr, a man with experience in both domestic and colonial hunger administration. Under Orr's directorship, between 1945 and 1948, the FAO initially pursued what Frank Trentmann describes as a 'globally integrated picture of food supply' in which 'the coordination of food supply and demand were reconceived as a shared global project of social justice'.[75] But Orr's internationalist vision was rapidly side-lined within the FAO, his visions of food security and relief compromised by both imperial and national interests.[76] While the polarising climate of the Cold War encouraged nations to prioritise their own interests, the British government was reluctant to cede British control in colonies to international organisations. In part because of these early failings, when Sen took the helm at the FAO in 1956 he was distrustful of the ability of national governments to act for the benefit of the wider world. In his role as director general he worked to ensure that the FFHC was not constrained by political influences, further promoting the depoliticisation of development discourses.[77] By the 1960s, therefore, the FAO had come to focus on improving living conditions rather than restructuring international systems in order to eliminate world hunger.

Within Britain, at the same time, an emphasis on rebuilding traditional family life after the ravages of war made for an unfriendly atmosphere towards radical views about issues such as gender, sexuality, and international relations.[78] Although many FFHC supporters were associated with politically active organisations, others showed considerable unease about the potential politicisation of the Campaign. Orpington's local FFHC committee turned down £40 donated by fifteen CND-supporting teenagers who had raised the money by fasting for four days on the corner of the high street. Explaining the decision, the chairman of the committee said that 'we have nothing against these young people, but we are not a political organisation. When they told us they wanted to collect money for us we had reservations. We did not know if they would raise the money illegally by causing obstructions in the town.'[79] This looks to have been a local decision – I have seen no evidence that FAO or the UK FFHC Committee demanded such caution in relation either to teenagers or CND supporters – but it is nevertheless reflective of the broader attempt to preserve non-politicised forms of international engagement discussed throughout this book. The antipathy towards protest shown by significant sections of the public created difficulties for the expanding humanitarian sector. This can be seen in internal debates about Oxfam's involvement in 'political' movements for change between those who prioritised fundraising and those who believed that the organisation ought to be campaigning for social justice. In Orpington, the local Oxfam committee accepted the £40 that the FFHC committee had turned away. But some supporters did not want Oxfam's image to be tarnished by pictures of young supporters taking part in CND marches or associating with anti-establishment organisations such as trade unions.[80]

The possibility of using the FFHC to critique colonialism or global power structures was further curtailed by the increasing surveillance of the Charity Commission in the 1960s. Throughout the decade, Charity Commissioners scrutinised and restricted any activities of organisations that were deemed too political.[81] Under the terms of the Commission, direct calls upon the government for a change of policy – such as the demand to increase aid expenditure – were declared uncharitable. While behind closed doors many supporters may have viewed the FFHC in explicitly anti-colonial terms, their opinions could never be more than tentatively embraced in public by organisations seeking to retain charitable status. In the 1960s many of these pragmatically minded NGOs eschewed more radical solutions in order to secure their seat at the technocratic table.[82] It was not until the end of the decade, after the adult-focused elements of the FFHC had wound down, that humanitarian NGOs developed a more stridently political voice. The public dimension of this political work was launched with the publication of the Haslemere Declaration in 1968. With this declaration, Oxfam, Christian Aid, War on Want, the Overseas Development Institute, and the NGOs connected to the Voluntary Committee for Overseas Aid and Development called for increased government aid and adjustments to international trade. One year later they worked to set up Action for World Development, an independent body free of UK charity legislation and focused on activism and lobbying.[83] The FFHC did not directly cause this politicisation – in fact, as I have suggested, some of its features actively hampered it – but, by increasing their publicity and by enabling Oxfam, Christian Aid, and War on Want to build up their portfolios of long-term development projects through the middle years of the 1960s it did help them to establish the firm footing necessary to launch their political activities.

Obscuring continuities: collaboration and person-to-person fundraising

The British government may have prioritised a narrative of continuing imperial benevolence; Christian Aid, Oxfam, and War on Want may have begun to critique neo-colonial structural inequalities; but for the majority of FFHC supporters the campaign was about people, not politics. In fact, the most enduring legacy of the FFHC is the precise way in which it mobilised discourses of internationalism to present development aid as a matter of people-to-people connections. Most supporters never openly explored or articulated the complex relationship between imperialism and international development. This apparent oversight should not necessarily be surprising. While the FFHC provided people with diverse opportunities to participate in everyday forms of international activism – attending fundraising events, running local committees and taking part in educational activities – there was very little onus on the actors and non-humanitarian institutions involved in the campaign to coherently define either internationalism or imperialism. This section discusses how Freedom from Hunger entered into the lives of the fundraising public and the influence this may have had on the relationships they imagined between themselves and people in the developing world.

Much of the recent literature on the campaigning and advertising strategies of humanitarian NGOs has focused on the problematic use of images of suffering to generate public sympathy.[84] These visual tropes have been criticised for mobilising ideologies of 'rescue' instead of addressing the causes of suffering, and for encouraging donor/recipient relationships that are premised on maximum distance between the spectator and the suffering other.[85] Rather than bridging the gap, as one might hope, these images tend to reinforce racial hierarchies and social dependencies. They exoticise distant others, fetishise affliction, and perpetuate a set of power relations where the victim is a passive recipient of aid.[86] In their efforts to mobilise public support, the FFHC and participating humanitarian organisations made use of similarly problematic images of suffering. When Philip Noel-Baker explained the need for the FFHC to the House of Commons he started with descriptions of suffering children, most vividly a baby with kwashiorkor who, he said, 'lives and soon dies, in tearless, inarticulate misery'.[87] Oxfam and Save the Children Fund advertisements used images of mothers and starving children in their FFHC-linked promotional material, while a widely distributed FAO commissioned poster – a striking illustration of a wheat sheaf and a child's visible ribcage – employed similar visual rhetoric.[88]

As a whole, however, the FFHC used comparatively few images of suffering in its advertising material, choosing instead to emphasise successful examples of productivity, cooperation and self-help. This was a conscious decision. B. R. Sen repeatedly cautioned against the temptation to rely on sensationalist slogans and superficial appeals; to his mind, for the FFHC to have lasting effects, the public needed to be made aware that the root of the problem was vast and complex.[89] In order to create this informed body of opinion, the FFHC made a great deal of information available to the public in the form of pamphlets, films and public speakers, seeking to capitalise on the expanding educational remits of organisations like the WI and Rotary Club. Local FFHC committees across the country were encouraged to form study groups and a monthly *Ideas and Action* bulletin kept readers abreast of conferences, published reports, and the progress that was being made on specific projects. More detailed information was also provided by the *Basic Studies* series, designed for use by NGOs cooperating in the campaign.[90] These studies aimed to use 'brief but authoritative language' to state the facts of important aspects of the campaign and explored topics such as 'Weather and Food', 'Animal Disease and Human Health', and 'Nutrition and Working Efficiency'. For those local committees that were particularly interested in the destination of their money, visits could sometimes be arranged by FAO advisers to help 'crystallise and clarify' the fundraisers' ideas about the projects they intended to support.[91]

As discussed in Chapter 2, representatives of humanitarian and development organisations were a common feature of associational educational programmes. More widely, affiliated organisations with their own resources also published further informational material for their members. Christian Aid, for example, provided detailed accounts of their £2 million-worth of anti-hunger schemes in a 16-page report that allowed members to locate the specific project that their committee or town had helped fund, as well as getting a sense of the broader scope of the campaign.[92]

Methods of participation varied significantly in ways that suggest that some members of the community were considerably more engaged with the educative aims of the campaign than others. Some engaged with the campaign through public debate, for example. Writing to the *Guardian*, one man criticised the FFHC for failing to address the increasing population by providing education about birth control; 'For all the effect the present campaign is likely to have on this terrible problem', he complained, 'its well-meaning exponents might just as well stuff themselves at the Savoy while the Malthusian catacylsm impends.'[93] Others came to the campaign's defence, claiming they were not 'a crowd of woolly minded philanthropists, ignorant of the demographic aspects of the problem'.[94] But while some embraced the educational components of the campaign wholeheartedly, for others, participation entailed little more than dropping a shilling in a collection box. Many areas even combined existing community interests with fundraising in ways that seemed to detract attention from the specific aims of Freedom from Hunger. For example, members of the Rydale Methodist Youth Club toured a kitchen sink religious drama through fourteen isolated villages on the North York Moors, donating the proceeds to the FFHC. The minister described the play as 'a very hard-hitting play about religion in a back street' – little to do, that is, with either hunger or development.[95]

Much more consistent were the ways in which the public emphasised the local dimensions of the projects that they supported. Many groups sought to foster personal ties with those in receipt of aid. Rather than raising money for a central fund, for example, most communities and organisations selected specific projects to support, increasing the sense of identification with those overseas. Bristol raised £48,000 for a Farm Institute in Nyasaland, Nottingham raised £40,000 to extend a training centre for Gwembe fisherman in Northern Rhodesia, and Reading contributed £12,310 to a crossbreeding scheme for dairy cattle in Allahabad.[96] Fundraisers often had a relatively clear idea of precisely how their money would be spent and what would be achieved: 26,000 gallons of milk would be processed daily at a plant in the state of Andhra Pradesh in India, for example, and an agricultural college in Swaziland would be capable of providing a two-year diploma course for twenty students per year.[97] By placing greater emphasis on the people-to-people nature of the campaign than on the roles played by various national governments, the FFHC actively encouraged the public to operate at a remove from state politics.

FAO publicity material promoted Freedom from Hunger as a *global* campaign, encouraging its participants to identify as international actors. Sen was very clear about his desire 'to create a climate of public opinion favourable to genuine international co-operation' and FAO publications encouraged a spirit of understanding that was grounded in 'goodwill and good neighbourliness'.[98] This statement echoes Rotary and the WI's emphasis on knowledge and education as the foundations of international understanding. In a reflection of the international frameworks of the campaign most of the press within Britain focused not on the paternalistic potential of the British government as a national (imperial) power but on the networked fundraising efforts of individuals, community groups and international charities. Organisations affiliated to the campaign also adopted a participatory vocabulary – with Oxfam, for instance, asking supporters to 'share in constructive work'.[99] The broader UN FAO structure meant that the FFHC frequently publicised the active participation of developing countries that would normally be identified solely as recipients of aid. A promotional pamphlet described how 600 Indian students had given up their autumn vacation to reclaim 45 acres of land, while 20,000 young Egyptians worked alongside 450 overseas volunteers to reclaim desert for agricultural use.[100]

Fundraising activities tapped into these same discourses, often seeking to empathise with those in need and show solidarity through personal sacrifice. Children acted out scenes of hunger in school plays, Scout troops ate a diet of plain rice and camped out under sheets to experience a night as 'refugees' and the students of Appleby Grammar School in Westmorland raised funds through a self-imposed Sweet Denial Week.[101] Some of these efforts were clearly more heartfelt than others. After reading about a particularly unmindful businessmen's 'Hunger Lunch' held to raise money for the campaign, Mrs G. V. Thompson was driven to write to the *Guardian* to express her disgust: '*Only* melon, veal, peas, potatoes, fresh fruit and coffee! And only one wine! ... One is filled with sympathy for them in such an ordeal and for their courage in undertaking it.'[102] Broadly speaking, however, these efforts positioned members of the public within wider global discourses of equality and internationalism that were exemplified by the FAO and by UNESCO's ongoing work to develop worldwide networks of cooperation and mutual understanding.

There were, however, significant limitations to the public's adoption of the FAO's ideals of global citizenship. While Freedom from Hunger made it possible for participants to transcend state boundaries, it did not necessarily overwrite national identification. The experiences of Somerset and Devon, while fundraising to support farm projects in Tanzania, illustrate how the FFHC could be used to assert membership of a wider international community while simultaneously affirming local and national identities. For Somerset and Devon, the FFHC was about more than just raising money for farmers' training centres in East Africa. At the heart of the two counties' involvement in the campaign was an exciting opportunity to forge links between their own 'largely rural community' and what Devon committee member Julia Canning Cook described as 'some far distant land'.[103]

During the campaign, Secretary for the Somerset Committee Hubert Fox flew out to see conditions at their sponsored projects in Tanzania, bringing back a filmed record of his journey and an exhibition of African arts and crafts, which toured the neighbouring counties in the back of a Mini.[104] Fox was also able to meet Julius Nyerere, the first prime minister of Tanzania, at a London airport. As Fox described it, Nyerere 'was most enthusiastic about the "people-to-people" aspect of the FFHC and even declared [that] it was much more valuable than anything a government could do'.[105] These clearly novel experiences led Canning Cook to conclude that from the FFHC

> Something quite new has emerged. A deep and lasting understanding by individuals in these two counties of the difficulties facing subsistence farmers in Tanganyika, and on their part a realisation that people here are interested in them as fellow farmers facing the mammoth task of conquering hunger.[106]

The particular globalisation experience of rural communities in developed countries is often overlooked, but, as this example illustrates, rurality could act as an important point of commonality across national boundaries. As discussed in Chapter 2, similar discourses of agricultural expertise also informed the WI's participation in the campaign. Having worked to increase agricultural production during the First World War, the WI was readily able to align its broader aims to improve the lives of rural women with the technocratic vision of agricultural development employed by the FFHC. Over the course of the campaign, the WI bought cows for young women in Jamaica, set up a 35-acre farm in Trinidad, and supported a tractor hire scheme to encourage crop rotation in Dominica.[107] Such schemes celebrated the particular experiences of the WI as a rural institution rather than prioritising Britain's national expertise as an imperial power.

In the 1970s, similar principles of people-to-people action would align with an increasingly politicised conception of global interdependence, informing calls for structural change and global economic reform.[108] During the first five years of the FFHC, however, they rarely moved beyond more shallow forms of empathetic but apolitical solidarity. National frameworks were still influential and often trumped internationalist imaginings. Indeed, the national advertising campaign sponsored by the central UK Committee promoted the FFHC under the banner 'A call to the nation', encouraging potential donors to think of themselves as members of a generous British community of givers.[109] The FFHC was not unusual on this issue; similar practices of national internationalism occur across wide range of transnational campaigns. For example, contemporaneous supporters of the CND professed to be concerned with 'humanity' as a whole while remaining firmly embedded in their national political traditions.[110] The following account from Somerset and Devon clearly expresses the sense of local *and* national pride that these counties invested in their participation in the FFHC.

> Local rivalries have played a major part, from a friendly game of one-upmanship scored in tennis between the two county committees, to a

ding dong battle between two extremely enthusiastic borough councils who have trebled their original targets. This fact was not unnoticed by four Tanganyikan journalists who visited us recently and went home to describe the people of Somerset and Devon as 'a grace to the whole of the British Isles' but went on to say they found 'our tribal differences intriguing.'[111]

As this account illustrates, the reputation of the British nation remained central to the way the public thought about their humanitarian activity.

In the British context, the people-to-people discourses promoted by the FAO made it possible to reframe Britain's relationship with the outside world. The WI's support for the campaign is illustrative of how this reframing worked. Over five years it raised over £182,000 for projects that fell almost exclusively within the Empire-Commonwealth, financing schemes in Uganda, Trinidad, India, East Pakistan, Botswana, Northern Rhodesia, Ceylon, Sarawak, and Fiji.[112] Yet none of their promotional, published or internal records show any acknowledgement of this geographical bias. Their silence on the matter of empire is particularly striking given that a number of these countries underwent dramatic political changes over the course of the campaign: Trinidad and Uganda gained independence in 1962, Sarawak in 1963, and Northern Rhodesia in 1964.

This wasn't simply a matter of being ill informed about the destination of their money. The WI wholeheartedly embraced the educational component of the campaign. Alongside typical fundraising activities, such as bring-and-buy sales and whist drives, institutes organised talks and film screenings about the countries in which they supported projects. Over 4500 members attended a touring lecture about the Ugandan farm institute supported by WI funds and frequent features in their magazine *Home and Country* discussed the achievements of the FFHC.[113] Instead, their silence reveals how they imagined Britain's relationship with the decolonising world. For the WI did not simply overlook the processes of decolonisation occurring throughout the campaign, they also spoke about the countries they supported in ways that actively obscured their imperial pasts. In the context of the FFHC, former colonies of the New Commonwealth such as Uganda, Sarawak, Botswana, and East Pakistan came to be understood collectively either as 'the undernourished side of the world' or as 'newly emergent' countries.[114] No obvious thought was given to the complicated and uncomfortable histories of colonisation from which these new nations were 'emerging'. Through selective silence and euphemism, the WI simultaneously configured poverty as a 'new' global challenge and the British public as an important part of a new global solution. This process was symptomatic not only of what many have characterised as imperial amnesia, but also of the wider discourses of internationalism that framed the FFHC and helped to create the 'Third World'.[115]

The campaign makes clear that, despite the rise of discourses of international aid in the 'under-developed' or 'third' world, the transition from imperial to international humanitarianism was not quick, smooth, or all-encompassing. Rather than replacing colonialism, Frederick Cooper suggests, the development concept allowed for its 'internationalization', a process by which the one-to-one relationship of metropole to colony was transformed into a generalised economic subordination of South to North, of Africa and Asia to Europe and North America.[116] In the FFHC, development was still predicated on the assumption that some people are more 'developed' than others and therefore have the knowledge and expertise to help those who are not.[117] As with the WI and Rotary's use of familial metaphors and philanthropic frameworks to describe their hospitality work, this inevitably reproduced the social hierarchies that had prevailed between both groups under colonialism.

The nature of the public's support for the FFHC shows that habits of mind associated with imperial philanthropy and trusteeship did not end with decolonisation either. Instead, they developed in this period to coexist alongside and within newer international discourses of humanitarian aid and development. Maggie Black has argued that the FFHC helped Britain to recast its own humanitarian interventions in the mould of the UN, whose unbiased machinery was comparatively free from the taint of self-interest and assumed superiority that clung to old colonial powers.[118] This new discourse of international development certainly offered an alternative language.[119] But the extent to which it actually replaced the habits of imperialism was considerably more limited. While each of the narratives discussed in this chapter offered a different interpretation of Britain's humanitarian vocation, they all shared an unshakeable belief in the value of the work being done and of Britain's suitability to carry out that work. As Hartley diagnosed in 1963, even those who were critical of imperialism and 'fled with horror from the idea of being colonialists' could not resist the allure of 'technical assistance' and 'aid to underdeveloped countries'.[120] More self-reflexive critiques of Britain's complicity in the global structural inequalities that determined the poverty of distant strangers did not gain traction until the 1970s.[121]

Notes

1 Sections of this chapter have previously been published in Anna Bocking-Welch, 'Imperial legacies and internationalist discourses: British involvement in the United

Nations Freedom from Hunger Campaign, 1960–70', *The Journal of Imperial and Commonwealth History*, 40:5 (2012), 879–96.

2 Barnett, *Empire of Humanity*, p. 227.

3 'Britain's £7m for Hunger Campaign', *Guardian* (20 November 1964).

4 Peter Gatrell, *Free World?: The Campaign to Save the World's Refugees, 1956–1963* (Cambridge: Cambridge University Press, 2011).

5 For further discussion of the FFHC's legacies to international development see Matthew James Bunch, 'All Roads Lead to Rome: Canada, the Freedom From Hunger Campaign, and the Rise of NGOs, 1960–1980' (PhD Dissertation, University of Waterloo, 2007).

6 *Freedom From Hunger Campaign News* (October 1963), p. 9.

7 James Vernon, *Hunger: A Modern History* (Harvard University Press, London, 2007), p. 3.

8 Vernon, *Hunger*, p. 4.

9 *Ibid.*, p. 273.

10 Frederick Cooper, *Africa Since 1940: The Past of the Present* (Cambridge: Cambridge University Press, 2002), p. 84.

11 TNA, MAF 252/243, Committee on Development Policy, United Nations Development Decade, 15 October 1963.

12 TNA, OD 11/72, Earl De La Warr, *Gazebo* (c.1963), p. 24.

13 Hodge, *Triumph of the Expert*, p. 12; Frederick Cooper and Randall Packard (eds), *International Development and the Social Sciences: Essays on the History and Politics of Knowledge* (Berkeley, CA: University of California Press, 1997), p. 13.

14 SOAS, CA/I/3/3 'What Every Non Governmental Organisation Should Know About FFHC', FFHC May 1960.

15 'Britain's £7m for Hunger Campaign', *Guardian* (20 November 1964).

16 'Who will adopt a herd of Buffaloes?', *Guardian* (21 November 1962).

17 'Freedom From Hunger Week wins wide support', *Manchester Guardian* (19 March 1963); see also *Guardian* (1 August 1963) and (23 May 1964).

18 RALSS, 358/F Box 3, 'Widow (Pensioner)' to Charles Chislett, 20 March 1963; Anonymous to Charles Chislett, 1 May 1963.

19 This treasurer happened to be the Rotarian and amateur filmmaker Charles Chislett, discussed in Chapter 2.

20 RALSS, 358/F Box 3, Various Freedom from Hunger Campaign donation letters to Charles Chislett.

21 SOAS, CA/I/3/3 'What Every Non Governmental Organisation Should Know About FFHC', May 1960.

22 Haskell, 'Capitalism and the origins of the humanitarian sensibility', 357.

23 David Lambert and Alan Lester, 'Geographies of colonial philanthropy', *Progress in Human Geography*, 28:3 (2004), 323.

24 *Ibid*, p. 320.

25 Pedersen, 'The maternalist moment', 201. See also John Stuart, 'Overseas mission, voluntary service and aid to Africa: Max Warren, the Church Missionary Society and Kenya, 1945–63', *The Journal of Imperial and Commonwealth History*, 3 (2008), 527–43; R. P. Neumann, 'The post-war conservation boom in British colonial Africa', *Environmental History*, 7:1 (2007), 37.

26 Cooper, *Africa Since 1940*, p. 31; Hodge, *Triumph of the Expert*, p. 8; Charlotte Lydia Riley, 'Monstrous predatory vampires and beneficent fairy-godmothers: British post-war colonial development in Africa', PhD dissertation, University College London, 2013.

27 John Darwin, 'Imperialism in decline? Tendencies in British imperial policy between the wars', *The Historical Journal*, 23:3 (1980), 657–8.

28 Wm Roger Louis, 'The dissolution of the British Empire', in Judith M. Brown and Wm Roger Louis (eds), *Oxford History of the British Empire, vol. V The Twentieth Century* (Oxford: Oxford University Press, 1999), p. 329.

29 SOAS, CA/I/3/2, Prince Philip, 'Service Overseas by Volunteers,' *World*, March 1965.

30 *Ibid.*
31 SOAS, CA/I/3/2, Voluntary Societies' Committee for Service Overseas, 'Service Overseas By Volunteers 1966'.
32 'Points from Parliament', *Daily Mail* (5 March 1963).
33 TNA, MAF 252/241, Notes for the Prime Minister's Speech FFHC Public Launching Ceremony, Festival Hall, 27 June 1962.
34 TNA, MAF 252/226, JD Anderson (FO) to John Wyndham (Private Secretary to PM) 15 March 1962.
35 SOAS, CA/I/3/2, Duke of Edinburgh, 'Service Overseas By Volunteers 1966'.
36 TNA, MAF 252/243, 'Committee on Development Policy, United Nations Development Decade,' 15 October 1963.
37 'Who will adopt a herd of buffaloes?', *Guardian* (21 November 1962).
38 'Freedom from Hunger: A call to the nation', *Daily Mail* (23 October 1962).
39 'How the Freedom from Hunger Campaign is helping strengthen the British Commonwealth', *Commonwealth Journal* (April 1963).
40 'Peer's World Food Plea', *Daily Telegraph* (5 March 1963).
41 Hartley, *State of England*, p. 70.
42 Hodge, *Triumph of the Expert*, p. 262.
43 Kothari, 'Authority and expertise', 433.
44 Hodge, *Triumph of the Expert*.
45 TNA, OD 11/71, FFHC Note of a Discussion held on 15 January 1963.
46 TNA, MAF 252/213, AJD Winnifrith to Mr Bishop, 2 February 1962.
47 TNA, MAF 252/226, FFHC UK Committee Newsletter, April 1962.
48 *Guardian* (18 March 1963).
49 TNA, MAF 2552/213, *The First Five Years: Freedom From Hunger 1960–65* (1965).
50 *Food and Agricultural Organisation Report, Number 53* (Rome: FAO, 1969); *Food and Agricultural Organisation Report, Number 66* (Rome: FAO, 1970); *Food and Agricultural Organisation Report, Number 63* (Rome: FAO, 1970).
51 TNA, OD 11/70, Freedom from Hunger Campaign brief for Overseas Development Secretary Alan Dudley for his meeting with Earl De La Warr, 25 October 1961.
52 TNA, MAF 252/226, FFHC UK Committee General Secretary's Report, 29 May 1962.
53 TNA, OD 11/70, Memorandum from Freedom from Hunger Campaign United Kingdom National Committee, November 1961.
54 Lester, 'Imperial circuits and networks', 124–41.
55 TNA, DO 189/335JW Howard to Miss J Owtram, 14 November 1963.
56 TNA, MAF 252/226JD, Anderson to John Wyndham, 15 March 1962.
57 Hodge, *Triumph of the Expert*.
58 TNA, DO 189/355TW, Aston to Mr Bottomley, 21 June 1963.
59 Louis, 'Public Enemy Number One', pp. 692–5.
60 *Ibid.*, p. 702.
61 *Ibid.*, p. 709.
62 *Ibid.*, p. 709.
63 Mark Mazower, *No Enchanted Palace: The End of Empire and the Ideological Origins of the United Nations* (Oxford: Princeton University Press, 2009), p. 185.
64 *The Basic Freedom: Freedom from Hunger* (Rome: FAO, 1962), p. 11.
65 Bunch, 'All roads lead to Rome', p. 27.
66 *Ibid.*, p. 24.
67 'The Basic Freedom: Freedom from Hunger' (Rome: FAO, 1962), p. 7.
68 SOAS, CA/I/3/3, Speech delivered by Earl De La Warr to Institute of Rural Life at Home and Overseas, 20 April 1961.
69 SOAS, CA2/I/18/3, Memo Youth Against Hunger: The Politics of Aid, 1965.
70 'Call for 1% of income: Hunger relief', *Guardian* (6 August 1960).
71 Firoze Manji and Carl O'Coill, 'The missionary position: NGOs and development in Africa', *International Affairs*, 78:3 (2002), 574–6.
72 Vernon, *Hunger*, pp. 41–54.
73 Hodge, *Triumph of the Expert*, p. 19.

74 Power, 'The Commonwealth', 16.
75 Frank Trentmann, 'Coping with shortage: The problem of food security and global visions of coordination, c.1890s–1950', in Frank Trentmann and Flemming Just (eds), *Food and Conflict in Europe in the Age of the Two World Wars* (Basingstoke: Palgrave Macmillan, 2006), pp. 27, 32.
76 *Ibid.*, p. 34.
77 Bunch, 'All roads lead to Rome', p. 29.
78 Lent, *British Social Movements Since 1945*, p. 8.
79 'Famine fund turns down money from CND fast', *Daily Mail* (26 August 1963).
80 Alan Leather, 'Guest Editorial: Trade Union and NGO Relations in developmentand Social Justice,' *Development in Practice* 14:1 (2004), 15.
81 Hilton, 'Politics is ordinary', 256.
82 *Ibid.*, p. 266.
83 Hilton, 'International aid and development NGOs', pp. 452, 455.
84 See, for example, Kate Manzo, 'Imaging humanitarianism: NGO identity and the iconography of childhood', *Antipode*, 40:4 (2008), 632–57; Heide Fehrenbach and Davide Rodogno (eds), *Humanitarian Photography* (Cambridge: Cambridge University Press, 2015).
85 Laura Briggs, 'Mother, child, race, nation: The visual iconography of rescue and the politics of transnational and transracial adoption', *Gender & History*, 15:2 (2003), 180.
86 Denis Kennedy, 'Selling the distant other: Humanitarianism and imagery – ethical dilemmas of humanitarian action', *The Journal of Humanitarian Assistance*, 28 (2009), 1–25; David Morgan, 'The look of sympathy: Religion, visual culture, and the social life of feeling', *Material Religion*, 5:2 (2009), 132–54; Heather D. Curtis, 'Picturing pain: evangelicals and the politics of pictorial humanitarianism in an imperial age' in Fehrenbach and Rodogno (eds), *Humanitarian photography*, p. 43.
87 HC Deb 20 March 1963 vol. 674 col. 410.
88 *The Times* (10 September 1962); *The Times* (20 October 1962).
89 B. R. Sen, *Towards a Newer World* (Dublin: Tycooley, 1982), p. 123.
90 Food and Agricultural Organisation, Rome, RG12, Sec 4, B-067 B15, Box 3, No File Label 'Freedom From Hunger Campaign: Use of FAO Basic Studies', p. 1.
91 Freedom From Hunger Campaign News (October 1963), p. 8.
92 SOAS, CA/I/3/4, Christian Aid booklet of achievements in the FFHC.
93 Letters to the Editor, *Guardian* (22 March 1963).
94 Ibid.
95 'Tractor takes theatre to villages', *Guardian* (16 April 1963).
96 '£5.6 Million Raised for Hunger Campaign', *Guardian* (27 May 1964).
97 'Freedom From Hunger', *Guardian* (10 December 1962); 'Who Will Adopt a Herd of Buffaloes?' Advertisement, *Guardian* (21 November 1962).
98 *Freedom From Hunger Campaign News* (November 1962), p. 3.
99 'How does Oxfam act', *Guardian* (2 November 1962).
100 Bocking-Welch, 'Youth Against Hunger', 166.
101 *Freedom From Hunger Campaign News* (October 1963), p. 2.
102 Letters to the Editor, *Guardian* (22 March 1963).
103 *Freedom From Hunger Campaign News* (September–October 1962), p. 32.
104 *Freedom From Hunger Campaign News*, October 1963, p. 8.
105 *Freedom From Hunger Campaign News* (September–October 1962), p. 32.
106 *Ibid.*
107 *Home and Country* (June 1967).
108 Kevin O'Sullivan, 'A "global nervous system": The rise and rise of European humanitarian NGOs, 1945–1985', in Marc Frey, Sönke Kunkel, and Corinna R. Unger (eds), *International Organizations and Development, 1945–1990* (London: Springer, 2014), pp. 204–7.
109 'A call to the nation', *Daily Mail* (23 October 1962).
110 Nehring, 'National internationalists', 559–82.
111 *Freedom From Hunger Campaign News* (September–October 1962), p. 32.

112 Kaye, *International Countrywomen*, p. 7.
113 NFWI, 5/FWI/D/2/2/33, Report on a lecture tour of Britain's Women's Institutes by Ron. Baker, May 1968; *Home and Country* (June 1967).
114 For example, *Home and Country* (November 1968).
115 On imperial amnesia see Paul Gilroy, *After Empire: Melancholia or Convivial Culture?* (Abingdon on Thames: Routledge, 2004).
116 Cooper, *Africa since 1940*, p. 91.
117 *Ibid.*
118 Maggie Black, *A Cause for Our Times: Oxfam the First Fifty Years* (Oxford: Oxfam, 1992), p. 70.
119 Manji and O'Coill, 'The missionary position', 572.
120 Anthony Hartley, *State of England* (New York: Harcourt Brace and World, 1963), p. 72.
121 Black, *A Cause for Our Times*, pp. 132–203.

CHAPTER FIVE

Christian responsibility in a shrinking world

Christian Aid: the new face of Christian responsibility

Religion does not figure strongly in histories of British decolonisation. While scholarship does assess how Christian churches overseas adapted and adjusted to the declining empire, little attention has been paid to the changing relationship between religion and empire *within* Britain at this time. Sarah Stockwell's work on Archbishop Fisher has reinstated the upper Anglican Church hierarchy in our wider understanding of the political discussions and processes through which Britain divested itself of an Empire.[1] Yet the broader role of domestic religious life in shaping the public's engagement with decolonisation – reaching from the top of the institutional hierarchy to the local parish church, and including affiliated organisations and campaigns – remains shadowy and under-defined. This neglect is surprising given the important role that religion and, in particular, missionaries are seen to have played in the formation, expansion, and justification of the British Empire.

Missionary involvement focused churchgoers' attention on the Empire on a regular and passionate basis in the nineteenth and early twentieth centuries.[2] Pamphlets, travel accounts and sermons related first-hand imperial experiences to less mobile audiences, while church campaigns such as those against slavery formed bonds of care between the metropole and its imperial peripheries. Catherine Hall's account of growing up in a religious household in 1950s Kettering is indicative of how similar networks continued to act as important conduits during the period of decolonisation:

> At home the sense of a Baptist family stretching across the globe was always part of domestic life: missionaries from 'the field', on 'furlough', bringing me stamps for my collection; African students studying at the university who were invited for Christmas or Sunday tea; the small concerns we held to raise money for 'good causes' both near and far.[3]

But the fact that many others had similar experiences to Hall has been largely overlooked. As Jeffrey Cox suggests, historians of twentieth-century Britain – among them historians of decolonisation – have, for the most part, adopted a secular outlook and, in doing so, have overlooked the significant roles played by religion in shaping British life.[4] More recently, however, the narrative of post-war secularisation has come under increasing scrutiny.[5] Rather than focusing on what has allegedly been lost, historians have begun to shift their attention to the ways in which religion was being transformed, taking account of its changing visibility in political and public life and identifying the ways in which the institutions, practices, and discourses of the church continued to play a meaningful role in the lives of many Britons.[6] It is in the context of this shifting consensus that we need to rethink the role of religious institutions in relation to the domestic impact of decolonisation.

Humanitarianism was central to these transformations. In the 1960s discourses of Christian responsibility to those in need were a central tenet of religious international engagement. The idea of a Christian duty of care was not new. But where once these responsibilities had been met primarily through missionary work – and guided by the evangelising imperative to save souls – by the 1960s the emphasis had shifted to saving bodies through aid and development initiatives. In the Christian churches, as in the charity sector more broadly, there was also a move away from ad hoc donations to individual causes and towards fundraising for large professional organisations with broad humanitarian remits. This transition was made possible by the establishment of new religious humanitarian organisations in the decades following the Second World War and had a significant impact on the nature of religious international engagement.

The largest of these British organisations was Christian Aid, which operated as the humanitarian arm of the ecumenical British Council of Churches (BCC), an organisation founded in 1942 to continue the work done by earlier bodies concerned with international friendship, social action, and faith.[7] Christian Aid had started out as Christian Reconstruction in Europe in 1945, was renamed the Inter-Church Aid and Refugee Service in 1948 before finally settling on its current name in 1964.[8] It was not the only religious organisation working in this field. The Catholic Agency for Overseas Development (CAFOD) was founded in 1962, for example, and the Evangelical Alliance Relief Fund (Tearfund) in 1968. Collectively, these organisations raised the profile of religious humanitarianism in Britain. But they also had distinctive approaches that appealed to different constituents within the broader religious community. Like the BCC, Christian Aid was predominantly an Anglican organisation, but its ecumenical reach also included

Methodist, Reformed, Baptist and Free Churches, and the Society of Friends. By contrast, Tearfund's evangelical objectives appealed to many of those unwilling to support Christian Aid because of its association with the theologically more liberal BCC.[9] This chapter focuses primarily on the opportunities for international engagement fostered by Christian Aid because it was not only the largest of the faith-based humanitarian organisations working in Britain at this time, but also the most active at a local level.

In existing literature on post-war humanitarianism, Christian Aid has been discussed as one member of a professionalised cohort of aid and development NGOs based in Britain.[10] There are good reasons for this grouping; Christian Aid followed a similar trajectory to other key post-war humanitarian organisations. Like Oxfam and War on Want, it was established to provide relief work in Europe during and in the immediate aftermath of the Second World War. Like Oxfam and War on Want, it adjusted its priorities over the course of the next decade to support development projects and relief work in a much wider geographical field. And like Oxfam and War on Want, Christian Aid played a central role in debates about the purpose of humanitarian NGOs and the political nature of aid and development work in the second half of the 1960s, particularly through its membership of the Disasters Emergency Committee and the Voluntary Committee on Overseas Aid and Development.[11]

While it shared many of its key aims and strategies with other humanitarian NGOs, Christian Aid's explicit religious remit made it distinctive in ways that are important to understanding the impact of decolonisation on ideas of international responsibility. First, it linked the organisation to a particular set of religious imperial traditions and legacies. Though it was not itself a missionary organisation, Christian Aid was shaped by the impact of decolonisation on missionary work. On a practical level, many of the missionaries forced to leave their posts at the end of empire moved into the humanitarian sector and became part of Christian Aid's network of organisers and speakers. At a more discursive level, Christian Aid's connection to missionary infrastructures required it to engage with critiques about the imperial nature of missionary work and the broader role of the church overseas.

Having a religious remit also determined how Christian Aid related to its supporters. Julia Berger's analysis of religious NGOs emphasises that while secular NGOs must build their resource and support networks from the ground up, religious organisations already have access to networks and communities around the world.[12] Christian Aid was part of a long history of humanitarian and welfare initiatives organised and conducted through local religious bodies. In the late nineteenth and early twentieth centuries, local parishes and chapels became a focal point for middle-class Christians who wanted 'to do something' with their spare time.[13] Through the provision of social services including mothers' meetings, temperance societies, debating clubs, Boys' Brigades, sports clubs, and vocational education classes, churches constituted an important dimension of associational life and situated themselves as key providers of philanthropic assistance.[14] Simon Green has argued that local religious classes 'lost heart' in this 'associational ideal' of Christianity back in the 1920s.[15] While the extent of churches' activity may have diminished by the 1960s, Christian Aid illustrates how church-sponsored or organised activities continued to exist alongside newer dimensions of associational life. Janet Lacey, the first director of Christian Aid, was passionate about engaging with the public and in 1957 set up the first 'Christian Aid Week' to involve local communities in fundraising and educative activities. Across the country there were begging bowls, local MPs opening fetes, hunger luncheons, and student fancy dress processions. Through these initiatives Christian Aid embedded itself in the social world of Christian Churches and drew upon the organising power of local religious life.

The nature of Christian Aid's relationship with its donor public was also shaped in significant ways by broader post-war debates that sought to redefine Christian Britain according to ideals of active Christian citizenship and social responsibility. These debates helped to set the terms by which religious humanitarian international engagement could be promoted. Through reference to specifically Christian duty, Christian Aid was able to put pressure on its constituency in a manner not available to other secular organisations. Drawing on a language of responsibility, sacrifice, and active Christianity, Alan Brash (Lacey's successor as Director) declared that 'anybody who does not give – in a costly and disciplined way – in answer to the cry of human agony today – that man cannot do anything relevant – and he certainly cannot preach the Christian Gospel – because manifestly he does not care'.[16] As it had in the eighteenth and nineteenth century, religion continued to shape wider discourses about Britain's global responsibilities.

This chapter uses the work of Christian Aid to illustrate how religious institutions acted as conduits to the outside world. Starting at an institutional level, it charts the imperial and international frameworks that shaped Christian Aid's work and considers the discursive strategies that the organisation used to make sense of its connections to the imperial legacies of missionary work. Next, by treating Christian Aid as one dimension of domestic religious life, this chapter shows how national debates about religious responsibility and local traditions of religious participation were both determining factors for the nature of the public's participation in humanitarian activity.

Neighbours in need: from European relief to third world development

By the mid-1960s, Christian Aid carried out most of its overseas work in the former and declining British Empire, but the organisation did not have imperial beginnings. This is true of many forms of post-war international engagement, but it is particularly important to recognise here because it is otherwise easy to oversimplify the church's post-war involvement in the 'third world' as a straightforward adaptation of imperial missionary activity and, in doing so, to understate the other more 'internationalist' frames of reference through which Christian Aid and its participants understood the work that they did.

Like Oxfam and War on Want, Christian Aid started out working in post-war European relief. The scale of post-war reconstruction was immense. Bombing created widespread homelessness, over twelve million displaced persons needed repatriation, and the redrawing of boundaries in Eastern Europe in the second half of 1945 had created millions of refugees in need of food, clothes, and housing. Refugee work was the cause through which Christian Aid established itself as a key player among British humanitarian organisations. With Janet Lacey at the helm, Christian Aid supported the United Nations Relief and Rehabilitation Administration's (UNRRA) work with refugees, sending relief teams overseas and finding sponsors for those refugees who were accepted for resettlement.[17] UN-organised World Refugee Year (1959–60) was the first major campaign for Christian Aid Week. Externally funded promotional material for this campaign boosted public awareness of Christian Aid's work and, by the early 1960s, Christian Aid Week was seen as a regular fixture in the humanitarian calendar. The total funds raised during the third and fourth Christian Aid Weeks represented a dramatic increase in the organisation's revenue (from £90,000 in 1958 to £253,729 in 1959 and £600,000 in 1960).

In the mid-1950s, in close association with the Council for British Missionary Societies, the BCC set out a policy for action that reaffirmed their early European objectives while also extending their field of action to a global scale. While many members of the RCS had imagined European involvement as a move away from the Empire and Commonwealth, neither the BCC nor Christian Aid regarded the two geographical fields as in competition with one another. In the organisation's second decade, the internationalism that they encouraged was refracted through both European and imperial lenses. That said, the events and processes of decolonisation became an increasingly important backdrop to the organisation's relief work in this period, repeatedly calling attention to Britain's global role, and to the role of the churches in that rapidly shifting international context.

Janet Lacey's discussion of the Suez Crisis in her memoir *A Cup of Water* illustrates some of these resonances. For Lacey, the events in 1956 provided a crystallising moment in the way that she thought about Britain's international responsibilities. On the evening of the 31 October she sat next to the radio in a friend's flat in snowy Geneva and waited for the international news. For two days the world press had been full of the Suez Crisis and Hungarian Revolution; that night was no different. Lacey listened to leader of the Labour opposition Hugh Gaitskell's passionate condemnation of Eden's decision to attack Egypt without the support of the United Nations. She listened to cries of anguish from Hungarians screaming 'come now – we can't last much longer' as shots and explosions sounded in the background. And she sat in frozen horror wanting to 'tear the radio from its socket with the rage of frustration that there was nothing [she] could do for these people killing each other'.[18]

That day was a potentially difficult day for anyone to be British abroad, but it had been particularly hard for Lacey, who was representing Christian Aid at a meeting of the World Council of Churches Refugee Committee. She felt humiliated by Britain's actions in Egypt and, as news spread of the attack on Port Said, found it hard to look her international colleagues in the eye. While some in Britain found Suez embarrassing because it revealed the nation's dwindling global power, for Lacey it was a symbol of skewed priorities. At the same time that British and French armies attacked Egypt, Hungarian freedom fighters were crying for help that they would not receive. Britain did lift restrictions on refugee immigration to allow approximately fifteen thousand Hungarians into the United Kingdom between October and the end of that year, but their inaction when it was needed most was a bitter pill for Lacey to swallow. For Christian Aid, humanitarian objectives should have trumped attempts to preserve imperial power.

By the mid-1960s, the profile of Christian Aid's work was considerably different to that of its early years. The organisation now spoke in broad terms about global need, adding a religious gloss to the emerging tropes of international development discourse when they stated that, 'Although, to our shame, there are many earthly reasons, there is not one heavenly reason why sixty per cent of the world's population is without sufficient means of sustaining life.'[19] By 1964, seven years after the first Christian Aid Week, the organisation's project expenditure was heavily weighted towards former colonies, particularly those Africa.[20] As the geographical reach of Christian Aid shifted from Europe to the Third World, the organisation's focus also began to move away from refugee work and towards development initiatives instead. This transformation was encouraged in part by their participation in the development-focused FFHC; £572,271 – over half of the organisation's expenditure in 1962 – went towards agricultural schemes in Uganda, Northern and Southern Rhodesia, Nigeria, Madagascar, Pakistan, India, Sarawak, and Korea.[21] But there were two other important contexts to this transition.

First, the processes of decolonisation created humanitarian crises that exposed Christian Aid to the political and military dimensions of imperial decline and provided opportunities for the organisation to expand its work. Lacey oversaw Christian Aid's involvement in a series of imperial aftermaths: the crisis in Congo that followed Belgium's rapid retreat in 1960; the provision of relief to Algerians in the bitter winter months following the ceasefire of the war with France – a conflict Lacey described as 'one of the bloodiest episodes of the post-colonial era'; and the long term involvement with 'victims' of the Mau Mau uprising in Kenya.[22] Second, decolonisation changed the dynamics of the international Christian community to which Christian Aid belonged. As was taking place at the UN and within the New Commonwealth, the balance of membership to the World Council of Churches – to which the BCC belonged – shifted towards the 'Third World' in the decades following the Second World War. As newly independent countries joined the Council, the prominence of 'Third World' issues, in particular racial discrimination and support for liberation movements, also increased. As a Christian Outlook broadcast on the BBC explained, the needs of countries were being more dramatically projected to the world as they gained independence than they had been under colonial rule.[23] Decolonisation not only had a clear impact on the operational decisions made by Christian Aid, it also affected how the organisation sought to demonstrate the importance of its work to the British public.

The death of Christian missions and the rise of imperial critiques

Christian Aid may have started life as a relief agency in war-ravaged Europe, but it was also keen to lay claim to a much longer history of religious international intervention. This had important implications for how supporters conceptualised their relationship to the declining empire. Speaking in a BBC radio broadcast in 1963, William Clark told audiences that it was in fact missionaries who 'were the first form of Christian Aid, and indeed usually the first form of British technical assistance in developing countries'.[24] A pamphlet published by Christian

Aid on the politics of aid described how missionary societies had worked for 250 years to see that 'schools, hospitals and agricultural projects were part of the "new life" promised in the gospel'.[25] As Lacey saw it, these societies were the 'the real pioneers of the service agencies'.[26]

Much like the UK National Committee for the Freedom from Hunger Campaign had appropriated 300 years of imperial administrative expertise to explain Britain's unique ability to contribute to the development movement, so Christian Aid aligned itself with a long history of missionary work in order to claim seniority and experience in the crowded humanitarian arena. Supporters were reminded that 'the Churches are not just starting from scratch in this field', while Lacey acknowledged that 'without the overseas expertise of the Missionaries, it would have been difficult for the Christian Service Agencies to have made anything like the large contribution to world need which they have been privileged to do'.[27] Missionary networks were crucial to Christian Aid's expansion as an international development organisation. Their early work in Kenya, for example, was carried out through connections with missionary organisations and existing regional charities such as the Christian Council of Kenya and the Women's Association, Maendeleo Ya Wanawake.[28] But these connections entangled the organisation with imperial legacies in ways that required careful attention and negotiation.

While Christian Aid was happy to claim experience based on a long history of missionary work, in practice it often worked to differentiate itself from the contemporary missionary movement, particularly as the idea of the overseas mission became increasingly difficult to justify. In 1957 Max Warren, General Secretary of the Church Missionary Society, warned that much was said 'about foreign missions being a form of cultural or even spiritual imperialism' and many perceived them as 'a survivor of the colonial era'.[29] These concerns had grounding. The relationship between missionaries and empire has always been ambiguous.[30] From a church and missionary point of view, the advance and retreat of British rule had been seen as both a source of, and also a solution to, worldly sin.[31] Religious groups had regularly condemned violent imperial acts, but most also acknowledged the extent to which missionary activity was supported and made possible by imperial infrastructures and colonial presence. By the 1960s, however, the problems that it raised seemed to outweigh the usefulness of this association to Christian Aid.

Christian Aid's approach to the church's imperial past is indicative of the broader reappraisal of missionary work taking place at this time. At the start of the decade, President of the Church Missionary Society, Sir Kenneth Grubb, celebrated the advantage the missionary cause had reaped from its connection to the British Empire, but he also worried that it had become a cause for embarrassment, both at home and overseas. In the context of decolonisation, this embarrassment seemed somewhat inevitable; as Grubb observed, 'when those who organised the colonial society and those who preached the Heavenly society arrived on the same ship and formed part of the same civilizing enterprise there was naturally some confusion amongst the recipients of their attentions'.[32] By the 1960s, the church was under increasing pressure to adapt to demands for independence. As Stockwell has shown, Archbishop Fisher was convinced of the necessity of moving with the 'wind of change' and encouraged the church to pursue its own decolonisation project.[33] The transition from a 'mission' to an 'indigenous' church in Africa often took place in parallel with the process of decolonisation by which colonies became independent nations. As Grubb summarised, with considerable nostalgia, 'the heroic age of the Christian missions is over [...] there was a directness and simplicity about the labours of his predecessors which cannot easily belong to his own, for the world to which he goes out has changed'.[34]

Gone were career missionaries and opportunities for 'glittering careers with a governor's plumed hat at the end of the avenue' and in their place came aid workers, relief agencies and short-term volunteers. The relationships that developed between these different forms of intervention – between the old and the new – could often be productive, but rapid change also created tension. While missionary-based agencies struggled to fundraise and recruit in this period, church-based humanitarian organisations such as Christian Aid were clearly thriving – so much so that Max Warren worried that the mission was being subsumed into the provision of overseas aid and relief to African people.[35] Hugh Sampson, Christian Aid's publicity officer, observed that the missionary societies had a traditional suspicion and jealousy of Christian Aid.[36] This was often focused on the perceived paucity of religion in Christian Aid's work. Indeed, the BCC attracted criticism from some mission officials for 'sponsoring secular activity under Christian auspices' rather than 'giving the cup of water in Christ's name'.[37]

If, as Trevor Huddleston observed at the end of the decade, missionary work was no longer 'a fashionable thing to emphasise', Christian Aid needed to be careful about how they engaged with this dimension of their 'origin story'.[38] When he took over from Lacey as director in 1968, Alan Brash tried to tackle the awkward relationship by distancing Christian Aid from the ongoing fundraising efforts of missionary societies. He proposed a leaflet entitled 'Missions or Christian Aid or Both?' which outlined what he perceived as the key differences between Christian Aid and the missions. In a tone befitting his name, Brash wanted to ask donors to 'think before [they] give' and 'sort out' their priorities. Unsurprisingly, Sampson, as publicity officer, put a stop to Brash's plan. Not only could this exacerbate the ill feeling between the missions and Christian Aid, he warned, but putting the two in opposition distorted the nature of Christian Aid's own work. Christian Aid had spent nearly half a million pounds on British Missionary Society projects during the Freedom from Hunger Campaign and missionary infrastructure remained a vital part of the organisation's operations.[39]

Entanglement between humanitarian work and missionary infrastructures was not unique to religious humanitarian organisations like Christian Aid. Oxfam was similarly reliant on Christian agencies to distribute relief funds; they made extensive use of the existing networks of the Salvation Army, the United Free Church of Scotland, the Baptist Missionary Society, the Worldwide Evangelisation Crusade, and even the World Council of Churches. But the organisation's secular identity meant that they were under considerably less pressure to publicly address these dimensions of their work. As Cox suggests, their consistent use of secular rhetoric made Oxfam's religious origins invisible to many of its contributors and supporters.[40] In contrast, Christian Aid needed to find a way to acknowledge the legacies and structures associated with colonialism that made its own interventions possible, while also promoting their work as a new way of engaging with the spaces of the former empire. They did this, in part, through engaged and persistent critique of colonialism and the unbalanced power structures inherent within the international aid and development movement.

Christian Aid's political activity needs to be understood as part of a broader shift in British Christianity. As Gerald Parsons describes, in the decades after the Second World War the relationship between religion and politics shifted from one based on consensus to one of confrontation.[41] To date, most work on Christian activism has focused on the Anti-Apartheid Movement and the important role played by 'turbulent priests' like Michael Scott, Trevor Huddleston, and Canon John Collins.[42] But the shift towards confrontation can also be seen across a wider range of social interventions made by the church in this period, including in the work of Christian Aid. Although the development movement cannot be distilled into a single unifying goal or point of conflict, and although it never stirred the same sense of international solidarity as the Anti-Apartheid Movement, Christian humanitarian aid nevertheless became a focal point for politicised debate, much of which was focused on the declining empire.

Speaking to the BBC Home Service for Christian Aid Week in 1963, William Clark told listeners that 'Aid is one of the clichés of politics today. No speech on national purpose is complete without a peroration on the question of aid to underdeveloped countries.'[43] The narratives of British exceptionalism discussed in relation to the FFHC in Chapter 4 would certainly attest to this characterisation, but Clark was keen to emphasise that aid should be about more than clichéd national purpose. 'Aid to developing countries is not just a hobby,' he argued, 'nor is it just a form of conscience money to old colonies, or [sic] is it just a clever man in the cold war, or a form of trade promotion.' His awareness of the potential pitfalls of humanitarian aid within the context of the Cold War and decolonisation was shared by Janet Lacey, who stressed that it would be 'tragic' if recently independent nations were

> forced to accept offers of economic aid with hidden political strings attached, either from the East or the West, before they have time to begin to develop independent political maturity. In moving from one particular kind of colonialism they will perforce take on the mantle of another.[44]

Lacey was at pains to make clear that Christian Aid was not a passive participant in a form of neo-colonialism – a middleman for passing on funds from the wealthy West to the poorer countries of the world. Instead, by working to promote the indigenisation of Christian councils and development staff in newly independent countries, Christian Aid saw itself as an active part of the long-term process of decolonisation.[45]

In 1969, for example, Christian Aid sent a memorandum to each Commonwealth prime minister outlining the role that they felt the Commonwealth ought to be playing in global economic development. The memorandum argued that development required the cooperation of both developed and less developed nations and suggested that 'the Commonwealth provide[d] a unique context in which [this] might be attempted on a large scale'. With its emphasis on cooperation and understanding, this statement is strikingly similar to discourses in play at the RCS at this time: it stresses the exceptionalism of Commonwealth collaboration (as distinct from the aftermaths of other declining empires), while also implying that the Commonwealth might serve as an example to the rest of the world. But whereas members of the RCS were more inclined to emphasise the threads of tradition and kinship that linked the modern Commonwealth to its longer imperial history, Christian Aid took pains to stress that this 'cooperation' needed to be emphatically different from a traditional colonial relationship. In a statement that could be read as both a celebration of the achievements of the New Commonwealth and also a critique of what had gone before, Christian Aid suggested that the Commonwealth 'could demonstrate to the world a pattern of creative cooperation between developed and less developed nations which was free from the taints of exploitation, racism, paternalism and neo-colonialism'.[46]

As described in Chapter 4, Christian Aid's participation in political debate increased significantly at the end of the 1960s. Most significantly, from 1969 onwards it worked with other members of the Voluntary Committee for Overseas Aid and Development to establish Action for World Development, an independent body free of UK charity legislation that focused on activism and lobbying around issues of global justice.[47] For most of the 1960s, however, there were still significant limits to Christian Aid's willingness and ability to engage in critique and activism. These are particularly clear when we compare Christian Aid to the more radicalised protests of the Student Christian Movement, which in the 1960s promoted nationalist resistance movements and forms of popular revolt.[48] Christian Aid did not publicly condone violent struggles; indeed non-British members of the World Council of Churches came under harsh criticism in *The Times* for providing financial aid to violent nationalist groups in Zimbabwe and Mozambique.[49] They did, however, recognise that calls for pacifism needed to be backed with political change. Such an interpretation was in line with the strong fear shared by many church figures at this time that a failure to address the concerns of African nationalists would fatally undermine Christianity within Africa.[50] For the church, ceding authority became a crucial component of maintaining influence.

These ambiguities are borne out in Christian Aid's response to the Mau Mau uprising in Kenya, which Lacey discusses in her memoir published shortly after her retirement as director. In Lacey's opinion, the basic problem in Kenya, and one which the churches had failed to fully address, was not hatred but indifference: 'the multi-racial society desired by the British could only come about when sufficient people on both sides wanted to get to know one another'.[51] This indifference, she argued, set the stage for violent protest against colonial rule. Although Lacey argued that Mau Mau should be understood as a declaration of independence by a people who had 'lost their patience', she made no attempt to either acknowledge or condemn the violent acts committed by British officials during the emergency.[52] While Lacey's conviction that Christian Aid 'must be in a position to fight for the right of man to be free wherever he was' may have echoed the human rights discourses developing at this time, it was not always upheld in the work that Christian Aid carried out in the field.[53] When it came to Mau Mau, there was a significant gap between Lacey's rhetoric and some of the practices facilitated by Christian Aid funding. Most problematic among these were the state-endorsed 'rehabilitation programmes' that involved screening 'loyal Africans' for potential terrorists.[54] The discourse of community development used by Lacey in her 1968 memoir overwrote (or at least overlooked) the practices of social control that Christian Aid money supported in the 1950s.

Discrepancies between the public faces of NGOs and the complex, compromised, and/or misguided work that they carry out in the field are not unusual. But while NGOs' practices clearly have significant consequences for the communities they purport to be helping, they often have little impact on donors' impressions of the NGOs themselves. There was little public discussion of the specifics of Christian Aid's activity in Kenya, suggesting that the broader brush strokes of responsibility, human rights, cooperation, and human need mattered more to the public than the operational decisions made by Christian Aid on the ground. Supporters 'bought in' to the identity that Christian Aid presented to them and trusted that the rest would follow.

Even within this public identity, though, there were limits to Christian Aid's solidarity with those they sought to help. Throughout most of Christian Aid's promotional and archival material, the sense of responsibility that the organisation called upon was a duty of care and not an acceptance of British accountability for the situation prevailing in recently independent nations. This distinction is clear in their discussion of a soil conservation project in Botswana that was funded in association with the FFHC. The report mentioned an article published in the *Guardian* that attributed the country's current poverty to more than sixty years of British colonial neglect. But rather than agreeing with this accusation, Christian Aid actively avoided the issue, concluding that 'whether or not that statement was justified, the fact is that this new member of our Commonwealth of Nations is faced with serious economic problems and is in urgent need of help'.[55] Christian Aid's decision not to assign blame was no doubt influenced by the restrictive role of the Charity Commission and the pressure to retain neutrality. But this persistent focus on the present is nevertheless striking, particularly when contrasted with the strongly held belief at the end of the nineteenth century that Britain needed to make atonement for past evils (especially the slave trade). Speaking in 1885, Prebendary H. W. Webb-Peploe had declared that 'we may ask ourselves whether we are not indebted to every race for some tremendous injuries inflicted in days gone by'.[56] Christian Aid spoke of national responsibility, certainly, but they spoke of a duty to the future rather than atonement for past sins.

While their rhetoric may not have always aligned with their practices, Christian Aid presented itself as an organisation that was sensitive to the complexities of carrying out development work in the context of decolonisation. In taking steps to inform their donor constituency of (some of) the political implications of their participation in humanitarian aid, they provided an important framework for local activity. Janet Lacey's account of the organisation speaks repeatedly of the responsibility of professionalised charities to convey their message to 'ordinary people'. For Lacey, moving on from old imperial systems was as much about attitude as it was about exploitation. As she described, 'Whenever anyone says to me "but you see, I love people", I shudder. It usually means an attitude of paternalism or a form of therapy for overwrought men and women.'[57] Raising money for good causes was not enough; Christian Aid wanted those who gave to give for the right reasons. But the ways in which Christian Aid fostered public engagement in international affairs were shaped as much by the changing national context of Christian participation and worship as they were by the perceived needs of those overseas. As the next section shows, international engagement did not happen in isolation from the rest of associational life.

Changing ideas of Christian citizenship

The British public stopped going to church in unprecedented numbers in the 1960s. Confirmation rates plummeted and, according to Callum Brown, 'the British people stopped absorbing Christianity into their lives'.[58] This might seem then like a bad time to try to mobilise a national Christian charity, particularly one that relied, in the first instance, on the time and financial support of religious people across Britain. But church attendance and worship have only ever been a part of the picture of religious life, and ideas of religious practice were changing in the 1950s and 1960s in ways that intersected with, rather than undermined, the ambitions of Christian Aid. Although the societal pervasiveness of religion in the late nineteenth and early twentieth centuries would never be regained, the rapid growth of Christian Aid is one example of how the institutions, practices, and discourses of the church continued to play a meaningful role in the lives of many Britons.[59] In its first three years the number of villages and local communities participating in Christian Aid Week grew from 316 (in 1957) to 1200 (in 1960) and this figure continued growing throughout the decade.[60] As Jeremy Morris observes, 'it is a strange death that leaves churches amongst the largest voluntary organisations in the country'.[61]

While it may not have marked the death of Christian Britain, the apparent 'crisis' of Christianity did prompt many to re-evaluate the church's role in British life. For conservative members of the church this was a time to hunker down, embrace tradition, and defend the moral condition of Britain against the societal changes brought about by the affluence of the 1950s and early 1960s. Public debates centred on sexual permissiveness, obscenity, and moral decline. The Lady Chatterley trial in 1960, the 'holy rage' over a naked woman at a literary conference and Profumo scandal in 1963, and Mary Whitehouse's ongoing campaign against sex and nudity on British television all attracted media attention.[62] But despite the impassioned letters to *The Times* that scandals such as these could attract, the societal influence of these conservative sections of the church was declining. This was reflected, for example, in the changing of criminal laws against abortion, homosexuality, and gambling.

Morally conservative Christians did not represent the full spectrum of religious participation, however, and the haemorrhage of people from organised Christianity also prompted other kinds of reflection and response. For many, the conservative preoccupation with moral standards came at the expense of real Christian action. In the House of Lords in January 1960, Lord Winterton complained that the church spent a great deal of time in discussing questions of divorce and remarriage, 'almost to the exclusion' of factors that seemed to him more important from a Christian point of view: slaughter on the roads, refugee problems and the appalling amount of crime.[63] In the 1960s the issue of Christian social responsibility was at the heart of debates about secularisation, pluralism, and religious change. Increasing emphasis was placed on active Christian citizenship across the denominations. This was, in part, the continuation of a long-term growth in liberal Protestantism, quietly on the rise since the inter-war period and focused on action rather than theology. More fully, it represents the politicisation of a specific form of benevolent humanistic Christianity that took place in the late 1950s and throughout the 1960s.[64]

Christian protestors sought to bring a set of moral beliefs and community back to the centre of British politics which, they felt, had become 'absent from more mainstream religious theories and practices'.[65] The BCC was at the centre of this transformation. By 1967, in response to criticisms that the ecumenical movement had 'become part of the whole attempt of the churches to escape facing up to realities', Kenneth Sansbury told readers of *The Times* that the BCC had brought together Christians 'to do some hard thinking about such things as apartheid in South Africa, British responsibility in Rhodesia, the control of nuclear weapons, Vietnam, [and] immigrants'. Their purpose was not escape, he argued, 'but a more effective Christian witness in a strife-ridden and perplexed world'.[66] As Sansbury's list makes clear, circumstances relating to decolonisation dominated the BCC's concerns.

Christian Aid was at the heart of the BCC's internationalist vision, but debates about Christian responsibility also impacted the wider humanitarian sector. Meredith Veldman suggests that the 'Christian witness' flourished outside institutional Christianity in this period.[67] Christians were certainly not limited to the opportunities provided by religious institutions; many carried out their religious duties through support for secular humanitarian organisations including Amnesty International, War on Want, Oxfam, the Anti-Apartheid Movement and Shelter.[68] Holger Nehring's work on Christian Campaign for Nuclear Disarmament (CND) protestors between 1957 and 1964 shows how 'religion was no longer linked to the church as an institution, but focused on the distinction between "political" and "unpolitical"'.[69] The Christian subgroup of CND saw its task as not only working for unilateral disarmament but also leading the church back to its rightful mission. While more left-wing than most, their views were nevertheless representative of a growing belief that the social and political implications of Christian faith required more explicit expression within 1960s Britain.[70]

By 1968, Christian Aid made its political intent, directed not only at governments but also at the fundraising public, an explicit part of their remit. Speaking to the BBC, Alan Brash explained how Christian and national responsibility were intertwined: 'To cut off individual and church response from involvement in the national response', he warned, 'is to make ourselves increasingly irrelevant – of fiddling not while Rome burns but while the world falls apart.' Christian Aid saw it as its own failure if the nation ceased to care. This decision was emphasised in a 1969 report that described the 'renewed emphasis on our foundation in Jesus Christ on the one hand and the stressing of the challenge for a total response, by individual, church and nation on the other'.[71] By working towards political, ecumenical, and humanitarian ends, Christian Aid sought to provide leadership for the nation's Christian conscience. Working through the World Council of Churches (of which the BCC was a member), ideals of Christian citizenship were extended to require individuals to act as members of an international as well as national community.

It is important to note that this was not first time that the ecumenical movement was thinking in international terms; indeed, there were long antecedents to the ideas of international Christian witness that Christian Aid promoted. Ideas of universal brotherhood and sisterhood stretch back to the discourses of the anti-slavery movements in the late eighteenth century where campaign slogans imagined fundraisers and victims as part of an international community (albeit one that was strictly ordered by racial hierarchies). Fresh attempts at more equal

Christian partnership took place at the end of the nineteenth century and continued into the inter-war period. The World Young Women's Christian Association, for example, was founded in 1894 to coordinate national activity and foster a 'public conscience such as shall strengthen all the forces which are working for the promotion of peace and understanding between classes and races'.[72] This work expanded during the inter-war period when Willoughby Dickinson, one of the earliest supporters of the League of Nations, founded the World Alliance for Promoting International Friendship through the Churches. Prevailing scholarly interpretations of internationalism are secular, but work on Dickinson has revealed important links between progressive politics and ecumenical internationalism in the inter-war period.[73]

Although it established important precedents, inter-war ecumenical internationalism remained an elite rather than a popular project. In its early years the movement failed to establish much in the way of a grass-roots reception and few local councils were successfully encouraged to straddle the Free Church/Anglican divide.[74] Lacey argued that the official ecumenical organisations were becoming irrelevant to contemporary British society and she was vocal in criticising the 'narrowness' of those she saw as 'obsessed' with institutional affairs.[75] By contrast, Christian Aid felt that they 'perhaps more than any other Christian organisation [were] able to be a bridge between the Church and the community'.[76] Indeed, it was not until Christian Aid set out a clear humanitarian agenda that the BCC was finally able to become a more successful – albeit more narrowly focused – means to ecumenical international engagement. Reflecting on its ecumenical impact, a report on an early Christian Aid Week celebrated the fact that 'some local Councils of Churches will never be the same again' because they found in Christian Aid 'new fellowship and fresh impetus in their overall activities'.[77]

As well as breathing new life into existing religious communities, Christian Aid also saw itself as part of a broader effort to rehabilitate the image of the church in British public life. This was, in part, a pragmatic necessity for an organisation with an explicit religious remit. 'If', as Lacey warned, 'a door was slammed in a collector's face because the word Christian was on the envelope, then there was something wrong with the image of the Church.'[78] Scepticism towards the church – or towards religion more broadly – was likely to result in scepticism towards associated organisations. But it is also indicative of Christian Aid's belief that humanitarianism had a unique ability to act as a recruitment tool for the Christian churches. As a report on local activity described, 'many people not in active touch with a local Christian community have first been put in touch with the work of the Churches because they have cared for the hungry and the outcast and have helped Christian Aid'.[79] The following report on attendees of a local meeting illustrates the enthusiasm with which outsiders were greeted by Christian Aid organisers:

> a local resident who is a highly educated and qualified (and rich!) consulting engineer, who brought his wife and sister (expensive tweeds and pearls); the headmaster of the local primary school (an amateur cricketer of some repute and clearly a strong personality); and a large fully bearded sergeant of the newly amalgamated Devon and Cornwall Constabulary; all very different men of considerable local influence who never go to Church.[80]

Outsiders such as these were valuable not just for the money in their banks, but also for the networks of influence and experience to which they could grant Christian Aid access.

Religious networks of international experience

If Christian Aid's humanitarian and ecumenical objectives provided the discursive framework for local activity – a vocabulary of shared Christian duty, national responsibility, and, at times, solidarity with the political objectives of those in newly independent countries – then local networks of participants provided the organising structures through which individuals came into contact with the outside world. Christian Aid acted as a crucial nodal point at which the diverse life experiences of members of the religious community intersected. While we cannot easily recreate what took place at local meetings, building an understanding of the diversity of Christian Aid's membership does give us a basis from which to imagine the different kinds of conversations that could have taken place. There were bound to be differences, for example, between a community whose vicar was 'born and bred' in the local area and one such as Child Okeford in Dorset, whose Anglican rector was an ex-Royal Marines Commando Chaplain with personal experience of the Borneo jungle and 'some knowledge of the lives and problems of the hill peoples of that country'.[81] Meetings attended entirely by 'old ladies' – as many often were – likely differed from those in Burnham-on-Sea attended by a university-qualified agriculturalist who had spent time with VSO in Kenya, or those in Plymouth where a specialist on eye disease who had studied trachoma in Nigeria spoke about conditions from 'personal first hand knowledge'.[82]

Existing patterns of religious associational life had a significant impact on local Christian Aid activity. Women had dominated the social and communal dimensions of Christianity since the early twentieth century and this dynamic continued into the post-war period.[83] As a result, Christian Aid's community organisers typically came from a relatively small cohort. In the South West, for example, 'the majority were ladies of mature years who [were] regular church goers and [could] be relied on to support an effort of this nature', while in Hampshire the organisation of Christian Aid Week was 'left to the single handed efforts of one old lady'.[84] These women were essential to the local organisation of Christian Aid meetings and activities.

While for some supporters Christian Aid was a vital window out on to the wider world, for other more mobile members it was just one more dimension of their existing international engagements. These included men such as Robin Dixon whose experiences of travelling and working in Africa in the 1950s encouraged him, once back in England, to work for the BCC organising Christian Aid Week. In 1953 Dixon had decided to cycle around the world with a friend and ended up in Kenya, initially working as a printing estimator and then on a ranch as part of a multiracial staff where he witnessed the murder of a Mau Mau man who had stolen a prize animal.[85] Dixon's 'lived' experience of colonial and racial power hierarchies was a world away from the parish lives of many Christian Aid supporters. Despite being in the minority, these mobile members of Christian Aid acted as important conduits for first-hand information – much like the missionary or colonial administrator home on furlough in the nineteenth century.

Because of the variability of informal local networks of first-hand experience Christian Aid also encouraged groups to enrich their local activities by seeking information from established lending bodies such as the Commonwealth Institute, missionary societies and the Overseas Development Institute. The lists of speakers that Christian Aid drew up not only reveal the broad networks of specifically religious mobility to which the organisation had access, but also illustrate the multiple ways in which decolonisation affected church and religious life. As with the Colonial Civil Service, decolonisation forced many missionaries to leave posts across the British Empire, contributing to the broader movement of return-migration discussed in Chapters 1 and 2. The expatriate experience of these missionaries was not uniform, but it shaped the domestic experience of decolonisation in significant ways. Missionaries redeployed their energies in a range of geographic and employment fields: many returned to posts in small, rural English parishes; others travelled to evangelise in communist countries in Eastern Europe; some took up posts working with immigrant congregations in English cities; while others became involved in social activism such as the Anti-Apartheid Movement.

Christian Aid's lists of recommended speakers provide another example of the ongoing entanglement between humanitarian and missionary networks. They included Canon Wittenbach, the Candidates' Secretary for the Church Missionary Society who was recommended for his 'lengthy experience of Asia'; Rev. MacKenzie, who had extensive experience of nationalist movements in Central and East Africa; Eva Auerbach, who returned to England to work as a chaplain for overseas students after time as a missionary in India; and missionaries from industrial missions in Nigeria and Northern Rhodesia who moved into work in English industrial towns such as Birmingham and Sheffield.[86] Through Christian Aid, these diverse religious repatriate trajectories intersected and fed into one another.

Not all speakers had missionary backgrounds, however, and religious networks were not the only networks that Christian Aid tapped into. The recommendation of speakers from the Movement for Colonial Freedom, the Anti-Apartheid Movement, Amnesty International, the Student Christian Movement, and CND also affirmed Christian Aid's openness to more radical manifestations of Christian citizenship. One list even recommended Irene Jacoby from the Friend's International Centre for her 'good contacts with communist youth organisations'.[87] Local organisers were free to choose which speakers to invite, but were they to invite one of these speakers we can assume that they were open to the possibilities for political engagement that Christian Aid provided.

These networks had implications for how Christian Aid organised their supporters and helped to frame their relationships with recipients of aid. Speaking in 1966, before he took over from Lacey as director, Alan Brash argued that 'it is important to relate opinions about development and political goals to the aspirations of those whose development we are seeking'. To achieve this understanding, he suggested that it would be useful for local Christian Aid committees to make contact with 'militant "Black Power" groups' within Britain'.[88] This suggestion is striking for a number of reasons. First, it acknowledged members of the black population in Britain as political agents rather than simply as either immigrant workers or Commonwealth students in need of a warm welcome and a cup of tea. Second, it described these militant groups as a 'valuable stimulus' rather than a threat and, in doing so, granted legitimacy to their objectives and approaches. Third, it blurred the neat binaries of home/away and giver/receiver usually reinforced by humanitarian aid, emphasising instead a sense of global interconnectedness and partnership.

By engaging with these Black Power communities Christian Aid participated in a wider international movement in which African-American influences intersected with British Caribbean and Afro-British politics, transcending international borders. Where the WI tended to segregate Commonwealth hospitality from international aid, Christian Aid's efforts linked overseas need and political struggle to racial tension within the UK. This was facilitated by the BCC, which explicitly linked domestic race relations to their overseas work, warning that 'so long as race relations within this country are seen to be unsatisfactory the sincerity of our professions overseas will be called into doubt'.[89] In 1969 a decision was made to commit a maximum of 2 per cent of Christian Aid's resources to domestic projects with migrants – one funded scheme included a multiracial 'coffee-bar' youth club. Although Christian Aid remained an overwhelmingly white organisation, these efforts show some parallels with the more radical Anti-Apartheid Movement, which brought together coalitions of black and white activists, many of who were practising Christians.[90]

Brash's discussion of Black Power also disrupted prevailing assumptions about international development as the preserve of the white male expert, but it was not the only way that Christian Aid challenged this perception. The opportunities for women that the organisation provided – at a local and national level – also sent an important message about who could speak on international issues. Janet Lacey's own career trajectory is illustrative not only of the diverse life experiences that Christian Aid accommodated but also of the different routes to international engagement made possible through religious humanitarian engagement. When she took over as director of Christian Aid, aged 45, Lacey had no experience working outside of Europe. Born in Sunderland in 1903, Lacey grew up in a poor Methodist family. Her father, who was much older than her mother, died when she was 9 and at 15 she was sent by her mother to live with her aunt in County Durham. They had a fraught relationship – the aunt disapproved of Lacey's involvement in drama and of the 'intellectuals' she befriended at the local Wesleyan Church – but her time there was an important building block towards her eventual career. During the 1926 strike, Lacey worked with a keen socialist in nearby pit villages. She would 'sit in a miner's kitchen and talk books and politics while he bathed in the tin tub in front of the fire'. Shaped by her exposure to the miserable poverty of the strike, and eager to escape the claustrophobic atmosphere of her aunt's house, Lacey applied to be a trainee youth leader at the Kendal YWCA. From there she went on to work as a community organiser for the YWCA and YMCA in Dagenham.

In 1946, Janet Lacey travelled to Germany with the YMCA to develop educational programmes for demobilising British soldiers. She was 43 years old and it was her track record of religious community work, rather than any previous experience overseas, that qualified her for this job. Confronted with 'suffering beyond description', Lacey vowed to help in whatever way she could.[91] In 1948 she took over as director of Christian Aid (then called Inter Church Aid) to organise their contribution to European reconstruction. By building on a background in community work – as well as the belligerence needed to get things done – Lacey was able to take charge of a large religious organisation at a time when the church hierarchy was overwhelmingly male and offered few opportunities for women to hold positions of power or responsibility. In her two decades as director she travelled widely in Europe as well as in the declining and former empire, particularly Africa, which she visited fifteen times.[92] Lacey's international experiences while working for Christian Aid show how the impact of decolonisation could reverberate beyond those upper-middle class sections of society traditionally seen as being the only ones with anything at stake in the end of empire. They also sent an important message to Christian Aid's mostly female local organisers that the field of international development could be a 'woman's world'. This was similar to the example the WI's mobile leadership set for its members in this period.

The humdrum internationalism of parish life

By its own account, to be successful, Christian Aid needed not only to raise money to support projects overseas but also to 'devise a method whereby the ordinary mortal in his or her daily living can relate to the task of world development'.[93] The importance of the local church community to Christian Aid – as both the location of ecumenical activity and as its main source of finance – prompted them to supervise local activity closely. Touring Area Secretaries encouraged local participants to support the campaign in the 'right way', according to the expectations and ideology of the central administration. But putting systems of supervision in place by no means guaranteed that local religious communities would toe the party line. As Reverend L. Coates, Area Secretary for East and West Yorkshire summarised somewhat pessimistically, 'Christian Aid work is rather like the proverbial curate's egg – "good in parts".'[94] Where the previous section provided a picture of the possibilities for communication and critique offered by religious networks, this section assesses how participants made use of, or made sense of, the opportunities that Christian Aid provided. Christian Aid may have ascribed great importance to notions of Christian responsibility and social commitment, but these were not necessarily the same ideals that guided parishioners' participation.

Each Christian Aid Week the BBC Home Service broadcast a series of programmes in which representatives of Christian Aid gave sermons and interviews to promote the cause. One of the programmes Christian Aid prepared for broadcast described what the organisation meant to parish life. It started out describing the once parochial nature of Christian charity:

> In the old days of Barchester, Christian aid was just helping in the village. The parson visited, his wife took the calves-foot jelly, and the squire dipped into his pocket – if he was that sort of squire. The next village was ten thousand miles away over the hill, as remote as the man in the moon.[95]

This isolation was contrasted with the present day when 'the magic mirrors of television and photography' and the 'magic carpet of modern transport' put the English parish in touch with the 'needs of all God's children'. Although this juxtaposition emphasises the pervasive sense of connectedness that characterised humanitarian activity in the 1960s, it also obscures the way in which missionary activity had already breached the isolation of the parish, connecting its members to the outside world since the eighteenth century. The financial support and manpower demanded by the missionary project had always required missionaries to instil their cause into the religious life of local congregations. Under constant pressure to justify their work to supporters at home, missions were dependent on their ability to penetrate grass-roots society.[96] Susan Thorne shows how even in the most isolated rural villages the colonies could be encountered on a regular basis through the local institutions of organised religion.[97] Missionary sermons and publications mapped the Empire for their public, furnishing them with representations of people of different countries and shaping ideas of race, gender, and nation.

Magic carpets and mirrors may not have been new to parish life in the 1960s, but they had come to reflect a different image of the church's mission. As Andrew Porter contends, 'the manner in which missionaries both experienced empire and interpreted that experience for others at home and overseas varied under the shifting influences of racial perceptions, denominational politics, gender, class and theological fashion'.[98] Whereas, in the nineteenth century, Africa had been most frequently imagined as a 'heathen nation' 'shrouded in the gloom of barbarism', the key motif of the 1960s was hunger.[99] Even within Christian discourse the key needs of the majority world were understood to be material rather than spiritual. The traditional lanternslide lecture was replaced by a screening of Christian Aid's film *The Long March*, the missionary was replaced by an aid worker or development expert, and the Christian explorer by a young VSO volunteer.

But for some, despite these changes, the imagined relationship between metropole and periphery still bore many of the hallmarks of earlier missionary and imperial traditions. The same BBC broadcast on parish life gave an account of Christian Aid that differed dramatically from the sober and politically engaged pronouncements of the central administration discussed in the previous sections:

> English people find it astonishingly difficult to see beyond the Parish pump and so we try to look outward at the big world. We have visiting speakers to talk about outlandish places that I can't find on the map. We have a display at the back of our church: photographs of hospitals in unpronounceable parts of Africa, and of black doctors in white coats peering into highly technical microscopes. It is all very humdrum but occasionally we have our moments. Inter-Church Aid sent us a black priest from Africa for a month. He was supposed to learn from us but really we learned from him. This calm and courteous fellow Christian with frizzy hair that one wanted to stroke. This man of God one jump from the stone age, whose friends had just been murdered in a tribal massacre. This is what he wrote after he left us, I can hear his voice, smooth as black velvet, struggling with our outlandish English.[100]

This is clearly a different repertoire of representations to those that made up the daily diet of the missionary public in the nineteenth century; gone, for example, are descriptions of the 'horrible wickedness' and 'depraved character' of 'wretched men'.[101] Nevertheless, the account reveals a lingering colonial mind-set: Africa is exoticised as outlandish and unpronounceable; the black priest, 'one jump from the stone age', is situated in a different temporality to that of the English parish; and his physical difference emphasised through reference to his frizzy hair, black skin, and 'black velvet' voice. By describing how the parish 'learned from' the 'calm and courteous' African, the broadcast drew on a long tradition of the noble savage. Whereas other Christian Aid material also represented interaction between Christian brothers as a learning experience, it was more likely to emphasise the equal partnership of each encounter. This broadcast offered praise to the point of being patronising.

It is difficult to reconcile this kind of language with either the politically engaged analyses of the central organisation, or our knowledge of the diversity of first-hand experience within some local Christian Aid activity. But perhaps it better captures what Christian Aid offered to those living in more isolated communities. This was an account of fascination, emphasising the novelty and excitement of experiencing 'the other' at first hand and describing how these interactions broke the 'humdrum' of parish life. It willingly admitted the less than wholly philanthropic role that curiosity played in engagements with the outside world, and was unapologetic about the fact that some of the appeal of meeting an African priest might be getting to touch his frizzy hair. As well as expressing the novelty of international engagement, it also emphasised the importance of entertainment and sociability to parish fundraising:

> We run a fete. Hoop-la, Punch and Judy and stalwart ladies doing cream teas in plastic dishes. We have the fun, and people who haven't got hospitals get the money – an excellent arrangement.[102]

In this account there is no mention of the Christian duty to give and little sense of the Christian sacrifice that saturated committee files. If parishes were to use their leisure time to raise money for hospitals overseas, they were going to have fun while they did it. Similar principles have guided much of the associational activity discussed in this book. In many cases, the social elements of fundraising for Christian Aid look to have been more important to participants than the cause itself. It was perfectly possible to raise money for Christian Aid and know little about the cause, since being informed was not the same as being motivated. As one reporter suggested, some of the areas with the best fundraising had little in the way of an educational programme.[103]

The importance of sociability and entertainment is evident in the typical events that made up Christian Aid Week activities. This was the focal point of the Christian Aid calendar – the week in which the most fundraising activity took place, the most money was raised, and the most effort was made to promote the cause to the secular community. At its most basic a typical local Christian Aid Week included a public display of photographs, a public meeting and/or film screening designed to inform the community of Christian Aid's purpose, and house-to-house collections to raise funds. Christian Aid also encouraged a wider range of participatory fundraising activities and sent out a detailed list of suggested activities to all local area committees.[104] The events put on in Ruscombe and Twyford, Berkshire, for Christian Aid Week in 1966 are indicative of how this typical programme could be supplemented with additional activities and scheduled across local community venues, associations and denominations:

Saturday	CHILDREN'S FILM SHOW, New Junior School
	REFUGEE LUNCH, St. John's Convent, Kiln Green
Sunday	UNITED SERVICE, St. Mary's, Twyford
Monday	WHIST DRIVE, Church Hall, Ruscombe
Tuesday	CHRISTIAN AID SALE, The Orchards, London

	Road
	CAKE BRING & BUY, Malvern Way Play Group
Wednesday	BUFFET SUPPER BRING & BUY, Congregational Hall
Thursday	UNITED ASCENSION DAY SERVICE, St. John's Convent, Kiln Green
	BINGO, Station Hotel, Twyford (PENN association)
Friday	'MESSIAH', Choral Society, St. Mary's Twyford
	BARBEQUE, Youth Club, Polehampton School Canteen
Saturday	COFFEE MORNING BRING & BUY, Ruscombe House
	JUMBLE SALE, Church Hall, Ruscombe
Sunday	VSO TALK – AID IN ZAMBIA, Colour photos by Anton Schooley, Church Hall, Ruscombe
All Week	EXHIBITION ON NIGERIA BY CHILDREN OF POLEHAMPTON SCHOOL, Court Room (next to library).[105]

While sociability was at the heart of this programme, the events listed also offered a range of more 'involved' ways for people to participate. The religious services provided opportunities for the congregation to reflect on the link between Christian duty and humanitarian aid; the VSO talk and Nigeria exhibition may have engaged those interested in the educational material that Christian Aid could provide; and the refugee lunch provided an opportunity for supporters to show empathy towards those in need through a small act of symbolic denial. Not part of this particular programme, but an integral part of many Christian Aid Weeks was the sponsored walk, an activity that tied in neatly with the title of Christian Aid's touring promotional film *The Long March* (seen by thousands over a four-year period). Some 26,000 young people participated in 97 sponsored walks during Christian Aid Week in 1967.[106] In Rotherham, 1400 walkers registered to watch *The Long March* before being dropped off by coach for a 30-mile walk on the Yorkshire Moors.[107] Events like this combined the presentation of emotive information about the needs of those in developing countries with a shared act of fundraising that was both social and physically challenging. In this way, they were more closely aligned to the rhetoric of service and sacrifice espoused by the central organisation.

Christian Aid in the parish was shaped as much by local rivalries, individual enthusiasts, and incompetent committee members as it was by the planning and ideology of the central administration. Poor attendance at one meeting was attributed to the bad weather and a '"rival" meeting (plus apple pie contest) by the local Women's Institute'.[108] When baked goods were not luring people away from Christian Aid, community groups might be let down by their own rectors, ministers, and vicars. Little was achieved in Glastonbury where the dean, Hugh Knapman, insisted on remaining Christian Aid Secretary despite the fact that 'his greatest interest seem[ed] to be keeping up the tradition of sending to Her Majesty the Queen a spray of the famous thorn tree once a year'.[109] Area Secretaries vented frustration about those who disliked committee work and formal group action on principle, those who took issue with Christian Aid itself, and those who simply did not get along – the Anglican rector and Methodist minister in Shepton Mallet were described as having 'a remarkable facility for upsetting each other'.[110]

Christian Aid Week also needed to fit in alongside local and national campaigns for a whole host of causes. For some this was simply par for the course and many chose to contribute to multiple campaigns throughout the year, seeing little contradiction in the aims of various humanitarian organisations. Others took to heart the fact that they had to compete for attention. Janet Lacey might have been firm friends with Oxfam director Leslie Kirkby, but not all Christian Aid members felt the same spirit of cooperation. Some were exasperated by Oxfam fundraisers who 'quite shamelessly appeal to the churches around Christian Aid Week period'.[111] In Haslemere representatives of other humanitarian organisations repeatedly called down the wrath of Area Secretary and local resident Margaret Bywater. She reported how a man from Oxfam had made himself known to the local clergy by asking if he could help with Christian Aid Week. As Bywater described, 'that was his way of introducing himself – very subtle and disarming and clever. It ended by the Anglicans doing a giant jumble sale for Oxfam which raised about £150.'[112] Bywater also reported that 'a local committee of Help the Aged has been formed to help raise £2000 for Tibetan Refugees. As usual the clergy and the church people of the town have been roped in. [...] They are actually running a Gift Shop in Haslemere THIS week (Christian Aid Week) and have appealed to all the churches for help with goods and service.' Mrs Bywater's husband refused to make the announcement in their church, an act that does not seem in particularly Christian spirits.[113]

Such petty disputes may seem a world away from the discourses of Christian duty and critiques of colonial world systems that characterised the central administration and national public identity of Christian Aid, but they are crucial to understanding the organisation's significance. It is hard to deny that rivalry and gossip are signs of parochialism. But in the case of Christian Aid, the parochial was not necessarily opposed or resistant to the international. Rather than thinking about parochialism and internationalism as necessarily competing for attention we must recognise that the parochial in fact provided the very structures through which the international entered into the quotidian discourses and practices of everyday life. The very same people who gossiped and competed also made up the crucial local networks through which Christian Aid was able to thrive. Thought about in this way, the Cotswolds Area Secretary's report that 'London is a long way away and ninety percent of the Christian Aid supporters in my area are quite uninterested in what goes on there' should not be seen as evidence of a community distancing itself from the wider world, but merely from London.[114] This crucial distinction makes clear that experiences of the declining empire were not necessarily filtered through the capital; like the WI and Rotary, Christian Aid facilitated the formation of relationships between Britain and the world through local and often rural connecting points.

Christian Aid could not have functioned without being embedded in British associational life and it is precisely through embracing this associational world that the organisation was able to bring so many Christians into contact with the declining and former empire. It is not just in the institutional discourses of an organisation that expanded its international remit and changed the shape of religious humanitarian intervention, therefore, but also in the 'humdrum' of associational life that surrounded Christian Aid in the parish that we can and should read the organisation's impact on Britain's internal globalisation. Christian Aid used humanitarian and Christian discourses of need, brotherhood, and religious duty alongside networks of mobile speakers with 'first-hand' experience to bring the shrinking world into local communities across Britain. None of this would have been possible without the practical efforts of individual participants.

Notes

1 Sarah Stockwell, '"Splendidly leading the way"? Archbishop Fisher and decolonisation in British colonial Africa', *Journal of Imperial and Commonwealth History*, 36:3 (2008), 545–64.
2 Susan Thorne, *Congregational Missions and the Making of an Imperial Culture in Nineteenth Century Britain* (Stanford University Press: Stanford, 1999).
3 Hall, *Civilising Subjects*, p. 3.
4 Jeffrey Cox, 'From the empire of Christ to the Third World: Religion and the experience of empire in the twentieth century', in Thompson (ed.), *Britain's Experience of Empire*, p. 83.
5 Jane Garnett *et al.* (eds), *Redefining Christian Britain: Post 1945 Perspectives* (SCM Press: London, 2006).
6 See, for example, Holger Nehring, '"The long night is over" The Campaign for Nuclear Disarmament, 'generation' and the politics of religion', in Garnett *et al.* (eds), *Redefining Christian Britain*, p. 138.
7 SOAS, CA2/I/18/1, *Area Secretaries' Manual Notes*, p. 5.
8 I refer to the organisation as Christian Aid throughout.

9 Gerald Parsons, 'From consensus to confrontation: religion and politics in Britain since 1945', in Parsons (ed.), *The Growth of Religious Diversity: Britain since 1945* (London: Routledge, 1994), p. 131.
10 For example, Manji and O'Coill, 'The missionary position'; Jones, 'The Disasters Emergency Committee'.
11 Jones, 'The Disasters Emergency Committee'.
12 Julia Berger, 'Religious non-Governmental organisations: An exploratory analysis', *Voluntas*, 14:1 (2003), 20.
13 Cox, *English Churches*, p. 57.
14 *Ibid.*, pp. 78–9.
15 Simon Green, *Religion in the Age of Decline: Organisation and Experience in Industrial Yorkshire, 1870–1920* (Cambridge: Cambridge University Press, 1996), pp. 381–8. See also, Prochaska, *Christianity and Social Service*, pp. 2, 4, 11.
16 SOAS, CA/I/1/1, Alan Brash, Address to British Council of Churches, 1968.
17 Janet Lacey, *A Cup of Water* (London: Hodder & Stoughton, 1970), p. 49.
18 *Ibid.*, p. 60.
19 'Christian Aid Week', St James Church Report (c.1965).
20 SOAS, CA/I/1/5b, Allocation of Funding, 13 July 1960; SOAS, CA/I/3/1, British Council of Churches Christian Aid Department Balance Sheet, 30 September 1964; SOAS, CA/I/12/3, Memorandum on Christian Aid Week and the BBC, c.1963.
21 SOAS, CA/I/1/2, Report on Christian Aid for 41st Meeting of British Council of Churches, Autumn 1962.
22 Lacey, *A Cup of Water*, p. 92.
23 SOAS, CA/I/14/3, Christian Outlook broadcast for BBC, 7 February 1962.
24 SOAS, CA/I/14/3, William Clark, 'Lift Up Your Hearts' BBC Home Service, 1963.
25 SOAS, CA2/I/18/3, Memo, 'Youth Against Hunger: The Politics of Aid', 1965.
26 Lacey, *A Cup of Water*, p. 186.
27 *Ibid.*
28 Manji and O'Coill, 'Missionary Position', 572.
29 Stuart, 'Overseas mission', 537.
30 Andrew Porter, *Religion Versus Empire? British Protestant Missionaries and Overseas Expansion, 1700–1914* (Manchester: Manchester University Press, 2004), p. 13.
31 David Bebbington, 'Atonement, Sin, and Empire, 1880–1914', in Andrew Porter (ed.), *The Imperial Horizons of British Protestant Missions, 1880–1914* (Cambridge: Wm. B. Eerdmans Publishing Co., 2003), pp. 14–31.
32 'Missions in a changed world', *The Times* (6 May 1959).
33 Stockwell, 'Splendidly leading the way', 553.
34 'Missions in a changed world', *The Times* (6 May 1959).
35 Stuart, 'Overseas mission', 537.
36 *Ibid.*, 536.
37 *Ibid.*
38 Trevor Huddleston, 'The Christian Churches in independent Africa', *African Affairs*, 68:270 (1969), 45.
39 SOAS, CA2/I/46/1, Hugh Samson to Alan Brash, c.1968.
40 Cox, 'Empire of Christ', p. 108.
41 Parsons, 'From consensus to confrontation'.
42 Rob Skinner, 'Facing the challenge of 'Young Africa': Apartheid, South Africa and British decolonisation', *South African Historical Journal*, 54:1 (2006), 54–71.
43 Clark, 'Lift Up Your Hearts'.
44 Lacey, *A Cup of Water*, p. 150.
45 *Ibid.*, p. 106.
46 SOAS, CA2/I/46/3, 'The Commonwealth and Economic Development,' Memo to Commonwealth Prime Ministers, January 1969.
47 Hilton, 'International aid and development NGOs', pp. 452, 455.
48 Cox, 'Empire of Christ', p. 103.
49 'Churches and Terrorists', *The Times* (15 September 1970).
50 Skinner, 'The Moral Foundations of British Anti-Apartheid Activism', 407.

51 Lacey, *A Cup of Water*, p. 93.
52 *Ibid.*, p. 130.
53 *Ibid.*, p. 28; For a discussion of internationalism, human rights and post-war deconstruction see Tara Zahra, '"A Human Treasure": Europe's displaced children between nationalism and internationalism,' *Past and Present*, Supplement 6 (2011), 332–50.
54 Manji and O'Coill, 'Missionary position', 571.
55 SOAS, CA2/I/18/3, Report on Botswana Soil Conservation Project, no date.
56 Cited in Bebbington, 'Atonement, sin, and empire', p. 19.
57 Lacey, *A Cup of Water*, p. 33.
58 Callum Brown, *The Death of Christian Britain* (London: Routledge, 2000); Hugh McLeod, *The Religious Crisis of the 1960s* (Oxford: Oxford University Press, 2007).
59 Garnett *et al.* (eds), *Redefining Christian Britain*.
60 SOAS, CA/I/1/2, Report on Christian Aid for 31st Meeting of British Council of Churches, 1957 and Report on Christian Aid for 37th Meeting of British Council of Churches, Autumn 1960.
61 Jeremy Morris, 'The strange death of Christian Britain: another look at the secularisation debate', *The Historical Journal*, 46:4 (2003), 976.
62 Callum Brown, 'What was the religious crisis of the 1960s?', *Journal of Religious History*, 34:4 (2010), 468–79; Mark Roodhouse, 'Lady Chatterley and the Monk: Anglican radicals and the Lady Chatterley trial of 1960', *Journal of Ecclesiastical History*, 59:3 (2008), 475–500.
63 Kenneth Sansbury, Letters page, *The Times* (1 February 1960).
64 David Bebbington, *Evangelicalism in Modern Britain: A History from the 1730s to the 1980s* (London: Routledge, 1989), p. 264.
65 Nehring, 'The Long Night is Over', p. 144.
66 Kenneth Sansbury, letter to *The Times* (3 August 1967).
67 Meredith Veldman, *Fantasy, the Bomb and the Greening of Britain: Romantic Protest, 1945–1980* (Cambridge: Cambridge University Press, 1994), p. 160.
68 Parsons, 'Consensus to confrontation', p. 132.
69 Nehring, 'The Long Night is over', p. 144.
70 Parsons, 'Consensus to confrontation', p. 131.
71 SOAS, CA/I/1/4, Christian Aid Report to 54th Meeting of the British Council of Churches, 1969.
72 Cited in Iriye, *Global Community*, p. 17.
73 Gorman, 'Ecumenical internationalism', 51–73.
74 David Carter, 'The Ecumenical Movement in its Early Years', *Journal of Ecclesiastical History*, 49:3 (1999), 482.
75 Lacey, *A Cup of Water*, p. 34.
76 SOAS, CA/I/5/3, 'Training and Education: The Present Picture and our Opportunities for Development'.
77 SOAS, CA/I/1/4, Inter-Church Aid Report to 33rd Meeting of the British Council of Churches, 1958.
78 SOAS, CA2/I/18/3, Letter from Janet Lacey to Area Secretaries, April 1965.
79 SOAS, CA2/I/18/1, *Area Secretaries' Manual Notes*, p. 12.
80 SOAS, CA2/I/18/4, A. R Adams, Regional Organisation Report of South West, October 1967.
81 SOAS, CA2/I/18/4, A.R Adams, Regional Organisation Report of South West, April 1968.
82 SOAS, CA2/I/18/4, Miss B. Carpenter, Regional Organisation Report, Midlands, April 1965.
83 Cox, 'From the Empire of Christ', p. 82.
84 SOAS, CA2/I/18/4, A.R. Adams Regional Organisation Report of South West, October 1967 and February 1968.
85 Robin Dixon, interviewee, Wellcome Trust Oral History Interviews, British Library Sound and Moving Image Catalogue, http://cadensa.bl.uk/uhtbin/cgisirsi/?ps=q0o7Vueofl/WORKS-FILE/111740074/9 (accessed 21 August 2012).

86 SOAS, CA/I/13/5, Speakers on International Topics 1964/65, 30 September 1964.
87 *Ibid.*
88 SOAS, CA2/I/46/3, Alan Brash, 'Christian Aid and World Development', 23 October 1966.
89 'British Council of Churches Joint International Department Policy Statement', 1968 in Ernest Payne, *Thirty Years of the British Council of Churches, 1942–1972* (British Council of Churches: London, 1972), *Appendix V.*
90 Thörn, 'Solidarity across borders'; Rob Skinner, 'Facing the challenge', 54–71.
91 Lacey, *A Cup of Water*, p. 28.
92 *Ibid.*, p. 32.
93 SOAS, CA/I/5/3, 'Notes on Adult Training and Education Programme,' December 1966.
94 SOAS, CA2/I/19/6, Rev. L. Coates, Regional Organisation Report of East/West Yorkshire, September 1966.
95 SOAS, CA/I/14/3, Unknown Author, 'Christian Aid in a Parish', Radio Broadcast for BBC Home Service May 1963.
96 Thompson (ed.), *Britain's Experience of Empire*, p. 28.
97 Thorne, *Congregational Missions*, p. 157.
98 Andrew Porter (ed.), *The Imperial Horizons of British Protestant Missions, 1880–1914* (Cambridge: Wm. B. Eerdmans Publishing Co., 2003), p. 3.
99 John Angel James, 1819 cited in Hall, *Civilising Subjects*, p. 302.
100 'Christian Aid in a Parish'.
101 Hall, *Civilising Subjects*, pp. 304–8.
102 'Christian Aid in a Parish'.
103 SOAS, CA/I/5/3, 'Notes on Adult Training and Education Programme', December 1966.
104 SOAS, CA/I/4/2, Christian Aid Week Bright Ideas.
105 SOAS, CA/I/4/2, Ruscombe and Twyford Christian Aid Week, 1966.
106 SOAS, CA2/I/19/6, Rev. L. Coates, East/West Yorkshire Monthly Report, January 1967.
107 SOAS, CA2/I/19/6, Rev. L. Coates, East/West Yorkshire Monthly Report, July 1967.
108 SOAS, CA2/I/18/4, A. R. Adams Regional Organisation Report of South West, October 1967.
109 SOAS, CA2/I/18/4, A. R. Adams Regional Organisation Report of South West, November 1968.
110 SOAS, CA2/I/18/4, A. R. Adams Regional Organisation Report of South West, September 1967.
111 SOAS, CA/I/14/3, Memorandum on Christian Aid Week and the BBC, 1962.
112 SOAS, CA/I/14/3, Margaret Bywater to James E. Sexton, 7 May 1962.
113 SOAS, CA2/I/19/3, Margaret Bywater, Area Secretary Report, 24 May 1968.
114 SOAS, CA2/I/18/5, Rev. G. Bewley, South West Area Secretary Report, April to June 1965.

Conclusion

In 1964 Charles Chislett, retired bank manager, Rotarian, keen traveller, and familiar face in Rotherham civic society, delivered a speech to his local Chamber of Commerce on the difference between 'the world of Commerce during our "Empire" period and now'.

> We as a nation still retain a large degree of know-how in colonial government and administration, but without an empire to govern. We have those who are willing to take responsibility, and if the schools and the training which produced the men who ran the empire can be retained with a different slant to prepare the best human material to head the world in commerce, opportunities are both challenging and boundless.[1]

Chislett's speech serves as an important reminder of where we might look when seeking to understand the domestic impact of decolonisation. As with many of the towns and villages that I have touched upon in this book, Rotherham was not a conspicuously cosmopolitan place. A medium-sized industrial town with a population of approximately 220,000, it had never been a hub for networks of imperial trade or missionary work.[2] Yet, as Chislett's speech proves, Rotherham was not isolated from domestic cultures of decolonisation and globalisation. Those listening were encouraged to adopt an optimistic outlook: a vision of a global, post-imperial role that built on colonial 'know-how' while looking beyond the boundaries of the former Empire. They were reminded that a willingness to 'take responsibility' was an enduring British characteristic and told that the British population – the 'best human material' – were capable of taking on leading roles in a globalising world. Given Chislett's high level of civic activity, it is likely that he shared similar diagnoses and prescriptions in a wide range of associational settings over the course of the 1960s, including with his Rotary Club (where he served as Chair of the International Committee), in the Rotherham Celebrity Lectures Group, and at his frequent film screenings.[3]

Chislett's participation in Rotherham civic society illustrates how those with international experiences could act as instigators, using the networks of traditional associational life to engage the wider population in their interests. By studying the Royal Commonwealth Society (RCS), Women's Institutes (WIs), Rotary Clubs, and Christian Aid and Freedom from Hunger Campaign (FFHC) committees across the country, this book has shown that in the 1960s globalisation and decolonisation opened up new opportunities for international engagement not just for the young, or for those involved in politically engaged new social movements, but also for middle-aged members of middle-class society who had little interest in challenging the authority of the state. These associational experiences not only broaden our understanding of *who* had a stake in decolonisation, they call attention to the optimism and enthusiasm with which members of the British public developed visions for a citizen-led post-imperial global role.

For most of the people discussed in this book decolonisation did not represent a crisis. That is not to say, as some have suggested, that it didn't matter to them, that they did not notice it happening, or that it did not influence the way they thought about and interacted with the outside world. But rather that they understood the end of empire, and so must we, as but one of many significant changes in a world that was rapidly shrinking. For these people, the literal shrinking of Britain's empire was not inherently more important than the figurative shrinking of a world brought together by the forces of globalisation. The geopolitical interconnectedness that followed the Second World War, in conjunction with the expansion of international mobility in the 1950s and 1960s, produced a sense of global closeness that was at least as important as decolonisation in determining associational forms of international engagement. This book has shown that these two processes were interrelated and interacting; each contributed to a dynamic of anxiety and optimism that shaped ideas about civic responsibility in this period. Participants in associational life called upon experiences from the recent imperial past to mitigate anxieties about the globalising present while simultaneously using the increased opportunities for international communication and collaboration represented by the globalising present to mitigate anxieties about the loss of empire.

At the heart of this dynamic was the idea of a benevolent global role. Every aspect of the civic international engagement detailed in this book rested on the largely unquestioned assumption that Britain could and should maintain its global influence in the post-imperial era. As scholarship has already shown, this remained an orthodox position within political culture throughout the 1960s.[4] While empire might have come to been seen to be out of step with modern Britain, intervention in the name of 'great powerdom' was not.[5] What this book shows is that, at least within this middle-class associational sphere, members of the British public imagined themselves as key actors in this national story. The public have always occupied an important position in discourses about the preservation of British imperial influence and identity – as settlers, traders, missionaries, administrators, and promotors of the 'civilising mission'.[6] As the limitations of the British state's global authority became more conspicuous in the 1960s, the notion of individual agency took on a greater significance. In light of the apparent failings of the state, the public assumed for themselves increasing responsibility in the preservation of global stability. Within middle-class 'non-political' circles, the fulfilment of this responsibility took three mutually supportive forms: the pursuit of international friendship; efforts to know and understand the world; and the provision of assistance to those in need. Each activity, though distinct in its aims and ambitions, affirmed public belief in a narrative about Britain as a caring nation, perhaps not infallible but essentially good.

This benevolent image intersected in important ways with Britain's imperial past and decolonising present. As this book has shown, there were some situations in which civic associations imagined the Commonwealth as the best framework through which to enact this benevolent global role. However, with the exception of the Royal Commonwealth Society (RCS), which facilitated wide-ranging debates about the post-imperial possibilities of the New Commonwealth, the idea of the Commonwealth only really gained traction within associational organisations in the 1960s when linked to discourses about friendship. By contrast, ideals of international understanding and aid that may once have been imagined as 'imperial burdens' were typically reworked to apply to humanity as a whole. The decoupling of the Empire from benevolence that decolonisation allowed was not about a break with the imperial past so much as a way to establish a selective continuity with it. As Jordanna Bailkin argues, we ought to 'read this era not in terms of a withdrawal from empire, but rather as a reinvestment in a new internationalism in which the former empire played a significant part'.[7] Associational projects of international engagement were heavily reliant on both the imaginative structures and material networks of the British Empire. In the case of friendship, education, and humanitarianism, the former and declining empire provided a pre-established network of commitments and connections that could be put to uses that, if not always new, were reframed and repackaged for a changing world.

In 1969 A. L. Adu spoke at the RCS about the 'weight of [...] colonial history' that he saw weighing down the shoulders of the British public.[8] Yet this book has shown that members of associational life were remarkably adept at discarding those parts of the imperial past that did not serve their contemporary narratives about benevolent internationalism and preserving those that did. The discourses adopted by the associations discussed here support Webster's account of the declining salience of heroic, militarised narratives of empire in the late 1950s and early 1960s.[9] Members on the central committees of the RCS recognised the need to disassociate the Society from images of a conquering, racially exclusive empire and took steps accordingly to diversify their programme and regulate the behaviour of branches seen to be out of step with the collaborative language of the modern Commonwealth. Though they were less self-reflexive about the process, there is little evidence that there was much space for imperial adventure narratives on Rotary or WI's educational programmes in the 1960s, and nothing in their widely distributed magazines that explicitly mourned the end of imperial heroism or military prowess.

While associations showed little desire for embracing Britain's imperial past 'wholesale', they also showed little discomfort in using a range of imperial experiences as touchstones to justify contemporary modes of international engagement. Most significantly, the imperial past functioned as a useful repository of skill, experience, and expertise, called upon to support particular interventions: Rotarian J. E. Parry suggested that empire had given Britain skills in cross-cultural understanding that it could teach to the rest of the world; Christian Aid tapped into the missionary tradition of welfare provision to claim expertise in the humanitarian field; while the UK Freedom from Hunger Campaign committee claimed experience based on the exploits of colonial scientists and administrators. The value that associations placed upon certain kinds of imperial experience illustrates how those who had lived and worked in the Empire continued to act as important mediators, even after the end of empire.[10] The image of empire that associations called upon in the 1960s was historically contingent and determined by the perceived demands of the globalising world. The most common reference points – the development and welfare initiatives of the late colonial period – were called upon because they supported the projects of humanitarianism and associational understanding that were most popular in this period. They differ significantly, for example, from the narratives about pioneering settlers and adventurous (masculine) explorers that were popular in the 1940s and 1950s, and from the nostalgic reflections on colonial rule in India that dominated in the late 1970s and 1980s (parasols and gin and tonic in the heat).[11]

Though historically specific, the imaginative work of the 1960s – the remembering *and* forgetting – also established many of the terms on which British imperialism continues to be understood publicly in the twenty-first century. As unabashed enthusiasm ceased to be fashionable in the early 1960s, it began to be replaced by an 'on balance' approach to Britain's imperial past, one in which violent elements were not explicitly denied, but were seen as less significant than (and also compensated by) the positive legacies of imperialism. This approach has proven to be remarkably resilient, enduring in contemporary discourse despite the continuing exposure of the many violent and disturbing aspects of the imperial past.[12] It determines the framework through which opinion polls have sought to assess public attitudes towards the Empire. Asked in 2014 whether the British Empire is 'more something to be proud of or ashamed of', 59 per cent of respondents found that the balance tipped towards pride.[13] Asked 'overall do you think the countries that were colonised by Britain are better off or worse off for being colonised?' 49 per cent determined that the Empire had benefited the colonies (compared to 14 per cent who determined that it had harmed them).[14] In the twenty-first century, as in the 1960s, this 'on balance' approach to the Empire, which encourages broad reflections rather than attention to detail, has made it easy to downplay apparently isolated acts of violence against an overarching narrative of benevolent intent.

In the 1960s, the principles of international goodwill offered the British public a sense of power, agency, and utility that bolstered against pessimistic readings of the lost Empire. Each of the three forms of international engagement discussed encoded hierarchies previously found in imperial relationships – figuring Britons as 'givers', whether of knowledge or of resources, to the global South – but this tendency was most apparent in relation to humanitarian projects. It matters, therefore, that over the course of the 1960s, it was these humanitarian projects that came to dominate the field of civic international engagement, receiving considerably more time and energy than efforts aimed simply at knowing or befriending. Its ability to encode and detoxify this comforting hierarchy partly explains the pre-eminence of humanitarianism at a moment of imperial collapse. But this was not the only reason it proved so successful. Humanitarianism, through its association with discourses of both charity and development, was a broad church. Its ideological flexibility allowed for common ground between otherwise irreconcilable groups: those who wanted to celebrate Britain's imperial past, those who wanted to condemn it, and those who took no strong position on it. Through humanitarianism, the WI and Rotary found shared purpose with extra-parliamentary groups on the left.[15] While for those on the left, humanitarianism represented one element in a broader programme for global justice, for Rotary, the WI, and for many of those involved in fundraising for the FFHC and Christian Aid, humanitarianism aligned with an associational prioritisation of 'people' over 'politics'. However false were their claims to political neutrality, these associations displayed a deeply held conviction in the power of individuals to affect change in ways that governments could not. Humanitarianism was deemed to be an apolitical effort that relied on a faith in goodwill and expertise and, in these terms, did not require a systemic critique of the status quo.

To understand the popular appeal of humanitarianism in the 1960s requires us to recognise not only the malleability of its discourses but also the significant ways in which the structures of civic society were changing in this decade. This book has shown how the rapid expansion of professionalising humanitarian and developmental organisations (including Christian Aid and the umbrella FFHC) intersected with increased interest in international activity among traditional associational organisations (including the WI, Rotary Club, and many local church groups). For most of the decade these interests worked in tandem: both sets of organisations supported aims to raise public understanding and awareness of issues facing the developing world and both predominantly treated aid and development as an apolitical activity. This alignment meant that they were easily able to facilitate each other's aims and objectives: while associations relied on humanitarian organisations as a source of international expertise and to provide direction for their activities, humanitarian organisations drew on associations for practical support in fundraising activities and public awareness campaigns. By the mid-1960s, humanitarianism was fully integrated into the humdrum of traditional associational life: the small committee meetings in village halls, the evening talks by visiting speakers, the whist drives and coffee mornings that sustained rather than merely sat alongside this work.

This integration into pre-existing associational patterns was a marker of the wider appeal of humanitarianism. More importantly, it explains how post-war organisations and initiatives such as Oxfam, Christian Aid, and the FFHC were able to expand so rapidly in the most intense period of decolonisation. At the end of the 1960s, however, a series of significant changes in the humanitarian sector began that may have disrupted this symbiosis. Those humanitarian organisations that had driven international engagement within apolitical associational life became increasingly politicised over the course of the 1970s as they

CONCLUSION

aligned themselves more closely with the language of 'rights' and 'justice' employed by new social movements. Such changes undermined the self-avowedly apolitical narratives of 'goodwill' that sustained many forms of associational engagement in the 1960s. Over the next two decades, the financing of the humanitarian sector also changed considerably, changing the relationship between professionalised NGOs and their donors. Increasingly, humanitarian organisations worked within a 'mixed economy' in which NGO projects were sustained by government grants as well as public fundraising.[16] At the same time, new strategies were developed for collecting public donations that were less reliant on the kinds of community fundraising efforts previously organised through associations.[17] As all of these changes took place, public recognition of NGOs, and their work in Africa in particular, continued to grow.[18] More research is needed into the wider impact of these changes on the apolitical 'active-citizenship' model of international engagement widely adopted by traditional associational organisations in the 1960s and on public ideas about their own responsibility to understand and assist the wider world.[19]

Fundamentally, this book has sought to answer the question: what did the end of empire mean to those for whom it meant something but not everything? At its simplest, the answer is that decolonisation, even at its most intense moment, did not register primarily as a trauma – not because these individuals lacked interest in Britain's relationship with the outside world, but because they found new ways to situate themselves within a dynamic of personal responsibility and agency. They found ways to draw on the material and imaginative geographies of imperialism while also engaging with the problems and possibilities presented by globalisation and increased mobility. As I hope I have shown, the benefits of paying proper attention to the activities and beliefs of associational life in Britain in the twentieth century are considerable. We can see how a major subset of the British public (until now largely overlooked) understood their relationship with the outside world and the contributions they could make within the framework of Britain's changing global role. This book sheds light on the immediate impacts of decolonisation in Britain but its scope is necessarily limited. There is still considerable need for studies that extend the insights granted by close attention to these associational worlds into the later twentieth century. We may well find many of our presuppositions about associational life confirmed – I am sure there will be no shortage of jam, tea, or petty rivalry – but we may also find in the activities and attitudes of these groups new ways to challenge and complicate received histories about the enduring legacies of Empire.

Notes

1 Charles Chislett, 'Chamber of Commerce, President's Report 1964–5', RALSS, 358/5, Box 1.
2 'Rotherham Through Time, Standardized Industry Data,' *Vision of Britain* http://visionofbritain.org/data_cube_page.jsp?data_theme=T_IND&data_cube=N_INDUS-TRY_GEN&u_id=10084763&c_id=10001043&add=Y (accessed 12 May 2012).
3 The scope of Chislett's affiliations is evident from the papers in RALSS, 358/F.
4 Ward, 'Introduction', *British Culture and the End of Empire*, p. 7; on the popularity of the idea within left-wing organisations see Burkett, *Constructing Post-Imperial Britain*, pp. 19–72.
5 Thompson, 'Introduction' in *Britain's Experience of Empire*, p. 20. See also Murphy, 'Britain as a global power'; D. Sanders, *Losing an Empire, Finding a Role: British Foreign Policy Since 1945* (Basingstoke: Palgrave, 1990); A. Jackson, 'Empire and beyond: the pursuit of overseas national interests in the late twentieth century', *Economic History Review*, 123:499 (2007), 1350–66.
6 See, for example, Thorne, *Congregational Missions*; Pickles, 'A link in the "great chain of Empire friendship"'; Riedi, 'Women, gender, and the promotion of Empire'; Springhall, 'Lord Meath, youth and Empire'.
7 Bailkin, *The Aftermath of Empire*, p. 92.
8 Adu, 'The reality and potential capacity of the Commonwealth', 12.
9 Webster, *Englishness and Empire*.
10 Buettner, 'Cemeteries, public memory and Raj nostalgia', 17.
11 *Ibid.*; Buettner, *Empire Families*, pp. 252–70; Angela Woollacott, 'Making Empire visible or making colonialism visible? The struggle for the British imperial past', *British Scholar*, 1:2 (2009), 155–65.
12 Andrew Thompson, 'Afterword: The imprint of the Empire', in Thompson (ed.) *Britain's Experience of Empire in the Twentieth Century*, p. 333. For a discussion of 'on balance' discourses see Alan Lester, 'Time to throw out the balance sheet' (2016) https://blogs.sussex.ac.uk/snapshotsofempire/2016/01/26/time-to-throw-out-the-balance-sheet/ (accessed 21 August 2017); David Olusoga, 'Wake up, Britain. Should the empire really be a source of pride?' *Guardian* (23 January 2016).
13 YouGov survey results', http://cdn.yougov.com/cumulus_uploads/document/6quatmbimd/Internal_Results_140725_Commonwealth_Empire-W.pdf (accessed 1 November 2017).
14 'The British Empire is something to be proud of' https://yougov.co.uk/news/2014/07/26/britain-proud-its-empire/ (accessed 1 November 2017).
15 Burkett, *Constructing Post-Imperial Britain*.
16 On state-NGO relations see, Hilton *et al.*, *NGOs in Britain*, pp. 303–8, 355–7.
17 Hilton, 'Politics is ordinary'; Hilton *et al.*, *NGOs in Britain*, pp. 308–16.
18 Kevin O'Sullivan, 'Humanitarian encounters: Biafra, NGOs and imaginings of the Third World in Britain and Ireland, 1967–70', *Journal of Genocide Research*, 16:2-3 (2014), 303.
19 An excellent example of the possibilities in this area is Skelton, 'From peace to development', the final section of which looks at the international work of women's organisations in the 1970s.

SELECT BIBLIOGRAPHY

Archives consulted

Borthwick Institute for Archives, University of York, York
Department of Manuscripts and University Archives, University of Cambridge
The National Archives, Kew
Rotherham Archive and Local Studies Service, Rotherham
School of African and Oriental Studies, London
The Women's Library, London School of Economics and Political Science, London
Yorkshire Film Archive, York

Selected texts cited

Adams, Michael, *Voluntary Service Overseas: The Story of the First Ten Years* (London, 1968).

Ahmed, Sara, *Strange Encounters: Embodied Others in Postcoloniality* (London: Routledge, 2000).

Ambrose, Linda M., *A Great Rural Sisterhood: Madge Robertson Watt and the ACWW* (London: University of Toronto Press, 2015).

Andrews, Maggie, *The Acceptable Face of Feminism: The Women's Institute as a Social Movement, 1915–1960* (London: Lawrence & Wishart, 1997).

Arnold, David (ed.), *Imperial Medicine and Indigenous Societies* (Manchester: Manchester University Press, 1988).

Arnold, Guy, *Towards Peace and a Multiracial Commonwealth* (London: Chapman & Hall, 1964).

Arsan, Andrew, Su Lin Lewis, and Anne-Isabelle Richard, 'Editorial – the roots of global civil society and the interwar moment', *Journal of Global History*, 7:2 (2012), 157–65.

Ashton, S. R. and Wm Roger Louis (eds), *British Documents on the End of Empire*, Series A, Volume 5, East of Suez and the Commonwealth 1964–1971, Part II Europe, Rhodesia, Commonwealth (London: Institute for Commonwealth Studies, 2004).

Bailkin, Jordanna, *Afterlife of Empire* (London: University of California Press, 2012).

Beaumont, Caitriona, *Housewives and Citizens: Domesticity and the Women's Movement in England, 1928–64* (Oxford: Oxford University Press, 2013).

Barnett, Michael, *Empire of Humanity: A History of Humanitarianism* (Ithaca, NY: Cornell University Press, 2011).

Barnett, Clive and David Land, 'Geographies of generosity: Beyond the 'moral turn', *Geoforum*, 38:6 (2007), 1065–75.

Baughan, Emily, 'The Imperial War Relief Fund and the All British Appeal: Commonwealth, conflict and Conservatism within the British humanitarian movement, 1920–25', *The Journal of Imperial and Commonwealth History*, 40:5 (2012), 845–61.

Bebbington, David, *Evangelicalism in Modern Britain: A History from the 1730s to the 1980s* (London: Routledge, 1989).

Bebbington, David, 'Atonement, sin, and empire, 1880–1914', in Andrew Porter (ed.), *The Imperial Horizons of British Protestant Missions, 1880–1914* (Cambridge: Wm. B. Eerdmans Publishing Co., 2003), pp. 14–31.

Berger, Julia, 'Religious non-governmental organisations: An exploratory analysis', *Voluntas*, 14:1 (2003).

Black, Lawrence, *Redefining British Politics: Culture, Consumerism and Participation, 1954–70* (London: Springer, 2010).

SELECT BIBLIOGRAPHY

Black, Maggie, *A Cause for Our Times: Oxfam the First Fifty Years* (Oxford: Oxfam, 1992).

Bland, Lucy, 'White women and men of colour: miscegenation fears in Britain after the Great War', *Gender & History*, 17:1 (2005), 29–61.

Blunt, Alison, *Travel, Gender and Imperialism; Mary Kingsley and West Africa* (New York: Guilford Press, 1994).

Bocking-Welch, Anna, 'Imperial legacies and internationalist discourses: British involvement in the United Nations Freedom from Hunger Campaign, 1960–70', *The Journal of Imperial and Commonwealth History*, 40:5 (2012), 879–896.

Bocking-Welch, Anna, 'Ghost hunting: amateur film and travel at the end of empire', in Martin Farr and Xavier Guegan (eds), *The British Abroad Since the Eighteenth Century*, Volume 2 (Basingstoke: Palgrave Macmillan, 2013), pp. 214–31.

Bocking-Welch, Anna, 'Youth against hunger: service, activism and the mobilisation of young humanitarians in 1960s Britain', *European Review of History*, 23:1–2 (2016), 154–70.

Briggs, Laura, 'Mother, child, race, nation: The visual iconography of rescue and the politics of transnational and transracial adoption', *Gender & History*, 15:2 (2003), 179–200.

Brown, Callum, *The Death of Christian Britain* (London: Routledge, 2000).

Brown, Callum, 'What was the religious crisis of the 1960s?', *Journal of Religious History*, 34:4 (2010), 468–79.

Bu, Liping, 'Educational exchange and cultural diplomacy in the Cold War', *Journal of American Studies*, 33:3 (1999), 393–415.

Buettner, Elizabeth, *Empire Families: Britons and Late Imperial India* (Oxford: Oxford University Press, 2004).

Buettner, Elizabeth, 'Cemeteries, public memory and Raj nostalgia in postcolonial Britain and India', *History & Memory*, 18:1 (2006), 5–42.

Buettner, Elizabeth, '"Would you let your daughter marry a Negro?": Race and sex in 1950s Britain', in Philippa Levine and S. Grayzel (eds), *Gender, Labour, War and Empire: Essays on Modern Britain* (London: Springer, 2008), pp. 219–37.

Buettner, Elizabeth, '"We don't grow coffee and bananas in Clapham Junction you know!": Imperial Britons back home', in R. Bickers (ed.), *Settlers and Expatriates: Britons Over the Seas* (Oxford: Oxford University Press, 2010), pp. 302–28.

Buettner, Elizabeth, *Europe after Empire: Decolonisation, Society, and Culture* (Cambridge: Cambridge University Press, 2016).

Bunch, Matthew James, 'All roads lead to Rome: Canada, the Freedom From Hunger Campaign, and the rise of NGOs, 1960–1980' (PhD Dissertation, University of Waterloo, 2007).

Burkett, Jodi, *Constructing Post-imperial Britain: Britishness, 'Race' and the Radical Left in the 1960s* (London: Palgrave Macmillan, 2013).

Burton, Antoinette, *Burdens of History: British Feminists, Indian Women, and Imperial Culture, 1865–1915* (London: University of North Carolina Press, 1994).

Burton, Antoinette, 'Who needs the nation? Interrogating "British" history', *Journal of Historical Sociology*, 10:3 (1997), 227–48.

Burton, Antoinette (ed.), *After the Imperial Turn: Thinking With and Through the Nation* (Durham NC: Duke University Press, 2003).

Buzard, James, *The Beaten Track: European Tourism, Literature and the Ways to Culture* (Oxford: Oxford University Press, 1993).

Cannadine, David, 'Introduction: Independence Day ceremonials in historical perspective', *The Round Table*, 97:398 (2008), 649–65.

Carter, David, 'The Ecumenical Movement in its Early Years', *Journal of Ecclesiastical History*, 49:3 (1999), 465–85.

Chadwick, John, *The Unofficial Commonwealth: The Story of the Commonwealth Foundation, 1965–1980* (London: Allen & Unwin, 1982).

Christie, C. J., 'British literary travellers in Southeast Asia in an era of colonial retreat', *Modern Asian Studies*, 28:4 (1994), 673–737.

Clarke, Nick, 'Globalising care? Town twinning in Britain since 1945', *Geoforum*, 42 (2011), 115–25.

Collins, Marcus, 'Pride and prejudice: West Indian men in mid-twentieth century Britain', *Journal of British Studies*, 40 (2001), 391–418.

Conradson, David, 'Geographies of care: spaces, practices, experiences', *Social & Cultural Geography*, 4:4 (2003), 451–54.

Cooper, Frederick, *Africa Since 1940: The Past of the Present* (Cambridge: Cambridge University Press, 2002).

Cooper, Frederick and Randall Packard (eds), *International Development and the Social Sciences: Essays on the History and Politics of Knowledge* (Berkeley, CA: University of California Press, 1997).

Cox, Jeffrey, 'From the empire of Christ to the Third World: Religion and the experience of empire in the twentieth century', in Andrew Thompson (ed.), *Britain's Experience of Empire*, pp. 76–122.

Craggs, Ruth, 'Cultural geographies of the modern Commonwealth from 1947 to 1973' (PhD dissertation, University of Nottingham, 2009).

Craggs, Ruth, 'The Commonwealth Institute and the Commonwealth Arts Festival: architecture, performance and multiculturalism in late-imperial London', *The London Journal*, 36:3 (2011), 247–68.

Craggs, Ruth, 'Hospitality in geopolitics and the making of Commonwealth international relations', *Geoforum*, 52 (2014), 90–100.

Craggs, Ruth and Hannah Neate, 'Post-colonial careering and urban policy mobility between Britain and Nigeria, 1945–1990', *Transactions of the Institute of British Geographers*, 42:1 (2017), 44–57.

Crowson, Nick, Matthew Hilton and James McKay (eds), *NGOs in Contemporary Britain: Non-state Actors in Society and Politics since 1945* (London: Springer, 2009).

Cumming, Gordon, *Aid to Africa: French and British Policies from the Cold War to the New Millennium* (Abingdon: Routledge, 2017).

Curtis, Heather D., 'Picturing pain: evangelicals and the politics of pictorial humanitarianism in an imperial age', in Heide Fehrenbach and Davide Rodogno (eds), *Humanitarian Photography* (Cambridge: Cambridge University Press, 2015), pp. 22–46.

Darwin, John, 'Imperialism in decline? Tendencies in British imperial policy between the wars', *The Historical Journal*, 23:3 (1980), 657–79.

Darwin, John, 'The fear of falling: British politics and imperial decline since 1900', *Transactions of the Royal Historical Society*, 36 (1985), 27–43.

de Grazia, Victoria, *Irresistible Empire: America's Advance through Twentieth Century Europe* (London: Belknap Press).

Dickson, Mora, *A World Elsewhere: Voluntary Service Overseas* (London: Dennis Dobson, 1964).

Dierikx, M. L. J., *Clipping the Clouds: How Air Travel Changed the World* (Westport, CT: Greenwood, 2008).

Driver, Felix, 'Geography's empire: histories of geographical knowledge', *Environment and Planning D: Society and Space*, 10:1 (1992), 23–40.

Ellis, Sylvia A., 'Promoting solidarity at home and abroad: the goals and tactics of the anti-Vietnam War movement in Britain', *European Review of History*, 21:4 (2014), 557–76.

English, R. and M. Kenny (eds), *Rethinking British Decline* (London: Macmillan, 2000).

Fehrenbach, Heide and Davide Rodogno (eds), *Humanitarian Photography* (Cambridge: Cambridge University Press, 2015).

Ford, K. and S. Katwala, *Reinventing the Commonwealth* (London: Foreign Policy Centre, 1999).

Gandhi, Leela, *Affective Communities: Anticolonial Thought, Fin-de-siècle Radicalism, and the Politics of Friendship* (London: Duke University Press, 2005).

Garnett, Jane, Matthew Grimley, Alana Harris, William Whyte, and Sarah Williams (eds), *Redefining Christian Britain: Post 1945 Perspectives* (SCM Press: London, 2006).

Gatrell, Peter, *Free World?: The Campaign to Save the World's Refugees, 1956–1963* (Cambridge: Cambridge University Press, 2011).

Gilroy, Paul, *After Empire: Melancholia or Convivial Culture?* (Abingdon on Thames: Routledge, 2004).

Gibson, Sarah, '"Abusing our hospitality": inhospitableness and the politics of deterrence', in Jennie Germann Molz and Sarah Gibson (eds), *Mobilizing Hospitality: The Ethics of Social Relations in a Mobile World* (London: Routledge, 2016), pp. 159–76.

Glass, Ruth, *Newcomers: The West-Indians in London* (London: Centre for Urban Studies, 1960).

Goff, Brendan, 'The heartland abroad: The Rotary Club's mission of civic internationalism' (PhD dissertation, University of Michigan, 2008).

Goff, Brendan, 'Philanthropy and the "perfect democracy" of Rotary International', in David Hammack and Steven Heydemann (eds), *Globalization, Philanthropy, and Civil Society: Projecting Institutional Logics Abroad* (Bloomington: Indiana University Press, 2009), pp. 47–70.

Gorman, Daniel, 'Empire, internationalism, and the campaign against the traffic in women and children in the 1920s', *Twentieth Century British History*, 19 (2008), 186–218.

Gorman, Daniel, 'Ecumenical internationalism: Willoughby Dickinson, the League of Nations and the World Alliance for Promoting International Friendship through the Churches', *Journal of Contemporary History*, 45 (2010), 63–4.

Grant, Matthew, 'Historicising citizenship in post-war Britain', *Historical Journal*, 59:4 (2016), 1187–206.

Green, Jonathon, *All Dressed Up: The Sixties and the Counterculture* (London: Vintage, 1999).

Green, Simon, *Religion in the Age of Decline: Organisation and Experience in Industrial Yorkshire, 1870–1920* (Cambridge: Cambridge University Press, 1996), pp. 381–8.

Hall, Catherine, *Civilising Subjects: Metropole and Colony in the English Imagination, 1830–1867* (Cambridge: Polity Press, 2002).

Hall, Catherine, and Sonya O. Rose (eds), *At Home with Empire: Metropolitan Cultures and the Imperial World* (Cambridge: Cambridge University Press, 2006).

Hall, P. A., 'Social capital in Britain', *British Journal of Politics*, 29 (1999), 417–61.

Hall, Stuart, 'Interview', in Richard English and Michael Kenny (eds), *Rethinking British Decline* (Basingstoke: Macmillan, 2000).

Hammond, Parry, Kennetta, *London is the Place for Me: Black Britons, Citizenship, and the Politics of Race* (Oxford: Oxford University Press, 2016).

Hansen, Randall, *Citizenship and Immigration in Post-war Britain* (Oxford: Oxford University Press, 2000).

Harper, M., '"Personal contact is worth a ton of text-books": educational tours of the Empire, 1926–39', *Journal of Imperial and Commonwealth History*, 32:3 (2004), 48–76.

Hartley, Anthony, *A State of England* (New York: Harcourt Brace and World, 1963).

Haskell, Thomas, 'Capitalism and the origins of the humanitarian sensibility, Part 1', *The American Historical Review*, 90:2 (1985), 339–61.

Hilton, Matthew, *Consumerism in Twentieth-Century Britain: The Search for a Historical Movement* (Cambridge: Cambridge University Press, 2003).

Hilton, Matthew, 'Politics is ordinary: non-governmental organizations and political participation in contemporary Britain', *Twentieth Century British History*, 22:2 (2011), 230–68.

Hilton, Matthew, 'Ken Loach and the Save the Children film: humanitarianism, imperialism, and the changing role of charity in post-war Britain', *The Journal of Modern History*, 87:2 (2015), 357–94.

Hilton, Matthew, Nick Crowson, Jean-François Mouhot, and James McKay, *A Historical Guide to NGOs: Charities, Civil Society and the Voluntary Sector Since 1945* (Basingstoke: Palgrave Macmillan, 2012).

Hodge, Joseph, *Triumph of the Expert: Agrarian Doctrines of Development and the Legacies of British Colonialism* (Athens Ohio: Ohio University Press, 2007).

Hoefferle, Caroline, *British Student Activism in the Long Sixties* (Abingdon: Routledge, 2013).

Hoffenberg, Peter, *An Empire on Display: English, Indian, and Australian Exhibitions from the Crystal Palace to the Great War* (Berkeley, CA: University of California Press, 2001).

Honeck, Mischa and Gabriel Rosenberg, 'Transnational generations: organizing youth in the Cold War', *Diplomatic History*, 38:2 (2014), 233–39.

Hopkins, A. J., 'Rethinking decolonisation', *Past & Present*, 200 (2008), 211–47.

Hostetter, David, 'House guest of the AEC: Dorothy Hutchinson, the 1958 fast at the Atomic Energy Commission, and the domestication of protest', *Peace & Change*, 34:2 (2009), 133–47.

Hughes, Celia, *Young Lives on the Left: Sixties Activism and the Liberation of the Self* (Oxford: Oxford University Press, 2015).

Hunt, Lynn, *The Family Romance of the French Revolution* (Berkeley, CA: University of California Press, 1992).

Huzzey, Richard, 'Minding civilisation and humanity in 1867: A case study in British imperial culture and Victorian anti-slavery', *The Journal of Imperial and Commonwealth History*, 40:5 (2012), 807–25.

Iriye, Akira, *Global Community: The Role of International Organizations in the Making of the Contemporary World* (London: University of London Press, 2002).

Jeppesen, Chris, '"A worthwhile career for a man who is not entirely self-seeking": service, duty and the Colonial Service during decolonisation', in Andrew W. M. Smith and Chris Jeppesen (eds), *Britain, France and the Decolonisation of Africa: Future Imperfect?* (London: UCL Press, 2017), pp. 133–55.

Jones, Andrew, 'The Disasters Emergency Committee (DEC) and the humanitarian industry in Britain, 1963–85', *Twentieth Century British History*, 26:4 (2014), 573–601.

Jones, Max, Berny Sèbe, John Strrachan, Bertrand Taithe, and Peter Yeandle, 'Decolonising imperial heroes: Britain and France', *Journal of Imperial and Commonwealth History*, 42 (2014), 787–825.

Kaye, Barbara, *International Countrywomen: The Many Aspects of International Work Undertaken in the Women's Institutes* (London: NWFI, 1967).

Kennedy, Denis, 'Selling the distant other: Humanitarianism and imagery – ethical dilemmas of humanitarian action', *The Journal of Humanitarian Assistance*, 28 (2009), 1–25.

Kirk-Greene, Anthony, 'Decolonisation: The ultimate diaspora', *Journal of Contemporary History*, 36 (2001), 133–51.

Kothari, Uma, 'Authority and expertise: The professionalisation of international development and the ordering of dissent', *Antipode*, 37:3 (2005), 425–46.

Kothari, Uma, 'From colonialism to development: reflections of former colonial officers', *Commonwealth & Comparative Politics*, 44:1 (2006), 118–36.

Lacey, Janet, *A Cup of Water* (London: Hodder & Stoughton, 1970).

Lambert, David and Alan Lester, 'Geographies of colonial philanthropy', *Progress in Human Geography*, 28:3 (2004), 320–41.

Lee, J. M., 'British cultural diplomacy and the cold war: 1946–61', *Diplomacy and Statecraft*, 9:1 (1998), 112–34.

Lee, J. M., 'Overseas students in Britain: How their presence was politicised in 1966–67', *Minerva*, 36 (1998), 305–21.

Lee, J. M., 'Commonwealth students in the United Kingdom, 1940–1960: Student welfare and world status', *Minerva*, 44 (2006), 1–24.

Lent, Adam, *British Social Movements Since 1945: Sex, Colour, Peace and Power* (Basingstoke: Palgrave Macmillan, 2001).

Lester, Alan, 'Imperial circuits and networks: geographies of the British Empire', *History Compass*, 4:1 (2006), 124–41.

Levy, Roger, *Rotary International in Great Britain and Northern Ireland* (London: Macdonald and Evans, 1978).

Lewis, Joanna, *Empire State Building: War and Welfare in Kenya, 1925–52* (Oxford: Oxford University Press, 2000).

Lewis, Su Lin, 'Rotary International's 'acid test': multi-ethnic associational life in 1930s Southeast Asia', *Journal of Global History*, 7:2 (2012), 302–24.

Light, Alison, *Forever England: Femininity, Literature and Conservatism Between the Wars* (London: Routledge, 1991).

Louis, Wm Roger, 'The dissolution of the British Empire', in Judith M. Brown and Wm Roger Louis (eds), *Oxford History of the British Empire, vol. V The Twentieth Century* (Oxford: Oxford University Press, 1999), pp. 329–56.

Louis, Wm Roger and Ronald Robinson, 'The imperialism of decolonisation', *The Journal of Imperial and Commonwealth History*, 22:3 (1994), 462–511.

Low, Gail, 'At home? Discoursing on the Commonwealth at the 1965 Commonwealth Arts Festival', *Journal of Commonwealth Literature*, 48:1 (2013), 97–111.

MacKenzie, John, *Propaganda and Empire: The Manipulation of Public Opinion 1880–1960* (Manchester: Manchester University Press 1986).

MacKenzie, John M., '"Comfort" and conviction: a response to Bernard Porter', *Journal of Imperial and Commonwealth History*, 36:4 (2008), 659–68.

Manji, Firoze and Carl O'Coill, 'The missionary position: NGOs and development in Africa', *International Affairs*, 78: 3 (2002), 567–83.

Manzo, Kate, 'Imaging humanitarianism: NGO identity and the iconography of child-hood', *Antipode*, 40: 4 (2008), 632–57.

Marks, Shula, 'What is colonial about colonial medicine? And what has happened to imperialism and health?', *Social History of Medicine*, 10:2 (1997), 205–19.

Matos, Jacinta, 'Old journeys re-visited: aspects of post-war English travel writing', in Michael Kowalewski (ed.), *Temperamental Journeys: Essays on the Modern Literature of Travel* (Athens, GA: University of Georgia Press, 1992), pp. 215–29.

Mazower, Mark, *No Enchanted Palace: The End of Empire and the Ideological Origins of the United Nations* (Oxford: Princeton University Press, 2009).

McCarthy, Helen, 'Parties, voluntary associations, and democratic politics in interwar Britain', *The Historical Journal*, 50:4 (2007), 891–912.

McCarthy, Helen, 'The League of Nations, public ritual and national identity in Britain, c. 1919–56', *History Workshop Journal*, 70:1 (2010), 109–32.

McIntyre, W. David, *Commonwealth of Nations: Origins and Impact 1869–1971* (Minneapolis, 1977).

McKibbin, Ross, *Classes and cultures: England 1918–1951* (Oxford: Oxford University Press, 1998).

McLeod, Hugh, *The Religious Crisis of the 1960s* (Oxford: Oxford University Press, 2007).

Middleton, Victor and Leonard John Lickorish, *British Tourism: The Remarkable Story of Growth* (Oxford: Butterworth-Heinemann, 2007).

Midgley, Clare (ed.), *Gender and Imperialism* (Manchester: Manchester University Press, 1998).

Midgley, Clare, 'Bringing the empire home: Women activists in imperial Britain', in Catherine Hall and Sonya Rose (eds), *At Home With the Empire: Metropolitan Culture and the Imperial World* (Cambridge: Cambridge University Press, 2006), pp. 230–50.

Midgley, Clare (ed.), *Feminism and Empire: Women Activists in Imperial Britain* (London: Routledge, 2007).

Miller, Harry (ed.), *Royal Commonwealth Society Centenary, 1868–1968* (London: Royal Commonwealth Society, 1968).

Moores, Chris, *Civil Liberties and Human Rights in Twentieth-Century Britain* (Cambridge: Cambridge University Press, 2017).

Morgan, David, 'The look of sympathy: Religion, visual culture, and the social life of feeling', *Material Religion*, 5:2 (2009), 132–54.

Morris, Jeremy, 'The strange death of Christian Britain: another look at the secularisation debate', *The Historical Journal*, 46:4 (2003), 963–76.

Mort, Frank, 'The Ben Pimlott memorial lecture 2010: The permissive society revisited', *Twentieth Century British History*, 22:2 (2011), 269–98.

Murphy, Philip, *Party Politics and Decolonisation: The Conservative Party and British Colonial Policy in Tropical Africa, 1951–1964* (Oxford: Oxford University Press, 1995).

Natarajan, Radhika, 'Performing multiculturalism: The Commonwealth Arts Festival of 1965', *Journal of British Studies*, 53 (2014), 705–33.

Nava, Mica, *Visceral Cosmopolitanism: Gender, Culture and the Normalisation of Difference* (Oxford: Berg, 2007).

Nava, Mica, 'Sometimes antagonistic, sometimes ardently sympathetic: Contradictory responses to migrants in post-war Britain', *Ethnicities*, 14:3 (2014), 458–80.

Nehring, Holger, 'National internationalists: British and West German protests against nuclear weapons, the politics of transnational communications and the social history of the Cold War, 1957–1964', *Contemporary European History*, 14:4 (2005), 559–82.

Neumann, R. P., 'The post-war conservation boom in British colonial Africa', *Environmental History*, 7:1 (2007), 22–47.

Norris Nicholson, Heather, 'Through the Balkan States: home movies as travel texts and tourism histories in the Mediterranean, c.1923–1939', *Tourist Studies*, 6:12 (2006), 13–36.

Oliete-Aldea, Elena, *Hybrid Heritage on Screen: The 'Raj Revival' in the Thatcher Era* (London: Springer, 2015).

O'Sullivan, Kevin, 'A "global nervous system": The rise and rise of European humanitarian NGOs, 1945–1985', in Marc Frey, Sönke Kunkel, and Corinna R. Unger (eds), *International Organizations and Development, 1945–1990* (London: Springer, 2014), pp. 196–219.

O'Sullivan, Kevin, 'Humanitarian encounters: Biafra, NGOs and imaginings of the Third World in Britain and Ireland, 1967–70', *Journal of Genocide Research*, 16:2–3 (2014), 299–315.

Owen, Nicholas, 'Critics of Empire in Britain', in Judith Browne and Wm Roger Louis (eds), *The Oxford History of the British Empire*, vol. 4 (Oxford: Oxford University Press, 1999), pp. 188–211.

Parpart, Jane L., 'Deconstructing the development "expert": Gender, development and the "vulnerable groups"', in Jane L. Parpart and Marianne H. Marchand (eds), *Feminism/Postmodernism/Development* (Abingdon: Routledge, 1995), pp. 221–43.

Parsons, Gerald (ed.), *The Growth of Religious Diversity: Britain since 1945* (London: Routledge, 1994).

Paul, Kathleen, *Whitewashing Britain: Race and Citizenship in the Post-war Era* (Ithaca, NY: Cornell University Press, 1997).

Pedersen, Susan, 'The maternalist moment in British colonial policy: the controversy over 'child slavery' in Hong Kong', *Past and Present*, 171 (2001), 161–202.

Perraton, Hillary, *A History of Foreign Students in Britain* (Basingstoke: Palgrave, 2014).

Pietsch, Tamson, 'Many Rhodes: travelling scholarships and imperial citizenship in the British academic world, 1880–1940', *History of Education*, 40:6 (2011), 723–39.

Phillips, R., 'Decolonizing geographies of travel: reading James/Jan Morris', *Social &Cultural Geography*, 2:1 (2001), 5–24.

Pickles, Katie, 'A link in the "great chain of Empire friendship": the Victoria League in New Zealand', *Journal of Imperial and Commonwealth History*, 33:1 (2005), 29–50.

Porter, Andrew (ed.), *The Imperial Horizons of British Protestant Missions, 1880–1914* (Cambridge: Wm. B. Eerdmans Publishing Co., 2003).

Porter, Andrew, *Religion Versus Empire? British Protestant Missionaries and Overseas Expansion, 1700–1914* (Manchester: Manchester University Press, 2004).

Porter, Bernard, *The Absent-Minded Imperialists: Empire, Society, and Culture in Britain* (Oxford: Oxford University Press, 2006).

Power, Marcus, 'The Commonwealth, "development" and post-colonial responsibility', *Geoforum*, 40 (2009), 14–24.

Pratt, Mary Louise, *Imperial Eyes: Travel Writing and Transculturation* (London: Routledge, 1992).

Prochaska, Frank, *Christianity and Social Service in Modern Britain: The Disinherited Spirit* (Oxford: Oxford University Press, 2006).

Riedi, Eliza, Ian C. Fletcher, Laura E. Nym Mayhall, and Philippa Levine (eds), *Women's Suffrage in the British Empire: Citizenship, Nation and Race* (London: Routledge, 2000).

Riedi, Eliza, 'Women, gender, and the promotion of Empire: The Victoria League, 1901–1914', *The Historical Journal*, 45:3 (2002), 569–99.

Richards, Jeffrey, 'Imperial heroes for a post-imperial age: films and the end of empire', in Stuart Ward (ed.), *British Culture and the End of Empire* (Manchester, Manchester University Press), pp. 129–44.

Richmond, Yale, *Cultural Exchange and the Cold War: Raising the Iron Curtain* (Pennsylvania: Penn State Press, 2010).

Riley, Charlotte Lydia, 'Monstrous predatory vampires and beneficent fairy-godmothers: British post-war colonial development in Africa' (PhD dissertation, University College London, 2013).

Riley, Charlotte Lydia, '"Tropical Allsorts": the transnational flavor of British development policies in Africa', *Journal of World History*, 26:4 (2016), 839–64.

Roodhouse, Mark, 'Lady Chatterley and the Monk: Anglican radicals and the Lady Chatterley trial of 1960', *Journal of Ecclesiastical History*, 59:3 (2008), 475–500.

Rose, Sonya, 'Sex, citizenship, and the nation in World War II Britain', *The American Historical Review*, 103:4 (1998), 1147–76.

Rosaldo, Renato, 'Imperialist nostalgia', *Representations*, 26 (1989), 107–22.

Ryan, James R., *Picturing Empire: Photography and the Visualization of the British Empire* (London: Reaktion Books, 2013).

Samuel, Raphael (ed.), *Patriotism: The Making and Unmaking of British National Identity*, vol. 1, *History and Politics* (London: Routledge, 1989).

Saunders, David and David Patrick Houghton, *Losing an Empire, Finding a Role: British Foreign Policy Since 1945* (London: Palgrave, 2017).

Schofield, Camilla, *Enoch Powell and the Making of Postcolonial Britain* (Cambridge: Cambridge University Press, 2013).

Schwarz, Bill, '"The only white man in there": the re-racialization of England, 1956–1968', *Race & Class*, 38:1(1996), 65–78.

Schwarz, Bill, *The White Man's World* (Oxford: Oxford University Press, 2011).

Seton-Watson, Hugh, 'Aftermaths of empire', *Journal of Contemporary History*, 15:1 (1980), 197–208.

Skelton, Sophie, 'From Peace to Development: a Reconstitution of British Women's International Politics, c.1945–1970' (PhD dissertation, University of Birmingham, 2014).

Skinner, Rob, 'Facing the challenge of 'Young Africa': Apartheid, South Africa and British decolonisation', *South African Historical Journal*, 54:1 (2006), 54–71.

Skinner, Rob, *The Foundations of Anti-Apartheid: Liberal Humanitarians and Trans-national Activists in Britain and the United States, c.1919–64* (London: Springer, 2010).

Smith, Andrea (ed.), *Europe's Invisible Migrants: Consequences of the Colonists' Return* (Chicago: University of Chicago Press, 2002).

Smith, Jean P., '"The women's branch of the Commonwealth Relations Office": The Society for the Overseas Settlement of British Women and the long life of empire migration', *Women's History Review*, 25:4 (2016), 520–35.

Smith, Vanessa, *Intimate Strangers: Friendship, Exchange and Pacific Encounters* (Cambridge: Cambridge University Press, 2010).

Springhall, J. O., 'Lord Meath, youth and Empire', *Journal of Contemporary History*, 5:4 (1970), 97–111.

Spurr, David, *Rhetoric of Empire: Colonial Discourse in Journalism, Travel Writing and Imperial Administration* (Durham, NC: Duke University Press, 1993).

Srinivasan, K., *The Rise, Decline, and Future of the British Commonwealth* (London: Palgrave Macmillan, 2015).

Stockwell, A. J., 'Leaders, dissidents and the disappointed: Colonial students in Britain as empire ended', *Journal of Imperial and Commonwealth History*, 36:3 (2008), 487–507.

Stockwell, Sarah, '"Splendidly leading the way"? Archbishop Fisher and decolonisation in British colonial Africa', *Journal of Imperial and Commonwealth History*, 36:3 (2008), 545–64.

Stoler, Ann Laura, *Carnal Knowledge and Imperial Power: Race and the Intimate in Colonial Rule* (London: University of California Press, 2002).

Stoler, Ann Laura, 'Imperial debris: reflections on ruin and ruination', *Cultural Anthropology*, 3:1 (2008), 1–34.

Stuart, John, 'Overseas mission, voluntary service and aid to Africa: Max Warren, the Church Missionary Society and Kenya, 1945–63', *The Journal of Imperial and Commonwealth History*, 3 (2008), 527–43.

Teo, Hsu Ming, 'Wandering in the wake of Empire: British travel and tourism in the post-imperial world', in Stuart Ward (ed.), *British Culture and the End of Empire* (Manchester: Manchester University Press, 2001). pp. 163–89.

Thompson, Andrew (ed.), *Britain's Experience of Empire in the Twentieth Century* (Oxford: Oxford University Press, 2012).

Thompson, Andrew, *The Empire Strikes Back? The Impact of Imperialism on Britain from the Mid-Nineteenth Century* (Harlow: Longman, 2005).

Thörn, Håkan, *Anti-Apartheid and the Emergence of a Global Civil Society* (Basingstoke: Palgrave Macmillan, 2006).

Thörn, Håkan, 'Solidarity across borders: The transnational anti-apartheid movement', *International Journal of Voluntary and Nonprofit Organizations*, 17:4 (2006), 285–301.

Thorne, Susan, *Congregational Missions and the Making of an Imperial Culture in Nineteenth Century Britain* (Stanford: Stanford University Press, 1999).

Trentmann, Frank, 'Coping with shortage: The problem of food security and global visions of coordination, c.1890s–1950', in Frank Trentmann and Flemming Just (eds), *Food and Conflict in Europe in the Age of the Two World Wars* (Basingstoke: Palgrave Macmillan, 2006), pp. 13–48.

Trentmann, Frank, 'Before "fair trade": empire, free trade and the moral economies of food in the modern world', *Environment and Planning D: Society and Space*, 25 (2007), 1079–102.

Veldman, Meredith, *Fantasy, the Bomb and the Greening of Britain: Romantic Protest, 1945–1980* (Cambridge: Cambridge University Press, 1994).

Vernon, James, *Hunger: A Modern History* (Harvard University Press, London, 2007).

Vion, Antoine, 'The institutionalization of international friendship', *Critical Review of International Social and Political Philosophy*, 10:2 (2007), 281–297.

Wainwright, David, *The Volunteers: The Story of Overseas Voluntary Service* (London, 1965).

Ward, Stuart (ed.), *British Culture and the End of the Empire* (Manchester: Manchester University Press, 2001).

Waters, Chris, 'Dark strangers' in our midst: Discourses of race and nation in Britain, 1947–1963', *Journal of British Studies*, 36 (1997), 207–38.

Webster, Wendy, *Imagining Home: Gender, 'Race' and National Identity, 1945–1964* (London: Taylor & Francis, 1998).

Webster, Wendy, '"There'll always be an England": Representations of colonial wars and immigration, 1948–1968', *Journal of British Studies*, 40:4 (2001), 557–84.

Webster, Wendy, *Englishness and Empire, 1939–1965* (Oxford: Oxford University Press, 2005).

Wiesen, Jonathan S., 'Service above self? Rotary Clubs, National Socialism, and transnational memory in the 1960s and 1970s', *Holocaust and Genocide Studies*, 23:1 (2009), 1–25.

Whitehead, Clive, 'Miss Freda Gwilliam (1907–1987): a portrait of the "great aunt" of British colonial education', *Journal of Educational Administration and History*, 24:2 (1992), 145–63.

Whittal, Daniel, '"In this metropolis of the world we must have a building worthy of our great people": race, empire and hospitality in imperial London, 1931–48', in Eve Rosenhaft and Robbie Aitken (eds), *Africa in Europe: Studies in Transnational*

Practice in the Long Twentieth Century (Liverpool: Liverpool University Press, 2013), pp. 76–98.

Whittle, Matthew, 'Hosts and hostages: mass immigration and the power of hospitality in post-war British and Caribbean literature', *Comparative Critical Studies*, 11 (2014), 77–92.

Woollacott, Angela, *To Try Her Fortune in London: Australian Women, Colonialism and Modernity* (Oxford: Oxford University Press, 2001).

Zelinsky, Wilbur, 'The twinning of the world: sister cities in geographic and historical perspective', *Annals of the Association of American Geographers*, 81:1 (1991), 1–31.

INDEX

Action for World Development 142, 165

amateurism 11, 16, 62–6, 71, 129
  see also know how

amnesia 4, 27, 81, 148–9, 189

Amnesty International 169, 173

Anti-Apartheid Movement 8, 13, 115, 163, 169, 172, 173, 174

anxiety 4, 41, 53, 60, 82, 105, 186

apartheid 4, 58, 115–17, 168
  see also Anti-Apartheid Movement

apolitical 9, 13–14, 81–2, 115–16, 118, 140–2, 147, 190–1

Associated Countrywomen of the World (ACWW) 73, 79, 95, 97, 98

Australia 34, 40, 43, 57, 79, 96–8, 100–1, 107

Barbados 63

Beaverbrook, Lord (Max Aitken) 28

benevolence
  imperial 5–6, 70, 131–5
  global role 5–6, 15–16, 134, 186
  national characteristic 4, 14, 82, 118, 187

BOAC 26, 52
  see also tourism

Botswana 148, 166

British Council 61, 73, 78, 82, 92, 105–7, 112

British Council of Churches 106, 155–6, 158, 162, 168–70, 174

Bryant, Arthur 25–7

Campaign for Nuclear Disarmament (CND) 13, 115, 141–2, 147, 169, 173

Canada 57, 58, 79, 98, 117, 136

Carrington, Charles 33, 44–5

Casey (Lord), Richard 34, 43–5

Central African Federation 28, 42

Central Office of Information 33, 105

Chamber of Commerce 26, 185

Charity Commission 142, 166

Chislett, Charles 63–7, 96, 130, 185

Christian Aid
  Area Secretaries 175, 179–81
  and the Commonwealth 164–5
  and education 172–5
  fundraising 176–80
  and local churches 175–81
  and politics 164–7
  projects 158–60
  supporters 171–2

Christianity
  Christian citizenship 157, 168–9, 173
  Christian witness 168
  crisis of 167–8

citizenship
  active 6–8, 11, 13–14, 83, 191
    see also service
  and belonging 7
  Commonwealth 45
  cultural 30
  international/global 29, 146
  and legal status 7
    see also Christianity, Christian citizenship

Cold War 52, 58–61, 67, 91, 101, 137, 141, 164

colonial administrators
  see Colonial Civil Service

Colonial Civil Service 9, 69–72, 74–6, 112, 136–7, 172
  see also imperial careers

Colonial Office 28, 36, 60, 73, 104–6, 138
  see also Commonwealth Relations Office; Foreign Office